D0961248

THE UNUSUAL SUSPECT

THE UNUSUAL SUSPECT

MY CALLING TO THE NEW HARDCORE MOVEMENT OF FAITH

STEPHEN BALDWIN

WITH MARK TABB

New York Boston Nashville

FaithWords
Hachette Book Group USA
1271 Avenue of the Americas
New York, NY 10020

Visit our Web site at www.faithwords.com.

Printed in the United States of America

First Edition: September 2006
10 9 8 7 6 5 4 3

The FaithWords name and logo are trademarks of Hachette Book Group USA.

The Library of Congress Cataloging-in-Publication Data
Baldwin, Stephen.
    The unusual suspect: my calling to the new hardcore movement of faith / by Stephen Baldwin with Mark Tabb. — 1st ed.
        p. cm.
    "Warner Books."
    ISBN-13: 978-0-446-57975-9
    ISBN-10: 0-446-57975-0
    1. Baldwin, Stephen, 1966 May 12- 2. Christian biography. 3. Actors—United States—Religious life. I. Tabb, Mark A. II. Title.
    BR1725.B3328A3 2006
    277.3'082092—dc22

                                                    2006006846

to
jesus
the
christ

for
augusta

Acknowledgments

God . . . thank You for waiting . . . giving me the choice . . . now I get it! I need You now . . . more than the air I breathe . . . I am yours . . . I will do ANYTHING . . . !

Kennya, Alaia, Hailey . . . my gifts . . . my earthly joy . . . my friends . . . my angels . . . ! God knew what I needed . . . to see Him . . . !

Mom, Dad, and all of my brothers and sisters and their families . . . I love you all . . . more than any words can say . . . see you all in heaven!

Carl Johnson & my New City Gospel Fellowship family . . . thanks for all the spiritual food, worship, love, support and prayers for me & the girls.

Luis Palau Association . . . Luis, Pat, Kevin, Keith, Andrew, Steve and all of your families . . . & the entire staff at LPA . . . The Lord has blessed me . . . with all of your love, support, prayer and guidance.

Pastors . . . A. R. Bernard, Ravi Zacharias, John Carter, Michael Hayes, Michael Fletcher, Floyd Nichols, Zane Anderson, Chuck

Swindoll, Raul Ries, Jay Hazlip, Zeny Tinouco, Bob Coy, Shelly Sampson, Matt Potterbin.

Fellow Soldiers . . . Jonathan Spinks, Carl Ritter, Paul Rodgers, Todd Hendricks, Tom Maharis, Gary Heavin, Michael Esposito, Michael Smith, Daniel & David Gonzalez, Hill Bowman . . . thank you and all your families.

The Skate Family . . . Paul Anderson . . . yo bro . . . thanks for starting it all, Darren Wells, Christian Hosoi, Jay Alabama, Rick Weigele, Lance Mountain, Ray Barbee, The *Livin' It* Crew, listed at Livinit.com.

Gary Terashita . . . thank you for believing . . . your passion . . . and most of all . . . your strong gutsy vision . . . so God would speak through this book.

Special thanks to the Warner Faith family, particularly David Young, Maureen Egan, Rolf Zettersten, Chip MacGregor, Chris Murphy, Harry Helm, Jean Griffin, Lori Quinn, Jana Burson, and Cara Highsmith.

Mark Tabb . . . aka "Tabby" . . . Praise the Lord for bringing together . . . a wild fire . . . and beautifully gifted wisdom . . . you said it best . . . "This ain't work . . . this is fun!" Thanks again.

Friends . . . Pat Reaves, Michael Kingman, Lawrence Holdrige, Alex d'Adrea, Lawrence Fishburn, Paul McCormick, Corey Kilgannon, Matt Greacen, Sam Rockwell, Keith Diamond, the Bevilacqua family, Dan Martineau & family, and all other friends listed at stephenbaldwin.com.

Louis & John Greacen & family . . . thank you for your example, perseverance, faith & prayers that our Lord has honored . . . you are with me always . . . I love you guys . . . !

The Body of Christ . . . please keep praying . . . learn His word . . . never take yours eyes off "JESUS" . . . let's kick some butt . . . for His kingdom . . . ! ! !   God Bless.

Contents

Faith

Main Entry: **faith**[1]

Pronunciation: 'fāth

Function: *noun*

Inflected Form(s): *plural* **faiths** /'fāths, *sometimes* 'fā<u>th</u>z/

Etymology: Middle English *feith*, from Old French *feid, fei*, from Latin *fides;* akin to Latin *fidere* to trust — more at BIDE

1 a : allegiance to duty or a person **: LOYALTY b** (1) **:** fidelity to one's promises (2) **:** sincerity of intentions

2 a (1) **:** belief and trust in and loyalty to God (2) **:** belief in the traditional doctrines of a religion **b** (1) **:** firm belief in something for which there is no proof (2) **:** complete trust

3 : something that is believed especially with strong conviction; *especially* **:** a system of religious beliefs

synonym see BELIEF

- in faith : without doubt or question **: VERILY**

Introduction
An Unusual Experience

The weirdest part of being a celebrity is the awkward moment when someone stops me on the street and says, *You look familiar. Where do I know you from?* I usually play along and say, "I don't know." They keep staring at me, and it's hilarious because I can see they are doing a Google search of their brain trying to figure out how they know me. *Did we go to high school together,* they will ask. I play along, smile and say, "I don't know, dude, where did you grow up?" *Saskatchewan.* "Huh. I'm from Long Island." So they start Googling some more, but they keep coming up with more wrong information because they typed a wrong word into their search engine.

After a while they finally hit the right key and this funny kind of embarrassment comes over them as they start to realize I'm a celebrity. *Wait a minute*, they say, *are you a Baldwin?* "Yeah, how are you? Pleased to meet you, Stephen Baldwin, always a pleasure," I stick out my hand and say. This is followed by a long pause and more often than not they come back with, *No you're not!* I tell them it's really me, but they stand there and argue with me. This has even gone on to the point where people ask to see my driver's license. When it reaches that point I excuse myself and tell them I really don't have time to argue over whether or not I am in fact STEPHEN BALDWIN.

Now, however, I get this version where I'm walking down the street and a young lady will stop me and say, *Are you Stephen Baldwin!?* I say "Yeah, nice to meet you." She will let out a little screech and say something like, *Oh my gosh! I can't believe it's you.* Then she will say, *Are you _really_ a Christian?* I go, "Yeah, giving my life to Christ is an awesome experience." And then she will take a half step back, look at me with a look of total shock and say, *No you're _not_.*

I can't win, but I can understand her surprise because I have to say to all you people out there who can't believe Stevie B is now a *Christian*, no one is more shocked by this turn of events than me. I'm the last guy on this planet I ever figured would wake up every morning and say, "Thanks God, what do You want me to do today?" Now this faith defines who I am. Is that not the craziest thing you've ever heard?

BALONEY

The Bible says faith is being sure of what we hope for and certain of what we do not see (Hebrews 11:1). Up until a few years ago that sounded like a bunch of baloney to me. How could anyone in their right mind buy into that? It wasn't until after I became a Christian that I remembered how much I loved bologna when I was a kid. Growing up on Long Island I ate bologna all the time, but then I grew up and my tastes became more jaded and I quit eating it. Only kids like that stuff. Me, I was too sophisticated, too refined, too grown-up to throw some bologna between a couple pieces of bread and chow down.

I think this same logic kept me from exploring God for so long. My parents drug me to church when I was little, but once I got old enough to choose for myself I never went back. Why should I? In my mind God was for kids, just like bologna. It wasn't until I was willing to dial back the clock and have the mind-set of a child that I was able to understand what this faith was all about.

What I didn't know then but I now know is that everyone must do the same thing. According to Jesus, the only way anyone will ever understand what appears to the grown-up mind to be nothing but baloney is to stop looking through the cynical eyes of an adult and embrace it with the heart of a child.

Yeah, that was easy for you to do, Stephen, because you never grew up. I'll give you that. But my lifelong unwillingness to kick to the curb that innate playfulness we have when we are kids didn't make me any more likely to be a candidate to sign on to the whole Jesus movement thing. If anything, it kept me from getting too close to it. I remember growing up watching the adults around me. Most of them appeared to be so caught up in being responsible citizens that they forgot how to enjoy life. They acted like you might as well stick your head in an oven the day you turn forty. And a lot of those people were the very ones who talked about God in their lives. Why would I want to become a part of that?

I didn't then and I still don't want to today. Stephen Baldwin, the *fun* Baldwin, refuses to become part of something old and stale and boring. That's part of what has surprised me about this thing called faith. Through it God replaced my jaded, cynical, been-there-done-that eyes with a whole new way of seeing the world. Further and perhaps even more surprising is I've come to this faith in a more intense and hardcore way than I could have possibly imagined.

I feel like I have gone skydiving and I'm falling from the sky toward earth at 120 miles per hour. The wind is howling in my ears and whipping across my face. But somehow, I feel calm and at peace. I'm not afraid. In fact, I'm absolutely positive that I am free from any danger. I feel all these things all at once with the full knowledge that I chose to jump out of a perfectly good airplane *without a parachute*!

This skydiving experience is what this book is all about. Listen, I'm not trying to come off like some kind of expert on the Christian faith. I'm just a guy from Long Island who had all his preconceptions about God blown away when I took a chance and embraced faith. In the pages that follow I'll tell you how and why I took such a radical step.

I also invite you into the mind of Stevie B as I let you in on what I have come to understand during my first few years on this path called Christianity. There's stuff in this book that will make you laugh, and stuff that will make you mad. I may use some language you're not used to, and I ask your forgiveness now if any of it offends as that is not my intent. One of my discoveries about the faith community is that we can often be more concerned about the inconsequential than the eternal. My prayer is that by the time you close the back cover you will be willing to take a chance, drop your guard, and enter into an experience like the one I'm having with God.

Sure, it might all sound like a pile of baloney, but bologna never tasted so good.

Purpose

Main Entry: **¹pur·pose**

Pronunciation: 'pər-pəs

Function: *noun*

Etymology: Middle English *purpos*, from Old French, from *purposer* to purpose, from Latin *proponere* (perfect indicative *proposui*) to propose — more at PROPOUND

1 a : something set up as an object or end to be attained : **INTENTION**

b : RESOLUTION, DETERMINATION

2 : a subject under discussion or an action in course of execution

synonym see INTENTION

CHAPTER 1

Celebrity vs. Reality

People constantly ask me for details of my "Damascus Road" experience (see Acts 9) that made me give my life to Jesus Christ. Most assume I hit bottom and had nowhere else to turn. They're wrong. Nothing in my life made me say, *Oh God I can't live like this anymore. I can't do this, I'm going to kill myself. Help me!* I've got to admit, my life was pretty awesome. When I woke up one morning and realized some studio had just paid me eighty times what my old man made a year to play Barney-freaking-Rubble, how could I not pinch myself and say, *"Is this a great country or what!"*

Don't get me wrong. There were things about who I was that I didn't like, and these things caused problems for me that I didn't want to face. I had a reputation as one of Hollywood's bad boys and living up to it led to behavior that was seriously questionable for a married man. But that didn't make me turn to Jesus. Overall, life was good. I just didn't realize it could be better.

Yeah, but you had it made, Stevie B. No argument here. I did have it made, at least according to the world system. You name it and I've been there, done that. Being a celebrity opened doors for me that were beyond anything I could have ever imagined. I've been on 250-foot yachts. I've hung out with billionaires and flown around on their private jets. I've been all over the world and experienced things 99.9 percent of people have never imagined in their wildest fantasies.

Of course a lot of guys assume I've done even more. They come up to me and ask, "Hey dude, by the way, in all those sex scenes in your movies, were you really doing it?" If they only knew what it takes to film those scenes they would understand how funny that question is. Movies are all about creating an illusion, and that is especially true of the sex scenes. But guys still want to know if I had sex with all the starlets I've worked with. The short answer is no, but I could have with a lot of them. The Hollywood life is a place that gives you license to do anything you want. Once you are in the club, celebrity gives you an all-access, no limits pass in the physical world. I could go wherever I wanted and do pretty much anything I wanted, and the hilarious part is that most of the time I didn't even have to pay for it.

But even as I let myself be swept along on this ride, something deep down inside me kept telling me none of this really made any sense. For me, celebrity was never reality. I thought, okay, I'll take the money and I'll have a good time while I do this acting thing. I wanted to see how far it would take me, but even as I did, I knew I didn't want to become part of the fabric of the Hollywood "reality." Deep down I was never completely comfortable in that world. Of course, that didn't stop me from diving pretty deep.

GROTTO A GO-GO

How far did I go? Deep enough to know which steps on the spiral staircase down into the wine cellar at the Playboy mansion would trigger the silent alarm. When you know that, baby, you're in pretty deep. I didn't learn this little secret until my third trip to the mansion. The fact that I made it there once was a really big deal. There are producers and a bunch of other studio execs that can't get in, so when I was invited there for the first time it was one of those moments in my celebrity life that made me say, "Hey baby, I've arrived. I'm legitimate because I'm going to the Playboy mansion."

As the youngest son of a social studies teacher, the mansion was awesome, not so much because of the decadence of the place but because of the mystery of it. Growing up I looked at enough *Playboy* magazines that I should be blind, so to be invited to the Mecca of the whole empire was unbelievable. The fact that I was a married man didn't keep me from going.

I remember walking into the Playboy mansion the first time and looking around and thinking to myself, "Wow, this place is crawling with sexy chicks," but I could feel something else deep down inside. I felt the presence of evil. Of course, most anyone in Hollywood would have responded to my little observation by saying, "Yeah, so? What's the problem? Enjoy it, man."

Keep in mind I wasn't anywhere close to becoming a Christian at the time. Yet even then I could sense the true nature of the place. The paganism that hangs in the air and the sexual exploitation of women gives the place an energy and power that is just pure evil. I don't know how else to describe it. That sense of evil should have made me turn tail and leave, but I didn't. Nor did it keep me from going back.

I learned the secret of the staircase on my third visit. I hadn't planned on going to the mansion, but the word got out that I was in town from my home in Tucson. Some people called and invited me to a party there, and I said, sure, why not. When I arrived I ran into Robert Downey, Jr. Now, in the old days, Downey *really* knew the mansion and he offered to give me a full tour. He wanted to make sure he showed me the grotto, which is this underground pool down in a cave. When you access the grotto you have to go down a long, very small, very narrow stone hallway. We were walking down this hallway and just as we came to the mouth that opened into the pool I saw some guy kind of stooped over what looked like a fuse box. I assumed it was a maintenance worker, but as I started to excuse myself and walk past him, he turned around and it was Hef himself. I was blown away. I was like, wow, it's the legendary Hugh Hefner in all his stereotypical glory: robe, slippers, pajamas, and pipe.

Hef turned around, and keep in mind it was pretty dark down there, and he said, "Good evening, gentlemen. Good to see you Robert. Stephen." Then he said, "Please forgive me, gentlemen, I was just adjusting the lights here in the grotto so that the mood is perfect. Enjoy yourselves." This blew me away. All I could think was, *How weird is it that Hef himself adjusts the lights in the grotto.* Talk about the personal touch. I mean, this guy was really into his whole deal. That set the tone for me that night.

After my tour I walked around the mansion doing my whole Hollywood routine. For me, hanging out at the Playboy mansion was part of the "fun" of being in the fast lane of celebrity and the Hollywood lifestyle that was completely acceptable. It was my rite of passage as Stephen Baldwin "THE TALENT." Of course I didn't tell my wife I was going to the Playboy mansion. If she had happened to ask I would have told her, but I didn't volunteer the information. To me, as long as I wasn't misbehaving I figured my being there was no big deal.

Later that evening Downey came up to me with this little grin on his face and he said, "Follow me." I asked where we were going and he just said, "Shhhh, I want to show you something." Now I know when I get to the end of this story you are not going to believe me, but folks, it's true.

Downey led me to what looked like a closet, but inside was a spiral staircase that went down about fifteen or twenty steps. We started down the staircase, and as we did, Downey stepped down the first two steps but skipped the third. I was coming down right behind him when he turned around and told me, "Don't step on that one." Then about halfway down he skipped another step and told me the same thing. Now, in retrospect, I don't know if he was just a kook and was joking around with me, but at the time he told me that these two steps would trigger the silent alarm.

When we got to the bottom of the staircase I found myself in a beautiful, vast wine cellar. Four playmates were already down there, hanging out and smoking pot. There was a time I would have joined in, but that's another chapter. At this point I had already been sober for years and I wasn't going to blow it. I immediately excused myself, thanked Robert for the good time, and got out of there.

I went back upstairs and stayed for maybe another ten minutes. There were a bunch of stars hanging out with the Playmates and everyone was drunk and high. Since I stopped drinking several years earlier, I felt disconnected from the whole scene. I glanced over at a couple of people whose names you would immediately recognize and they were all giggling and flirting with the Playmates. That's when it hit me. I looked around the room and said to myself, *Wow, what am I doing here? If you think about it, all of this is pretty meaningless. This isn't working for me anymore.* I thought there had to be more to life than this. And if there wasn't, I was really screwed. I had officially done it all, and still it left me with a question somewhere in the back of my mind that I couldn't answer. But more on that later.

BIRTH OF A DYNASTY

So how did I go from Stevie B, the youngest of six kids from a middle-class family in Massapequa, New York, to Stephen Baldwin, part of the most successful brother dynasty in Hollywood history and insider to the hidden mysteries of Hef's Playboy mansion? And how can I honestly say all I experienced through the journey wasn't enough? I'll get to that last question later because the answer lies in the story of my rise from small-town jock to playing Michael McManus in the double Oscar winning film, *The Usual Suspects.*

The story is pretty simple. My mom and dad met at Syracuse University and got married. They later moved to Long Island, New York, where my dad started teaching at Massapequa High School. Between 1955 and 1966 they had six kids, the last of whom was little ole me. I will go into much more detail about all this in the next chapter, but for now it is enough to say that who my siblings and I became was in large part due to how this school-teacher and his wife raised us. The genetics of our driven personalities pushed us to excel and the boldness of our character made us popular overachievers in athletics, art, academics and anything else we put our minds to. That's just how we were raised and that's how we Baldwins still are. Anything we do, we do full bore.

Then my big brother Alec decided to get into acting. After high school he started at George Washington University and majored in political science. Later he lost one of the largest student body elections in the history of George Washington University by a single vote. This made Alec reevaluate his future which led to him transferring to NYU and the Lee Strasberg Theatre Institute. While waiting tables at Studio 54 someone told him about an audition the next day for some movie. He tried out, but they told him he wasn't right for the role. However, the cast director told him about a role on a soap opera called *The Doctors*. Alec auditioned, landed the role, and did the show for a couple of years.

So what does all that have to do with me and the making of the Baldwin Brother Hollywood dynasty? On the show *The Doctors*, homeboy was making more in a month than daddy-o made in an entire school year as a teacher. So my dad gets this brilliant idea that the world does not need more doctors or lawyers, but actors. What a genius concept! Now Daniel, William, and little Stevie B sit down to dinner one night, and while we are sitting there my dad tells us how much Alec is making per soap opera episode. We react to this tidbit of information by projectile spewing our tuna casserole across the room. The three of us wipe the tuna from our chins, look at one another and say, *If that schmuck can weasel his way into a situation like that, we might as well give it a try.* This was the catalyst for the Baldwin brothers taking Hollywood by storm. True story. Or at least how I remember it.

After this, Daniel and Billy started playing around with acting. The two of them did some commercials, and auditioned for other parts. Before long the word started to get out about the Baldwin boys, especially as Alec started landing better and better parts. Billy went on to get into a very serious modeling career which led to bigger and better things, including major roles in movies like *Backdraft*.

My turn at the plate came after I graduated from Berner High School with a C average and not a lot of college options. Knowing no school in its right mind would let me in based on my scholastic potential, I figured I better try a different approach. I auditioned for the American Academy of Dramatic Arts in New York and got in. They didn't care about grades, which was a good thing for me because I didn't care about them either. But I knew I had talent. Of the four of us, I did the most community theater growing up. I also had success as an opera singer, which you will read more about later.

All of this helped me get into this very prestigious institution with very high standards for professionalism, standards I was eager to break in every way, shape and form I possibly could. It didn't take them long to come to the very intelligent deduction that perhaps inviting Stevie B to enter their institution wasn't the brightest decision they had ever made. This place was crawling with a bunch of artistic intellectuals and ballerinas, and if that ain't a candy store for a kid like me, I don't know what is.

Now don't get me wrong. I was anxious to pursue this drive inside me, this artistic desire. However, I would be lying if I said I didn't walk around that place with a little extra juice knowing I was Alec Baldwin's kid brother. I used this to my full advantage every chance I got. I even offered my own private acting lessons within the institution itself, and trust me, you can let your imagination run wild with that one.

Needless to say, my time at the American Academy of Dramatic Arts was pretty much one and done. They did not invite me back for a second year. So I left college and started pounding the pavement. I got a place in Manhattan, found an agent and a manager, and started going through the audition process. At the same time I met a drop-dead knockout Brazilian hotty on a New York bus, asked her out, and we've been together ever since. Anyone who doesn't believe in miracles after that is a complete idiot.

The Baldwin brother success in Hollywood, however, is not miraculous. The four of us simply figured out on a common-sense level what we would have to do to be successful in this business, and we did it. Obviously we possessed innate talent and ability, but we also had that drive to succeed. Everything just lined up for us and however many years later it is now, we're still doing it.

I landed my first professional acting job on the old sit-com, *Kate and Allie*. The part was a real stretch. I played a high school troublemaker who had one line, "So, is this an open book test?" Find the DVD. You'll see real genius at work. I had a few other bit parts on shows like *Family Ties* and did a few commercials.

My first serious role came in a feature film about the Soviet invasion of Afghanistan called *The Beast*. William Mastrosimone wrote it and Kevin Reynolds from *Waterworld* was the director. I'd been out of the American Academy of Dramatic Arts maybe a year, slinging pizza on the Upper West Side while scratching for any small part I could find, and suddenly I'm off to Israel for three months to make my first movie. How weird is that? That job led to several more which finally led to my playing Buffalo Bill Cody in *The Young Riders* television show from 1989 to 1992.

The notoriety from the show, along with the Baldwin brother hype, catapulted me into full-bore celebrity status.

Then, in 1995, I landed the role of Michael McManus in *The Usual Suspects*, written by Christopher McQuarrie and directed by Bryan Singer. The film went on to win two Academy Awards along with high praise from all the critics.

Now when I tell the rest of this story most people think I am full of crap. Whatever. Don't believe me if you want, but it is true. The buzz and critical acclaim surrounding *The Usual Suspects* placed me and the other guys in the film in a position to become very, very big. It worked for Kevin Spacey and it worked for Benicio Del Toro. And if I had played the game according to the rules it would have worked for me as well. I could have gone on to become an A-list actor. Like I said, you can say I'm full of it if you want, but I know myself and that old Baldwin drive to succeed. I can't say for certain that I would have made it to the top, but I guarantee you there's a pretty good chance I would have.

There was just one problem with that whole equation called RULES. I didn't want to play by their rules, not because I am some sort of self-defeatist whack job, but because I didn't want to pay the personal price that kind of success demands. I didn't want to become Brad Pitt. I didn't want to be Tom Cruise. Part of me did, but another subconscious part of me knew that if I reached that level of success I couldn't do whatever I wanted anymore. Once you reach the top, once you hit that pinnacle of success, your whole life becomes focused on staying there. Every cell of your body becomes all about that next $100 million movie and keeping yourself squarely in the public eye. People are fickle beings. They'll forget you overnight unless you devote your entire life to making sure they don't. Call me nuts, but from my perspective, that ain't living. I know there are people in Hollywood who will read that statement and think I am a moron. To which I say, think whatever you will, but I had a choice. I refused to choose a lifestyle that demanded I sacrifice my life for my career. I didn't then and I never will.

So instead of playing by the rules I agreed to be in a movie called *Bio-Dome* with Pauly Shore. Some of the people representing me told me to hold off on the picture even though the studio was offering me a ton of money. Instead of listening to them I read the script and nearly wet myself laughing over what I knew I could do with the part. At the time Pauly Shore was hot, he was funny, and I thought we would work well together.

But that wasn't even my logic for doing the movie. All I wanted to know was whether it was funny and could I have a good time making it. I didn't do the movie for any other reason than Stephen's own personal will and desire to serve himself. My attitude was: I want to have a good time, so take a hike, it's my career. That's why I did it.

Did *Bio-Dome* keep me from reaching the pinnacle of Hollywood? I don't know. Maybe. But it also had some far-reaching positive effects that I'm even now just discovering.

BEEN THERE, DONE THAT

Now this is the place where people expect to hear me say that even as I was climbing the stairway of success I was never happy, that my life was empty and horrible and I hated my very existence so much that I had no choice but to turn to Jesus Christ or jump off the George Washington Bridge. Nice story, but that wasn't me. I'll admit that in the beginning I partied too much, drank too much, and snorted enough cocaine to throw the entire population of a small South American country into anaphylactic shock. All of that led me to a twelve-step program, not to the born-again experience I'm having with Jesus Christ now. I didn't even go to a twelve-step program until Kennya gave me no other choice.

Like I said at the beginning of this chapter, God didn't knock me flat on my back and hit me with a spotlight from heaven. Nor did I lie awake at night contemplating the tragedy that was the life of Stephen Baldwin. Instead, throughout my Hollywood existence I pretty much laughed at the whole thing. I mean, give me a break. My dad made something like twenty-five grand a year and I made $2 million to play Barney Rubble. Are you kidding me? That's the dumbest thing I've ever heard. Did I deserve it? I don't know. I guess. Should I have saved some of it? You bet. Did I? NO. But that's not even the point, although most people think it is.

Come on, Stevie B. What's the problem? That's just the way it is. Don't knock it. Get what you can. Take. Take. Take. That's the world system. I was never completely comfortable with that way of thinking. Instead, a question kept bouncing around in the back of my head. I kept wondering why this success kept coming. Now I know the answer to that question was God. I think I suspected it then. At the time, none of what was happening to me and my career made any sense. The fact that four brothers with no background in the business, no ties to Hollywood whatsoever, could make as many films as we have and achieve the level of success we've attained just didn't make any sense to me. Some call it dumb luck. I don't think so. I always knew there had to be something more to it. Always in the back of my mind I knew some higher authority had to be behind this. But why? Why would God want to make me famous?

The question running through my mind affected my career even before I came to faith. First, the question kept me from taking myself too seriously, which means my career never came before my happiness. I always tried to put my wife and my children before my career. Always. This is rare in Hollywood, or any other field for that matter. Everyone knows the career has to come first if you want to make it. Before relationships. Before fatherhood. Nothing is as important as achieving success. I didn't want to play that game.

Second, the deep, inner knowledge that something greater had to be behind this kept me from equating my celebrity with reality. I never connected the two. I knew better.

Even though I never took the ride too seriously, even though for me if it wasn't going to be any fun I wasn't going to do it, and even though I was pinching myself all along the way because I knew I was unbelievably lucky or blessed, I knew something was missing. The question of why this was happening had to be answered. What I now understand—that I didn't understand then—is that the answer to that question comes down to one little word: Purpose. Yes, I was happy, at least to the degree that I understood happiness at that point in my life. But I didn't understand the purpose behind it all.

Everyone has to wrestle with this same question, and most people don't even realize it. We work. We get married. We have children. We make money. We do this whole life thing and most of us have no idea why we do it. To me, that's scary. Millions of people scurry around out there on a journey they don't even know they are making. I was blessed because God made me wonder. He kept making me look for the purpose behind everything going on in my life. I couldn't stop wondering if there wasn't supposed to be something more.

I have to tell you, that sense of holy discontent was a gift, because without it I would have been just like the other fried lives in Hollywood that think the MTV awards and Miami Beach and making money and having sex and giving a little to charity is enough. They just accept the fact that all of that is enough. I couldn't. Something inside me made me search for more.

Yes, I lived an amazing life. I had experiences that go beyond most people's wildest dreams, and I can honestly look you in the eye and say the experience I am now having with Jesus Christ blows away everything I did before. But the bigger thing is this: Once I gave control of my life to Jesus, all of the stuff that came before finally made sense. For the first time in my life all the pieces fit. I knew why Stephen Baldwin was born and why God took me on this wild ride. The answer comes down to the purpose He had for me when the sperm hit the egg inside my mother's womb. He designed me to seek Him first. Everything else I now do comes down to this simple purpose God has for me and everyone else who has ever been born.

Life isn't so complicated. Not anymore. Yeah, I had a good life. A blessed life. A lucky life. Call it what you will. But now I've discovered the ultimate reality that I always wanted and could never find.

Unusual

Main Entry: **un·usu·al**

Pronunciation: -'yü-zhə-wəl, -zhəl; -'yüzh-wəl

Function: *adjective*

: not usual : **UNCOMMON, RARE**

- **un·usu·al·ly** *adverb*

- **un·usu·al·ness** *noun*

CHAPTER 2

Growing Up Baldwin, or *The Brady Bunch* on Crack

The story you are about to read is true. The names have been changed to protect the innocent. Namely me. If I disclose too many details about my family I am a dead man. It will be, do not pass go, do not collect $200, we're going to kill you now, little Stevie.

Not long ago my oldest sister Beth and my big brother Alec were talking about their ages and how hard it is for them to believe they are as old as they are now. In the middle of the conversation Beth turned to Alec and said, "You think it is hard to believe we are as old as we are, think about this: Stephen's about to turn forty." To which Alec responded in that very dramatic, Alec Baldwin way, "Stephen's going to be forty? My God, I never thought he'd make it past thirty." I think that says it all about who I was growing up, and my role in the family.

So what was it like growing up as the youngest of six kids in a working-class Catholic family in a middle-class neighborhood in Massapequa, Long Island, New York? About what you would expect, I guess. That is, if you were nuts and your brothers were as well.

As hard as it is to believe, I had a smart mouth when I was a kid. My brother Daniel had to kick so much butt back in the day because of my big fat mouth. He still has the scars from having to defend me when I would mouth off to someone and start a fight. Like an idiot, I usually mouthed off to someone older and bigger than me. So I would run to my big brother and he would defend the family honor. That's one of the perks of being the baby in the family.

The other perk is that the baby is always Mom's favorite. Ask anyone who's the youngest kid in a large family. They will tell you. Of course I never used this to my advantage, unless I really had to, which would be like every day. My brother Billy is only three years older than me and there were days when he would come after me verbally, and I would go right back at him. But, since I was the baby of the family, my parents never thought I would use bad language. So when Billy and I went after each other as brothers do, I would flip him off and then turn around and run as fast as I could. He would chase me all over the house so he could beat me up, which he could do easily. In fact, he still can.

Knowing Billy would succeed in his attempt to inflict great bodily harm on me, I used a perfect defense strategy: I ran straight to Mom and hid behind her. Billy would come to her and say, "Mom, he's hiding behind you and you're protecting him. That's not fair. I smacked him in the head because he flipped me off. That's wrong." My mother would reply, "What else is he supposed to do to defend himself, he's a poor, little, innocent thing?" Now this would really set Billy off because my mom was always getting on him for using bad language. But in her eyes I never did anything like that. Not sweet little ole me. I know I am still her favorite. At least I think I am. Maybe.

STEVIE HOUDINI

Before you feel sorry for my brothers, you need to know they got their shots in. About the time that I was ten or eleven years old, I did my own version of Harry Houdini. To get attention in my family I allowed myself to be bound and gagged, and I would escape. They hung me from trees, stuffed me in small spaces, whatever, and I always weaseled my way out of it.

One day I got this bright idea for my ultimate escape. Thinking back, I'm not sure if it was really my idea or if William and Daniel came up with it. The plan was this: Billy and Danny would roll me in two bedsheets mummy style. Then, they would roll me up in a throw rug, and secure it with three of my father's belts pulled as tight as they could get them. Me, being little Stevie Houdini, told them to go for it. I knew I could escape. However, my siblings didn't tell me of the bonus feature to this trick. Once they had me mummified in the sheets and throw rug and my dad's belts, they carried me upstairs, threw me in the bathtub with my feet sticking up and my head down in the tub, and turned on the water. They left me there and went downstairs to watch reruns of *Gilligan's Island* or engage in other activities that I cannot mention due to the disclaimer at the beginning of this chapter.

Now as they threw me in the bathtub, I just laughed and told them I would show them. I'm Stevie B Houdini. I can escape from anything these two dorks come up with. However, like the real Houdini in his water chamber, I now faced a time constraint I had not previously taken into consideration. Once my brothers went downstairs and began engaging in activities which I cannot mention or they will come to my house and finish me off, they quickly forgot all about me. They made themselves some peanut butter and jelly sandwiches and started digging Mary Ann and Ginger and having a good ole time. Not until a Tidy Bowl commercial came on the screen did they remember their kid brother upstairs, wrapped in sheets and a rug, stuffed head down in the bathtub with the water running.

I have to say I think there may be some deep Freudian issues I still haven't dealt with from this episode. While my brothers were downstairs doing God knows what, I quickly came to the realization that for the first time in my life, my brothers had finally devised a method of entrapment from which I could not escape. And the water kept getting higher. I think the rug absorbed a lot of the water; otherwise my two brothers might have ended up in the state pen for killing their little brother rather than making it big in Hollywood.

By the time they finally came back upstairs, my neck was stretched as high as it possibly could to keep my nose above water. To take a breath I had to blow the water away from my face. The weight of the waterlogged rug and sheets kept making that harder and harder for me. When my brothers threw the bathroom door open, I let them have it, all the while still blowing the water away from my face so I could breath. Instead of pulling me out, they ran to another room, grabbed a Bic pen, pulled the insides out of it, then shoved it in my mouth like a straw and ran out of the bathroom laughing. I failed to see the humor in the situation. I screamed some profanities at them, all the while holding on to my Bic snorkel. Finally I started pleading with them to come and save me. "I'm sorry, I'm sorry," I yelled, "just get me out of here." The two of them were right outside the door the whole time. After a few more minutes of letting me suffer they came in and pulled me out.

That was life in the Baldwin household. I'm sure it's not too different from any other home in America, if, of course, that home is filled with psychos.

KEEPERS OF THE ASYLUM

Our parents managed the madness the best they could. My mom was the typical stay at home mom, and my dad was a high school history teacher and football coach. By the time I came around my dad seemed tired from the whole parenting routine. Alec told me that Dad changed a lot when his parents both passed away in the late sixties. My dad was a star football player at Boy's High in Brooklyn and went to Syracuse University on a football scholarship. That's where my parents met.

After they graduated from Syracuse, my dad took a job teaching in Massapequa. He was a real teacher. This was his calling. He poured his life into his profession twelve months a year. At a time when other teachers had side jobs where they made their real money, my dad took on extra responsibilities at the school. They made him a football coach because of his background, but he was an anomaly as a coach. Academics came first for him. He didn't have the same shortsighted, "sports are everything" attitude a lot of other coaches have. My dad also worked as a youth council advisor to students, and did summer recreation and autumn recreation on the weekends during school. He was so involved in everything going on at the school that only the janitor carried around more keys than he did.

By the time I came around my dad had changed. He became much quieter and more withdrawn than he once was. The deaths of his parents played a big part in this, but so did the financial pressure of trying to make it with six kids on a teacher's salary. Even so, the guy pulled some surprises on us every once in a while.

One of those times came during my brother Alec's senior year of high school. My dad taught at Massapequa High School, while all of us kids went to the crosstown rival school, Berner High. When Alec was a senior he ran for—prepare to be shocked—senior class president. Hard to believe about him, huh? So my dad came up with this genius idea of how to help my brother get elected.

Even though he taught at the other high school in town, my dad had keys to both schools. Immediately prior to the election he helped my brother make a banner twenty feet across with a campaign slogan my dad thought up. Keep in mind, my brother is the third Alexander in our family. Back in the day, everyone called him Xander, not Alec. That came later. So late one night, my old man and Alec went over to the school and hung this campaign banner inside the cafeteria. The next morning, when the students filed into Berner High School, the first thing they saw was this twenty foot banner that said in huge, bold letters: S-E-X, Students Elect Xander. He won in a landslide.

FAMOUS BEFORE WE WERE FAMOUS

Episodes like this didn't come as a complete surprise to most people. Growing up in a big family in a relatively small town, most people knew who we were. My brothers and I all played sports, which gained us a bit of notoriety. Massapequa is one of those towns where youth sports on every level are a huge deal. Throw in the fact that my dad coached football, and everyone knew who the Baldwins were. That made the stakes even higher when our high school played against my dad's school. When Berner played Massapequa, everyone in town turned out for it.

One year when Alec was in school my dad made a bet with him over the big crosstown rival game. The loser had to push the winner through the town in a wheelbarrow. Alec won and my dad, being a man of his word, pushed my big brother up Merrick Road in a wheelbarrow holding a sign declaring his victory.

Having people in town know who we were wasn't always a good thing. When I finally made it to high school, the Baldwin family reputation preceded me. That is why my first day in ninth grade Algebra class at Berner High was the first day of the rest of my Algebraic career. What I didn't know was that it was also the last day of my Algebraic career. If I knew then what I know now I would have had a lot less turmoil in my Algebraic existence which stretched out over four years and never resulted in a passing grade.

On that first day in ninth grade when my teacher, let's just call him Mr. Napoleon Complex, did roll call and said, "Stephen Baldwin," and I raised my hand and yelled, "Yo!" I didn't fully understand why he then asked, "Is your brother Daniel Baldwin?" I, of course, thought of that as a purely complimentary question and said with a certain amount of pride in my voice, "Yes, sir." Mr. Napoleon Complex then made a slight notation next to my name that changed my Algebraic career forever.

What I never could have known then was that Mr. Napoleon Complex's history with the Baldwin family went back much further than my brother Daniel. In 1968 when I was two years old, the teachers' union went on strike for pay hike reasons. My father was not a member of the union for personal reasons, and he crossed the picket line. When he did, Napoleon Complex jumped out and assaulted him. My dad could have wiped the floor with the guy, but he restrained himself. I guess he figured Mr. Napoleon Complex wasn't worth the trouble. I didn't know any of this on that fateful day of the first day of ninth grade Algebra during roll call when I said "Yo!" gleefully. I had no idea what I was getting myself into.

I also didn't know that my brother Daniel had made a little of his own history with my Algebra teacher. Now Daniel was over six feet tall and weighed 200 pounds in the sixth grade. Mr. Napoleon Complex did not share my brother's genetic good fortune. He was, how do I put this, not a large man. But that didn't stop Mr. Napoleon Complex from calling my brother out into the hall one day and physically assaulting him. He punched my brother in the stomach and smacked him in the face, and even though Daniel could have handed Mr. NC his head, he didn't. Instead he called my mother with the news of this altercation.

I never could have known on that first fateful day during roll call in Mr. Napoleon Complex's ninth grade Algebra class that my mother called my father at the rival high school to inform him of the exchange between their son and Mr. Napoleon Complex. So again, I could never have known that my father, with news of this, excused his current class for the rest of the day, climbed in his station wagon and drove across town. He walked into Berner High School unannounced, and, without knocking, walked into Mr. Napoleon Complex's class and asked all the students to leave the room. What happened next is a mystery, actually, except to say, my dad didn't restrain himself this time.

So a few years later when little Poindexter Stevie B walks in and says "Yo!" on my first day of high school to one of my teachers who broke my father's jaw in 1968, beat up my brother Daniel three years before I walked into class, and then got his clock cleaned by my dad, well, suffice it to say my Algebraic experience was interesting.

That, in a nutshell, was what it was like to grow up Baldwin. Yeah, I could tell more stories, but I think you get the general idea. Besides, I figure I better shut up before I say too much and provoke my brothers into coming by my house in the middle of the night and kicking the crap out of me.

Predestine

Main Entry: **pre·des·tine**

Pronunciation: (ˌ)prē-ˈdes-tən

Function: *transitive verb*

Etymology: Middle English, from Middle French or Latin; Middle French *predestiner,* from Latin *praedestinare,* from *prae-* + *destinare* to determine — more at DESTINE

: to destine, decree, determine, appoint, or settle beforehand; *especially* :
PREDESTINATE

CHAPTER 3

My Life,
the Greatest Production of All Time

Before I say anything else, I need to explain the title of this chapter. No, I'm not tripping on my ego here. My life isn't the greatest production in the history of the human race as though I think of myself as the pinnacle of western civilization. I may have an ego, but it isn't that big. Instead, this title comes from my perspective as an actor and entertainer.

All my life I've played different roles in various productions. But when I separate my life on screen from my real life, I see how my life is like a movie. From the time I was born, I've played different roles: child, student, musician, athlete, actor, husband, father. It is as though my life is a production, written, produced, and directed by the hand of God. All the roles He's had me play and all the paths He's taken me down all worked together to prepare me to receive my greatest role and fulfill His purpose for creating me in the first place.

When I read back over the script God wrote of my life, I understand everything that's happened in this story has all come about to bring me to a place where I could understand who God is and how He wants to use me. That's the greatest production.

This role I'm now playing in the drama God penned that is my life, is the greatest role I will ever play in my life. And it is my life.

This may sound a little confusing. I hear a lot of people say they believe God is in control of everything and His timing is perfect. The Bible says the same thing, so I know it is true. That's what this chapter is about. It is a celebration of how God worked in my life even when I didn't care about Him. I believe God had a plan for my life before I was even born.

Before you throw this book down and tell me I'm the biggest egomaniac in the history of egomaniacs, you need to know that Paul said the same thing in the Bible. He said God chose him to be his spokesman even before he was born (see Galatians 1:15). Here's the wild part: Paul didn't become a believer until late in life. He spent his early adult years as a bounty hunter for the Jewish council in Jerusalem. Instead of hunting down outlaws, Paul tracked down and killed Christians.

One day while he was on the trail of a herd of them in Damascus, Jesus knocked Paul to the ground and struck him blind. That's when Paul became a believer. To me, the best part of the story is this: Even though Paul spent all those years fighting against God, he could still say that God had a plan for his life, and that He'd devised that plan before Paul was even born. That means that all of Paul's experiences before coming to Christ weren't a waste of time. God orchestrated his entire life to bring him to that moment on the Damascus road when Jesus would reveal God's master plan to him. That blows my mind.

Guess what? I don't think God only did this with Paul. I believe He did the same thing with my life. When I look back on my life I can see God all over the entire production. I see my life as a movie, and if that's true, God is Spielberg to the infinite power.

From the moment I was conceived, on through my childhood and on to my journey to Hollywood, God perfectly orchestrated every nanosecond of my life. That's how big I believe

God is. He left nothing to chance. My parents, the values they instilled in my brothers and sisters and me, the way we were raised, none of it just happened. Every event that shaped me and made me who I am, from my father's death when I was seventeen, to leaving home and meeting Kennya, even the bad choices I made that led me to a twelve-step program, I can see God's hand in all of it. If He hadn't been there I would easily have ended up dead, or diseased, or left lying and bleeding in the street from a gunshot wound. I think about the night I took my Suzuki RF 900 down Interstate 10 at 150 miles per hour. If I'd hit a nickel in the road at that speed I would've been toast. But I didn't. Why? Because God's hand was there even though I wasn't yet a believer. He had a plan for my life, and He wasn't about to let my stupidity get in His way.

ACT I: LEONARD BERNSTEIN'S "CHICHESTER PSALMS"

God has a way of speaking to you even when you aren't listening. Most of the time we don't even realize what happened until we look back on the events years later. I know I didn't understand everything taking place on a spiritual level when I toured with the Long Island Symphony Orchestra as a ten-year-old, singing the Twenty-third Psalm in Hebrew. But God did.

Yeah, little Stevie B had an opera career when I was a kid. Hard to believe, isn't it? I wasn't one of those obnoxious kids with overbearing parents on some lame amateur hour talent show. I never even knew I could sing until Mrs. Deacos had me and everyone else in my fourth grade choral class march up to the piano and sing scales. She wanted to find the sopranos and altos and basses in the class. My friends and I spent most of the time punching one another while waiting for our turns. When I stepped over to the piano, I thought it was no big deal when she played some scales and I sang every one of them perfectly. I didn't know I had a natural four octave range. Heck, I didn't even know what that meant. Mrs. Deacos did.

That day of singing scales led to me auditioning in front of the director of the Long Island Symphony for the boy's part in their production of Leonard Bernstein's "Chichester Psalms." The second movement of "The Psalms" begins with a huge production of the Twenty-third Psalm. Even though the music is in a woman's alto range, Bernstein insisted that a young boy always sing the part. For this production, that young boy was me. Basically, I played the part of David, the guy who wrote the psalm, as a young man singing his most famous song accompanied by David's own instrument, the harp. I didn't really know what I was singing since the lyrics were all in Hebrew. During the performance I walked out onto the middle of the stage in front of 3,000 people, dressed in a little tuxedo, while the orchestra built up behind me. Then I belted out in my best operatic voice:

Adonai ro-i, lo echsar.
Bin'ot deshe yarbitseini,
Al mei m'nuchot y'nachaleini,
Naf'shi y'shovev,
Yan'cheini b'ma'aglei tsedek,
L'ma'an sh'mo.
Gam ki eilech
B'gei tsalmavet,
Lo ira ra,
Ki Atah imadi.
Shiv't'cha umishan'techa
Hemah y'nachamuni.

The voices of the women's choir would come in behind me, singing the refrain. Then the men's voices boomed in with words from Psalm 2 which says in English, "Why do the nations rage?" Bernstein wanted the men to sound threatening as they sang about conflict, which clashed with the women who celebrated God's peace and care for His people. The men and women went back and forth, until the men's jeers died out. Then I would return and finish singing the rest of the words to Psalm 23. At the very end, when I hit my last note, the orchestra would very quietly play the men's Psalm 2 music.

The whole thing was very dramatic with all kinds of symbolism about the state of the world and God's power. Front and center of it all was me, this little fourth grade kid who cared more about getting to first base with the girls than I cared about some Hebrew poetry. I didn't know it at the time, but the words coming out of my mouth declared, "The Lord is my shepherd, I have everything I need."

On a purely human level I was doing nothing more than letting sounds I didn't understand fly out of my mouth, but on a spiritual level I was singing to God. In retrospect, I understand none of this happened by chance. God's hand orchestrated these events just as surely as the conductor of the symphony guided that orchestra. I may not have understood the words I sang in Bernstein's "Chichester Psalms," but I saw the power of those words.

I toured with the Long Island Symphony for several months. Every time I sang I watched the reaction of all the Jewish grandmothers in the front row. The words moved them in a way the performance of some kid singing opera never could. Then one night I saw the effect this song had on my dad.

My dad and I had a very unusual relationship. Like I said in the last chapter, by the time I came along, the last of six kids, I think the whole fatherhood thing had worn him out. Or maybe I was just such a goofball that he never really knew how to take me. I don't know. But I will never forget the night he came backstage after watching me perform Bernstein's "Chichester Psalms" for the very first time. Keep in mind my dad was a football coach, a real man's man. He never showed a lot of emotion, or at least I don't remember him showing much. That night was different, however. He came backstage with a look in his eye that I never saw before. He looked almost dumbfounded.

Of course, me being me, I didn't catch on at first. I said something stupid like, "Hey Dad, did you see how I made all those old women cry? Cool, huh?" When he didn't respond I caught on that my dad wasn't here to listen to me crack some stupid joke. Something had touched him. He stuck out his hand to me and shook my hand like I was a man. Then he said something I've never forgotten. He looked down at me like I was a space alien, like he didn't even know me, and said, "You're going to be okay."

My dad didn't have to say anything else. I caught it. As I've replayed that conversation over and over in my head in the years since, I realize this was the only real, spiritual conversation I ever had with my dad. In a sense I think he wanted to say that he had experienced something beyond him; he'd experienced God's touch through his own kid. The only words he could find to convey what he'd experienced were, "You're going to be okay." It was an odd choice of words, but to me it totally made sense. In the Bible fathers laid their hands on their sons to place a blessing on their lives. This was my blessing moment from my dad. It didn't happen by chance. God was right in the middle of it.

ACT II: *GODSPELL*

Singing opera with the Long Island Symphony lit a fire inside me. I started doing community theater here and there, and a thought started forming deep inside me that this might be something I could really get into long-term. However, being a kid, I also liked fooling around and having a good time. As you can see, nothing has changed much in thirty years. Back then, if I could find a way to get on stage and have a good time at the same time, I was one happy camper. Again, nothing much has changed. I'm not trying to make excuses for immaturity when I say this, but I firmly believe God created this childlike playfulness inside me. Not only does it serve me well as an actor, but it has also planted me in places where God could speak to me.

That's how I ended up in a community theater production of

Godspell with a bunch of zany high school thespians. If you aren't familiar with *Godspell*, the musical tells the story of Jesus through rock music. How's that for a wild combination? The whole story is based on the Gospel of Matthew. Instead of the twelve disciples, the characters following Jesus around are all clowns—literally. None of the characters other than Jesus has a name. The program listed us as ourselves. Everyone had a solo, and everyone took turns telling one of Jesus' parables to the crowd. I was the soloist in the song "All Good Gifts." The lyrics, which come directly from an old Episcopal hymn, go,

> *We plow the fields and scatter*
> *The good seed on the land*
> *But it is fed and watered*
> *By God's almighty hand*
> *He sends the snow in winter*
> *The warmth to swell the grain*
> *The breezes and the sunshine*
> *And soft refreshing rain*

The chorus says,

> *All good gifts around us*
> *Are sent from heaven above*
> *Then thank the Lord*
> *Oh thank the Lord for all his love*
> *(Matthias Claudius, 1782)*

Over the course of two or three years we did around 125 performances, which means I got up in front of a crowd as many times and told people how great God is. I only got into this play by cracking everyone up as a kid with my original version of Shirley Temple on crack. That and I could sing. But, of course, all of this was probably just a coincidence. I just happened to get in this play, and I just happened to sing through the parables of Jesus, and I just happened to watch a re-creation of the crucifixion 125 times. That kind of stuff just happens. Yeah right.

You can call it a coincidence if you want, but I can now see my role in *Godspell* as part of God's hand working in my life. It's like a friend of mine told me the other day, "Stephen," he said, "there's no way you could be a part of proclaiming the Gospel over and over and it not have an effect on you."

ACT III: 79TH STREET CROSSTOWN BUS

As far as I am concerned, this was the best act of all. It all came about because, once again, I was acting like an idiot.

One day when I was nineteen I was on a bus in New York City. I think I may have been going from my job slinging pizza in the East Village back to my apartment. Some of the details are a little fuzzy. On this particular day I noticed that a little kid kept staring at me. I guess he thought I was a freak or something. Obviously the kid was a good judge of character. So this little kid is sitting next to his mother, but his mother isn't paying any attention to him. She had her head buried in a magazine or something.

When I noticed this kid staring at me, I thought I could have some fun with it. I started making faces and acting like a goof, and my little audience loved every minute of it. He'd start laughing, which annoyed his mother, which led to a constant barrage of shushes. To me, it was business as usual. Play to the crowd. Make 'em laugh. And have a good time doing it.

I was having such a good time entertaining my tiny audience that I didn't notice this hot, sort of exotic chick on the bus. For Stevie B at nineteen to not notice a hot woman was itself an act of God. For that matter, for Stevie B pre-conversion to not notice a hot woman at any age was pretty much miraculous. However, on this particular day I didn't notice this woman. But she noticed me. She didn't say anything, but she noticed.

Fast-forward one month. Same bus line. Same time of day.

I'm on the bus, only this time there aren't any little kids to entertain. That's when I noticed her. How could I not? She looked amazing. For the rest of that bus trip I kept trying to find some excuse to strike up a conversation with her, which didn't take too long. By the time the bus reached her stop I had her name, phone number, and I'd asked her out on a date. After the first date I asked her out again, then again, and again.

We'd seen each other about three weeks when she said to me, "I need to tell you something." My first thought was, *Oh great, she's going to tell me she's a lesbian.* Instead she told me how she watched me make silly faces at the little kid with his mother. She thought I was cute and funny and liked kids, so she decided that she might like to meet me someday. When she saw me on the bus the second time she decided not to get off at her stop because she noticed I was looking at her. She waited five stops to see if I would say hello, which I finally did.

No woman in New York City ever stays on any form of public transportation any longer than they absolutely have to. So for this woman, a student at the Parsons School of Design, who looked like she did, to make that kind of decision about a guy like me, that my friend, is an act of God. But that's how I met my wife.

Now here's the Spielberg part of all of this; here's the part you couldn't script in a movie because it would be too weird. This woman I happened to meet on the 79th Street crosstown bus, this woman who stuck with me in spite of all the garbage I put her through during the first ten years of our relationship, this woman just happened to be from Brazil.

And for some strange reason when she decided to hire a housekeeper to help around the house after the birth of our first child, she decided to hire someone from Brazil even though she hadn't lived there since she was three.

And the housekeeper that her extended family in Brazil helped us find just happened to be a Christian who, before taking the job, asked her church to pray for her.

And in that prayer meeting someone just happened to receive a word from the Lord that told of God's plan for Kennya's and *my* life. I'll fill you in on all the details in the next chapter, but for now let me just say, what I thought was a chance meeting turned out to be the single most important moment of my life for more reasons than you can imagine.

If I hadn't decided to have some fun making faces at a little kid one afternoon while riding home on the bus, my life would not be what it is today. But it did happen because it all fit into God's script for the production which is the life of Stephen Baldwin.

ACT IV: BIO-DOME

I can honestly say that part of God's plan for my life was for me to ignore the advice of my managers and make a movie that was universally panned by the critics. Yes, God wanted me to star in a film about two brainless slackers who spend their days watching television, making out with their girlfriends, and drinking large quantities of various substances. While driving down the road drinking bladder busters, my character had to find a bathroom and fast. Mistaking a high-tech science experiment for a new shopping mall, my character and Pauly Shore's character find ourselves locked inside for one year with a group of nerdy scientists. Of course, two of the women are really hot. They always are in movies like this.

The film was brainless and pointless and hilarious and God wanted me to make it. I didn't think that at the time. Making *Bio-Dome* played right into my usual, let's have a good time attitude. God had other plans, I just didn't know it at the time.

When I say God wanted me to make this movie, I do not mean to imply that He approved of everything in the film. The film contains stuff that does not reflect the life I now live. I haven't even allowed my own children to see it.

I know some people think the movie kept my career from really taking off in the way it could have after *The Usual Suspects*.

People who think that don't realize that without *Bio-Dome*, I could not have the career I have today, and I'm not talking about movies.

The critics may have hated *Bio-Dome*, but kids loved it. They loved it when we first made it and they still love it today. Everywhere I go I have some kid in his late teens or early twenties come up to me and tell me that this is their favorite movie. Most have never seen *The Usual Suspects*, or *8 Seconds*, or *Fled*, or *One Tough Cop* or any of my other sixty movies, with the possible exception of *The Flintstones in Viva Rock Vegas*. But they've seen *Bio-Dome* over and over again. That's why God wanted me to make the film.

I didn't know it ten years ago when I agreed to become Doyle Johnson, but God had already called me both to know Him personally and to impact the youth culture in America with the Good News of Jesus Christ. I didn't know it because I didn't know Jesus at the time. One of the reasons kids will listen to me today is because they recognize me from the movies. But not just any movie. One movie: *Bio-Dome*.

God had me make this film to give me the platform that would later become my life's work. At the time I just wanted to goof off with Pauly Shore for a couple of months. God knew that, and He also knew the plans He had for my life, plans He made sure came to pass.

IN RETROSPECT

Did I know what God was up to while these things were taking place? Not at all. I can only see it now. But as I look back I can see each act playing out just as God wanted. He created me to know Him and love Him and sing His praises with my life. That's why He had me sing Psalm 23 back to Him when I was ten. He sent His Son to earth to save me. That's why He exposed me to His Son's words, death, and resurrection through *Godspell*. God planned for Kennya and me to know Him and serve Him together. That's why He brought us together through a chance meeting on a bus in New York City. And God called me even before I was born to take the message of Jesus Christ to the part of the youth culture in America most people overlook. That's why He opened a door to that very culture through a movie many of my advisors told me not to make.

Like I said at the beginning, you couldn't write this script. Only God could. Only God could pull off this production that is my life. Now here's the part that blows my mind: He does the same thing for everyone who will just open their eyes to see Him at work.

Redeem

Main Entry: **re·deem**

Pronunciation: ri-'dēm

Function: *transitive verb*

Etymology: Middle English *redemen*, modification of Middle French *redemer*, from Latin *redimere*, from *re-*, *red-* re- + *emere* to take, buy; akin to Lithuanian *imti* to take

1 a : to buy back : **REPURCHASE b :** to get or win back

2 : to free from what distresses or harms: as **a :** to free from captivity by payment of ransom **b :** to extricate from or help to overcome something detrimental **c :** to release from blame or debt : **CLEAR d :** to free from the consequences of sin

3 : to change for the better : **REFORM**

4 : REPAIR, RESTORE

5 a : to free from a lien by payment of an amount secured thereby **b** (1) : to remove the obligation of by payment <the U.S. Treasury *redeems* savings bonds on demand> (2) : to exchange for something of value <*redeem* trading stamps> **c :** to make good : **FULFILL**

6 a : to atone for : **EXPIATE b** (1) : to offset the bad effect of (2) : to make worthwhile : **RETRIEVE**

synonym see RESCUE

- **re·deem·able** /-'dē-mə-bəl/ *adjective*

CHAPTER 4

If 9-11 Can Happen . . .

In 1992, my wife Kennya and I were living in Tucson, Arizona, while I was starring in the television series, *The Young Riders*. Our first child was on the way and Kennya came to me and told me she wanted to hire a housekeeper to help around the house. I said, "Sure, whatever you want to do, go for it."

Instead of hiring someone from Tucson, my wife called her family and asked for their help in finding just the right person to come into our home and be around our soon-to-be newborn daughter. This was not unusual since most women ask their mothers and family for advice when making big decisions. The fact that my wife's family lived in *Brazil* made this search for a housekeeper a little out of the ordinary. Kennya was born in Rio, and even though her parents moved to New York when she was three, her roots remain in Brazil.

AUGUSTA

Through her extended family, Kennya found a housekeeper who agreed to move to the United States and come work for the Baldwins. My part in this process was in my own special and supportive way to stay as absolutely clueless as possible. *You want to hire a housekeeper?* Fine. *She's from Brazil?* Okay. Whatever you want dear. I need to go to work to shoot my television show now. Just tell me who to make the check out to. It wasn't that I didn't care. I was busy. And I knew my wife. Believe me, if I had been involved in the process I would have just been in the way.

After a few weeks of searching my wife found a fifty-five-year-old, six-foot-tall, very serious woman named Augusta whom we invited to come be our housekeeper. Of course, being from Brazil, she only spoke Portuguese. Not a problem for my wife. Me, I couldn't understand a word she said. Every day I felt like I do when my wife and mother-in-law talk about me right in front of me in Portuguese, only this was worse because now these conversations took place every day in my own home. But Kennya was pleased with Augusta, which meant I was as well.

Our new housekeeper worked hard, kept to herself, and did exactly what my wife asked of her. She did, however, have this one minor quirk. For the entire first week Augusta was with us she walked around our house singing in Portuguese. When she did the laundry, she sang. When she cooked, she sang. When she cleaned, she sang. All day, every day, she sang and sang and sang.

For me, it was no big deal. If she wants to sing while she works, good for her. Yet every song she sang was about Jesus. She would sing along in words I couldn't understand and then in the middle of every chorus I would hear her sing, *Jeeesssuuussss.* That much I could make out. Again, this was all cool with me. I was too busy to pay that much attention to anything our new Brazilian housekeeper might be singing.

However, after about a week of hearing *Jeeeesssuuuussss* every seven minutes or so, Augusta's singing became just a little unnerving to my wife. That's when Kennya came to me and asked, "Honey, did you happen to notice Augusta singing?" Being clueless I said no or whatever or something like that. Kennya filled me in on what I'd missed. She said, "Well, she is literally always singing about Jesus." I responded with an eloquent, *Huh. Good for her. I'm sure she needs that. God bless her*, and went back to work.

And I meant what I said.
God bless her.
If she needs Jesus, good for her.

It wasn't like I was anti-Jesus at that point in my life. I grew up Catholic, and although my family wasn't exactly devout, my brothers and sisters and I had gone through catechism and all of that as kids. One of my brothers had even been an altar boy. Along the way I'd read a little of the Bible. I found it interesting, but hard to understand. Maybe that's why I didn't pursue God back then. I don't know.

By the time I hit early adulthood and Hollywood I'd stopped thinking about God and religion and got busy being Stevie B. They called me the fun Baldwin and believe me, I tried to live up to the name. I dove into the Hollywood party scene with the drugs and alcohol and anything else that would help me have a good time.

Eventually this part of my life started interfering with the rest of my pursuits. I slowly started to understand that I had to make a choice between focusing on my career and potentially succeeding, or letting the drugs and alcohol kill me. Then Kennya came to me, and keep in mind this took place long before we were married, and she told me, "Babe, I can't do this anymore. You're cute. You're funny. You're a great kisser. But you disappear for three days at a time and I don't hear anything from you. I can't live like this."

That's when I joined a twelve-step program and heard I needed God myself. Step three of the twelve steps says, "Make a decision to turn our will and our lives over to the care of God *as we understand Him*," and that's what I did. I didn't have a choice, not if I wanted to get sober. And I did want to get sober. I wanted to do it for myself because I was tired of what the drugs were doing to me, and I wanted to do it for Kennya because I didn't want to lose her. Chicks change things. They really do.

By God's grace I have now been clean and sober for over seventeen years. I didn't pursue any kind of deep relationship with God, but He played enough of a role in my life back then that having my housekeeper walk around the house singing about Jesus didn't make me mad or cause me to dismiss her. God was cool. He helped me clean up my life. I wasn't anything close to being born again, nor did I think I ever would be. But if our new housekeeper wanted to sing about Jesus all day, I wouldn't hold it against her. Live and let live. Whatever.

After a few more days of listening to Augusta's singing, Kennya had finally had enough. She went to her and said, "You're doing a great job, but I couldn't help but notice your singing. I was wondering why every song is about Jesus. Perhaps you know some other songs you could sing as well." As soon as my wife said this, Augusta burst out in hysterical laughter. Kennya failed to see the humor in what she had just said. "I'm your boss," she said. "What is so funny?"

Augusta quickly straightened herself up and told my wife, "I apologize. I don't mean to be disrespectful, but I'm just so happy you noticed my singing. I'm very excited that you came over to me and asked me this question." By this point Kennya started to wonder about this woman's sanity. Then Augusta said, "Again, I mean no disrespect, but I find it quite amusing that you think I am here to clean your house."

"Okay, you're kind of freaking me out here," Kennya replied. "What do you mean you find it amusing I think you are here to clean my house? Why else would you be here?"

Augusta then proceeded to tell Kennya how before she accepted the job with us, she went to her church in Brazil for advice. Moving to a new country and starting a new life at fifty-five is a frightening prospect for anyone. Augusta hesitated in making such a drastic change, at least until she sought God's direction on the matter. Rather than offer counsel, her pastor invited the rest of the church to pray over her. In the midst of that prayer meeting a member of the congregation stood and said he had a prophetic word, that is, a message straight from the Lord through the Holy Spirit. This person said God wanted Augusta to go ahead and move to the States and start working for us.

But that was only the beginning. Augusta went on to tell my wife that God had told her through her church that if she came and worked for us, we would one day come to Christ and eventually have our own ministry.

Now Kennya was really freaked out. She muttered something like, "Oh, that's interesting. Excuse me," and ran to find me. Kennya walked into my office and said, "Honey, guess what Augusta just said? *We're going to become born-again Christians some day and have our own ministry!*" Now it was my turn to double over in laughter. All of this took place in 1993, nearly four years after I became sober and eight and a half years before the prophecy given to Augusta came true.

JOURNEY THROUGH THE WORLDLINESS

Augusta only worked for us a little over a year, but throughout her time in our home she and Kennya had long talks about God, Jesus and Augusta's faith. Up to this time in her life Kennya had never had a good reason to give God much serious thought. The idea that God Himself would speak to someone in a Brazilian church service about us got her attention. She started wondering if there might be something to Jesus, which led her to investigate the faith even more. Not only did she discuss God with Augusta, Kennya started reading the Bible on her own and occasionally attended Bible studies. Even after Augusta left us, she and Kennya kept in touch. What started as a curiosity slowly grew into something more.

As for me, I was busy making movies. *The Young Riders* ended after three seasons, but the success of the show led to parts in movies like *8 Seconds*, *Threesome*, and *The Usual Suspects*. Since we lived in Tucson I also played a lot of golf between films. Finding a way to hit a two-inch ball into a four-inch cup from four hundred yards away in four strokes or less takes a lot of time. Squeezing my wife and family into my schedule was hard enough without bringing God into it.

When our second daughter was born, Kennya and I decided to move back to New York. Both of us grew up there and we wanted our girls to be closer to their extended family. Not long after we moved back, Kennya, as a result of the steps toward God she'd already taken, plugged into a Brazilian church. This wasn't just any church. It was an extremely charismatic Brazilian congregation. For those of you who aren't familiar with church jargon, this means this was a church that *got down* for Jesus. Kennya felt at home there and kept going back.

Two years later Kennya came home, sat me down, and uttered those words every man instinctively fears: "Honey, we need to talk." She then proceeded to tell me she had given her life to Jesus Christ that night and had been baptized in water. While I sat there trying to figure out exactly what that meant, she hit me with this, "Stephen, we've been around the world. We have two beautiful kids. We made a lot of money and we've hung out with all sorts of famous people, and in the natural all of this is exciting. But . . ." and a long time ago I learned to dread the word but, "but," she said, "because I have now given my life to Jesus Christ, I am going to focus all of my energy on how I can best serve Him."

As she spoke, I kept looking at this woman, my wife of ten years, and she just seemed . . . different. She had a confidence, this strength, like nothing I had ever seen in her before. I don't know how to describe it except to say that I felt like I was in a Clint Eastwood movie and Kennya was Clint Eastwood. *I will be serving Jesus now. You got that? Punk.* I hugged Clint, I mean her, and tried to encourage her by saying something lame like, "Oh that's wonderful. Great." I was fine with her decision. I really was. Like I said, God was cool. I just figured Kennya could go do her spiritual thing and I would keep on making money and being a worldly idiot.

There was only one problem: The movie didn't end and Clint didn't ride off into the sunset. The change in Kennya wasn't some emotional high that she got over in a few days. The woman had changed. Dramatically. When she said she planned on serving Jesus she wasn't kidding. She served Him, all right, and she did it right in front of my eyes. But she didn't try to push her Jesus on me. She never wagged a finger in my face and told me I had better get right with God or else. Nor did she pressure me to go to church with her or attend any of her Bible studies. No, she did something far more dangerous: She started praying.

Every morning Kennya would get out of bed and immediately hit the floor. She would stay there, face to the ground, praying, for a solid hour without moving. I'd never seen anything like it in my life. Then, after praying for an hour she would get back in bed, grab her Bible, and read for thirty to forty-five minutes. Only then would she get up and get on with her day. At night she would do the same thing before going to bed. This went on for the next twelve months. That's right. After giving her life to Jesus, my wife spent two hours a day in prayer and at least an hour reading the Bible for one year. I don't say any of this to brag on Kennya. She didn't do this for any kind of recognition. She did it simply because God told her to.

I didn't know it at the time, but spiritually I was toast. Not only was Kennya praying for two hours a day, she was praying for me. God had me in His sights, and I wouldn't get away. Of course, I was clueless. All I knew was my wife had found God. I did not know He would soon find me.

A YEAR IN THE LIFE

My wife's year of prayer was, for me, the most powerful year of my life to that point. It didn't start out that way. The first morning I got out of bed and found Kennya curled up on the floor I thought she might be sick or something. Once I figured out what she was doing my first thought was, *Isn't that cute? My wife now loves Jesus.* And I went on with my day. I guess part of me kept waiting for her to get over this. After three months went by and she hadn't slowed down I started to think this might well be a permanent thing. Yet, at this point I still didn't think too much of it.

After six months, I stopped thinking stepping over my praying wife when I got out of bed as cute and started to find it more than a little annoying. Praying every day was one thing, but did she have to pray for *an hour*!? Was this a normal part of every Christian's routine? If so, I wondered how they got anything done. Plus, I got tired of having to wait for Kennya to finish this whole prayer regimen before we could get going. I would get out of bed and find her on the floor, facedown, praying, again, and say, "Okay, honey, come on, let's go. I need to get an early start. Make me an omelet. Let's go."

I tried to be supportive. Heck, I'd been supportive for six months. I didn't complain about the time she spent at church or the money she gave away to people I didn't know. Yet the longer this went on the more it began to get under my skin. *If you want to love Jesus, great, but can you cook my breakfast now?*

Nine months into this process I got out of bed one day, looked over at Kennya lying facedown on the floor, and said, "How do you do that? How do you stay in one position like that for an hour? That's insane." That's when it hit me. Now I'm no rocket scientist, I'm just an actor, but I've studied human behavior and psychology as part of perfecting my craft. I know enough to understand that the only way my wife could have this much discipline for so long is if something more than lying facedown on the floor is happening. The wheels slowly started turning inside my head and I came to this brilliant conclusion: My wife is having some kind of experience. And I'm not.

For the first time since Kennya had announced her intention to serve Jesus I started to feel like I was missing out. Something real and powerful and beyond my limited ability to understand was happening in my wife's life, and I wanted to know what it was. Again, she hadn't done anything to push God off on me except live out her faith. That was enough.

When I tell this story people sometimes ask why she never sat down and explained to me the full story of who Jesus is and what it means to know Him, as if to imply she shirked her duties as a Christian. People who ask this are dummies. They do not understand the power God unleashed in my home for a year through the living Gospel of my wife's life. She didn't have to preach at me, and if she had it wouldn't have done any good. Her life did all the talking. After nine months I finally started listening.

From the ninth month to the twelfth month I started exploring this Jesus Who Kennya loved so much. I started reading the Bible a little bit and I started praying in my own silly way. On Sundays I would even get out of bed and go to church with her. Not every Sunday, at least not in the beginning, but more and more as time went by. I still hadn't made a decision to follow Jesus, although I did pray what is called "the Sinner's Prayer" a couple of times. That's a prayer that acknowledges all the crap you've done and asks God to forgive you and take control of your life. I said the words, but I still hadn't come to the place where I was ready for God to take over every part of my life.

However, He ignited a curiosity inside of me. I wanted to find out more about Him, and more about Jesus. For the first time in my life I started to seriously consider the possibility that God was real. Yeah, I knew He existed. I knew there was a God. But there is a huge difference between believing a God exists out there somewhere and understanding that He will actually get involved in your life right now.

THE IMPOSSIBLE BECOMES POSSIBLE

One morning, at the height of my curiosity about God, two planes took off from Boston, turned left, and slammed into the World Trade Center in New York City. A short time later both towers collapsed. If you had asked me on September 10, 2001, if I thought something like that was possible I would have laughed and said no way. Not in 2001. Not in America. Stuff like that only happens in movies, and I make movies.

There was only one problem. It happened. Not only did it happen, but it also happened in New York, my hometown.

As I watched the impossible unfold right before my eyes, it rocked my world. People said on 9-11 that the world would never be the same again. For me, that is the truth. I still haven't gotten over it, but not for the reasons you might think. The terrorist attacks against the United States did more than anger me as an American. They showed me that anything truly is possible, and not in a good way.

I had always been one of those crazy, philosophical, artistic guys who would say, "Hey, *anything's* possible" in a flippant way. But I didn't mean it. I didn't think *anything* was really possible. I did after 9-11. That which I, at the core of my being, considered to be a total impossibility had now happened. After the planes hit the Twin Towers, for me, the word impossible no longer existed.

Leading up to the morning of September 11, 2001, God brought together a string of events that I thought were just random happenings. My wife had been a Jesus freak for a year now, and she'd spent that year praying for me. I'd been kind of reading the Bible and praying even though I kept trying to keep a safe distance between me and God. As I explored this curiosity I kept hearing how all of history would one day come to a conclusion and Jesus Christ would return to judge the earth and set up His eternal kingdom. That always sounded impossible to me, until the day the word impossible ceased to have any kind of meaning.

As I tried to sort all these thoughts out in my head I had an epiphany: Anything's possible, which means, Jesus Christ could come back tomorrow. And if that is true, where am I in my walk and in my understanding about God and the Bible and Jesus? The answer to that question led me to take the final step in this process God started when He sent a fifty-five-year-old, six-foot-tall Brazilian housekeeper to help clean our house. I gave Jesus complete control of my life and made that decision public by being baptized in water.

That final step didn't go down quite as nice and neat as it sounded in that last paragraph. On the surface everything looked wonderful. I prayed the Sinner's Prayer, again, and set the date for my baptism. Kennya and I sent out invitations to our friends and family to join us for this day of celebration. Like I said, on the outside, everything looked like a Norman Rockwell painting.

However, on the inside, me and God had a gut level, down and dirty, gloves off, knock-down confrontation. You see, this wasn't just some religious decision. Nor was it an attempt by me to find something solid in a world that had been knocked off its foundation. When I do something, I go at it with nothing held back. The last thing I want to do is waste my time on a lie. So me and God had to have a little talk.

In my mind I went outside and climbed on top of the biggest, gnarliest looking boulder I could find. When I reached the top I looked up at heaven, shook my fist and yelled at God at the top of my lungs, "Okay, buddy, this is how this is going down. You win. You've got me. All of me. And I'm not going to play games with this. I plan on being the greatest believer in You that there has ever been, and if that sounds arrogant, praise the Lord, because that's what I want to be. But let me just tell You," I screamed at God, "You better be real because if You aren't, You will regret the day You ever messed with Stephen Baldwin. If all this turns out to be nothing but a lie I will spend the rest of my life waging war against You. But if all this is real, and it better be real, I will serve You with everything I've got even if it means dying for You. If that's what it takes, I'm ready. But don't hold out on me. I want all of You."

Yeah, I Stephen Baldwin, didn't just decide to follow Jesus. I actually challenged Him to a fight. I threatened God—that's how passionate I am about this faith. But when I did, I made a covenant with Him. From that point forward He now had everything I am.

I shared this story at Willow Creek Community Church outside of Chicago and afterward a little old lady in her eighties came hobbling up to me leaning on a cane and said something I will never forget. She asked me, "Young man, I was just wondering, when you talked about pumping your fist at God and challenging Him with all your threats, during all of that could you hear Him up in heaven laughing?"

God spoke through that woman. I heard Him say through her, *Who in the heck do you think you are, Baldwin?* He put all the details of my story into perspective. I made so much noise about choosing God, that I didn't realize it was God Who searched for me. Of course He was real. If He wasn't I wouldn't have been on that boulder. But more than that, He reminded me that just as He arranged the first thirty-five years of my life to bring me to Himself, He would take care of however many years I might have left.

Yeah, I could hear God laughing, but He wasn't laughing at me as if I was some kind of fool. Instead I heard the laughter of a proud Father Who said, "That's my boy." He wanted me to climb up on that boulder and shake my fist at heaven. He wanted me mad, good and mad, because He wanted me to become more passionate about Him than anything else in my life.

So when this little old lady asked if I could hear God up in heaven laughing, I heard God say through her, "Go boy!" In my mind I pictured a guy holding back a raging pit bull with a muzzle and a choke collar at one end of a football field. On the other end stood a guy holding a stinky slab of steak. The moment the muzzle and the leash come off the dog, he attacks. That's how I felt. I was God's pit bull. And that is still how I feel. By the way, when I took off I ran right past the steak because I saw a herd of cattle, and when I got to the herd of cattle I saw a ridge and now I want to know what's on the other side. Once I make it past that ridge with God I'm going to see another one and I already know there's something more beyond that, and even more beyond that because, when it comes to Jesus Christ, this pursuit is never going to end.

Copyright
Main Entry: ¹**copy·right**
Pronunciation: -ˌrīt
Function: *noun*
: the exclusive legal right to reproduce, publish, and sell the matter and form (as of a literary, musical, or artistic work)

CHAPTER 5

Who's on First?

Okay gang, let's have some fun. Stop reading, put down the book, go to www.abbottandcostello.net and listen to the comedy routine *Who's on First* by Bud Abbott and Lou Costello. I would have put it in the book for you but the people who own the rights wanted so much for it that we would have had to jack up the price of this book. Since I wanted to keep the cost down to whatever you had to pay for it, I had to go the cheap route. So put down the book, go over to your computer and click on this site. Once you get there, click on "Media" on the main menu. When the media screen opens up, click on "audio clips" and scroll down until you find *Who's on First*.

You really need to listen to the routine to get the full effect, but, if you own a dinosaur of a computer like the one my secretary insists on using, that may not be possible. You will need to click on "routines" in the media menu, scroll down until you find *Who's on First* and read it. Do not pick this book back up until you do. I mean it. Don't even think of trying it or I may have to reprise my role of Officer Bo Dietl in *One Tough Cop* and take care of you, if you catch my drift. If these instructions don't work, just keep Googling until you track the routine down.

MY INNER COSTELLO

What does a sixty-something-year-old comedy routine have to do with the life and times of Stevie B, born-again-hardcore-radical for Jesus (besides the fact that I think *Who's on First* is one of the funniest things I've ever heard in my life)? If you haven't caught on to this by now, my brain doesn't exactly work like everyone else's. I'm just a little, what's the right word? Off. When I listen to Bud and Lou do this routine, it reminds me of my own spiritual journey. For thirty-five years I was Lou Costello. I was the guy standing there asking the same question over and over again, because I couldn't wrap my brain around the answer I kept hearing.

Now just in case you don't like to follow instructions and you didn't put down this book and go to the Internet, the routine goes like this (and I can't go into too much detail since I didn't want to pay what I considered to be a very high royalty rate to print the whole skit right in here in this chapter). Bud Abbott, the skinny guy, is coach of a baseball team. Lou Costello, the short, chunky guy, asks about the players on the team. Now, Abbott warns Costello that a lot of the guys on the team have funny names, which is the whole premise of the gag. So he starts running down the list, "Who's on first, What's on second, I Don't Know is on third. . . ." Costello stops him because these names don't make any sense to him. They don't sound like names, they sound like questions.

I've watched this bit on video and it is hilarious to watch the little guy get more and more frustrated. He keeps asking "Who's on first?" and Abbott answers, "Yes." The longer the conversation goes, the more annoyed Costello gets. All he wants to know is who is on first base, which of course, he is.

But Lou never gets it. His mind cannot comprehend the reality that Who could be a name as well as a question. Believe it or not, a guy named Who might actually play in a ballpark near you sometime soon. Chin-Lung Hu doesn't play first base.

Instead he plays shortstop for one of the Dodgers minor league teams. His name may be spelled different, but it is still pronounced Who.

Can you imagine that guy playing for the Yankees and hitting a home run to beat the Red Sox? Fifty-five thousand people in Yankee Stadium would chant, "Hu, Hu, Hu." Some poor guy would walk out of the bathroom and ask, "Who hit the homer?" and his buddy would say, "Yes!" Then the other guy would say, "What do you mean? Who hit the homer?" only to hear again, "That's right." Man, I wish that could happen. It would be the funniest moment in the history of baseball.

I got in touch with my inner Lou Costello one day while walking down the street in New York City. Right there in the middle of the West Village I had an epiphany. A thought ran through my head which said to me, "Isn't it funny that the answer to the questions I've always asked has been right in front of me all along? And that answer is God! God through faith in Jesus Christ has been the answer to everything. Even though He stood right in front of my eyes, I never saw Him."

This thought wasn't funny ironic, but laugh out loud funny. That's what I did. I started giggling while walking down the streets of New York. Anybody walking by me at that moment probably thought I was nuts, but hey, I am so I didn't worry about it.

In that moment I realized I was Lou Costello. All my life I had been frustrated looking for some sense of fulfillment and satisfaction. I always knew there had to be something bigger and greater going on around me, but I never knew what that might be. I kept asking, "What does this all mean?" and "What is my purpose?" and "What is the bigger plan behind this success I've had?" It wasn't until I found myself walking down the streets of New York that afternoon that the answer finally hit me: God is Who and faith is first base.

So what took me so long to get this obvious answer through

my thick skull? The answer was too obvious! God didn't sound like an answer to me. Of course I believed in God. Only an idiot could think this big, complex universe could just show up one day without God's help. And I knew God was there to help me when I needed Him. I paid attention during my twelve-step program. I knew how important God was for overcoming addictions. But in my mind that didn't make Him *the* answer for all of the questions I kept asking. To me, only religious freaks went overboard with the whole God thing and dedicated their entire existence to serving Him. Where is the fun in that? So I kept trying to have my fun and I kept looking around wondering what the point of it all was, and all the while the answer was right in front of me.

THE LOU IN YOU

Who's on First is funny because Lou never gets it. When he hears the words who, what, I don't know, why, because, today, tomorrow, and I don't give a darn, his mind is wired to interpret this data in one way. Yet Abbott uses the words in a completely different way. It is as though they are speaking two different languages, which in a sense they are.

Guess what? I see a lot of spiritual Lou Costello's running around today. They're confused because they still don't get it. They still don't understand that Who is God and faith is first base. This is a crazy chapter, I know. But the only reason this all sounds nutty is because you need spiritual eyes to understand both this chapter and the true nature of reality. You laughed at *Who's on First* (or you should have unless you are seriously humor impaired) because it is a play on words. I have discovered the comedy routine of life is written on a script that is a play on life. Reality is not what you think it is. The truth is right in front of you, if you can only see it.

But that's the problem. Most people never move from their Costello perspective to the Abbott perspective because they've been duped. The devil has created an environment in which we live and breathe and work and exist in what we think is reality. But it isn't. We're like Lou Costello listening to Bud Abbott tell us the first baseman's name is Who. We keep responding, Who can't be a name, who's on first? Then we groan about our miserable lives and ask "What's the point of it all?" Then someone tells us the answer is God, but we say God can't be the answer. He's just the first half of a curse word. We look for some hope in life, and we hear Jesus can give it to us. But to our ears that sounds nuts because Jesus is something you say when you hit your thumb with a hammer. We don't understand He is the Messiah. Heck, we don't even know what a Messiah is, much less why we need one.

Abbott's words sound ridiculous to Costello because his experiences and understanding keep him from comprehending what he is hearing. The devil pulled the same trick on the human race and duped the world into thinking faith is nuts. He's convinced people that it's complicated. And it is. Faith in Jesus Christ is so complicated because it is so simple. The experience you can have as a result of faith in Jesus Christ is so awesomely complicated because it is so simple.

The reason comes down to what I've said over and over in this book: You don't get the experience until you become willing to submit to it. If you sit back and wait for it to make perfect sense before you dive in you will never take the plunge. You'll stay stuck next to Costello forever, all the time wondering, Who *is* on first base?

So you are telling me that your experience of faith is an old vaudeville comedy routine? Yeah, kinda sorta. At some point I had to stop asking who's on first and simply accept the fact that Who is on first. And Who is God and first base is faith. Now, no matter what life throws at me, no matter how the script changes, the answer is always the same: FIRST BASE! No matter what the experience may be, faith is the first thought because you can't get to second or third or slide into home unless you've gone to first base.

Come on, Baldwin, it can't be that simple. Why not? Everyone wonders why they exist and what the purpose of their life might be. The answer is simple: first base. Run to first base, run to God in faith, and you will find what you're looking for. Or you can keep wandering around in left field muttering "Why?" It's your choice.

ROUNDING THE BASES

I have to remind myself of my little epiphany every day. Otherwise the truth I know doesn't get through my thick skull. God is Who, and first base is faith. Okay, God, I've got it. And then I read in the Bible that I am supposed to give ten percent of my income to God. The Bible calls this the tithe. I've got to tell you, there are a lot of times that I don't want to give ten percent of my income to anyone, even God. There are weeks when I just don't have the money, or at least that's what I tell myself. "Yeah, God," I say, "about that whole tithe thing, the money's kinda tight right now. How about I cut You a check later? Right now I've got these other things I need to take care of." Then I wonder why things keep getting tighter moneywise. Is the Lord punishing me for not giving? I don't know. Maybe. Or maybe He's just trying to get my attention because He's screaming at me, "Hey Baldwin, FIRST BASE!"

My wife likes to remind me of first base especially with my career. I spend anywhere between twenty-five and forty weekends a year doing *Livin' It* events. You don't have to be a mathematician to figure out that this ministry is pretty much my full-time job. But I still have this other little job on the side called Hollywood. Acting gigs pay the bills. Beyond that, I love what I do and I'm pretty good at it.

So when my Hollywood manager calls with a part I will get pretty excited about the possibilities and I'll go home and tell my wife about it. Kennya always asks me the same question and it absolutely drives me crazy: "Did you pray about that, Stephen?" Did I pray about it? Quiet, woman. This is a good part. This is a great opportunity. This will be really good for my career. "Did you pray about it?" I could pinch her because she is right. That's why you didn't see me playing Jennifer Garner's love interest on *Alias*. The part sounded great until I went to first base. God told me not to pursue it.

In every decision I make, in any situation in which I find myself, I always have to remember: First base. Before I do anything else I have to go to God and ask, "Lord, is this Your will?" Abbott and Costello didn't teach me this. The Bible did. James 4:13-17 says we should never assume anything when we make decisions. Instead we should take every decision to God. Whatever the question, the answer is always the same: First base. I don't even wait until I have to make a decision. I start off my day running down to first. Just like I wake up in the morning and brush my teeth and take a shower and grab a Q-Tip for my ears, I start off asking God to show me His will for that day. I tell God I love Him and then I ask, "What do You have for me today?"

This is what keeps me on track. Who? Jesus. Where? First base. What is that? Faith. It is as simple as that.

But life isn't simple. Once in a blue moon a hot-looking chick will come walking down the sidewalk and look at me and say, "Ooo yeah, look it's a Baldwin." I look at her and I say, "Have a nice day." As I keep walking I say to myself, *First base*. First base, baby, is the key no matter what the situation. It all comes back to God is Who and first base is faith.

You've got to listen to Bud and Lou do this. It is hilarious.

Control
Main Entry: ¹**con·trol**
Pronunciation: kən-'trōl
Function: *transitive verb*
Inflected Form(s): **con·trolled; con·trol·ling**
Etymology: Middle English *controllen,* from Middle French *contrerouler,* from *contreroule* copy of an account, audit, from Medieval Latin *contrarotulus,* from Latin *contra-* + Medieval Latin *rotulus* roll — more at ROLL

1 a *archaic* **:** to check, test, or verify by evidence or experiments **b :** to incorporate suitable controls in <a *controlled* experiment>
2 a : to exercise restraining or directing influence over **:** REGULATE **b :** to have power over **:** RULE **c :** to reduce the incidence or severity of especially to innocuous levels <*control* an insect population> <*control* a disease>
synonym see CONDUCT

CHAPTER 6

I Wake with a Smile

Every morning when I wake up my body goes through the same routine. I stretch and moan and groan and scratch and do everything else the body does to shake the brain back into reality. Once my eyes finally open and the squirrels in my head climb back in their wheel and my thoughts start turning again, a smile always breaks out on my face. Every single day. I'm telling you the truth. I wake up every morning with a smile on my face, and it's not because I suddenly realized how much money they paid me to make a fool of myself with Pauly Shore in *Bio-Dome*.

I wake up with a smile because I wake up with the knowledge and the understanding that God loves me and I believe He has an incredible day lined up for me. That may sound kind of cheesy coming from a guy who's played so many tough guys in the movies, but it's the truth. Once my brain becomes coherent my first thought is always a prayer: "Hey, Lord, what do You have for me today?"

And get this. Some mornings I wake up to the sound of God whispering in my ear. He gets the conversation going by saying, "Good morning, my son. I love you so much. Are you ready to go out and have some more fun today serving Me?" When this happens, I can't even describe the feeling that comes over me. How can anyone not wake up with a smile when their day starts like this? With Jesus, there is no wrong side of the bed. Every day starts off great.

I know what you are thinking. Of course I greet every day with a smile because I'm one of the lucky ones. I have it made. After all, I've made over sixty movies, cashed more big money checks at the height of my success than any one guy should, married way over my head, and have two beautiful daughters. Okay, I'll admit it. God's been very good to me. But guess what? Counting your blessings won't put a smile on your face day in and day out.

Before I entered into this experience with God I knew how blessed I was, but I didn't wake up with a smile. I woke up with the weight of the world on my shoulders and the burdens of life bearing down on me. Blessings don't insulate you from reality, and the fact is we live in a tough world. We make the world even tougher when we walk through it with the mistaken idea that we are somehow in control of our own lives. That's the biggest lie Satan ever pulled on the human race.

My smile came when I stopped trying to be in control and chose instead to turn my will over to the Lord. I get up and ask Him what He has in store for me today because this day and my life belong to Him. Back when I stood on the boulder in my mind, I told Him I would follow Him wherever He led me and do anything He asked no matter what. Each day I remember that vow before my feet even hit the floor.

WHERE HE LEADS

Asking God where He wants to take me each day has led me to some unusual places. At least they felt unusual to me.

Early on in this faith experience I went into the largest Christian bookstore I could find in New York City. Now before I tell you the rest of the story you need to keep in mind that I have a rather excitable personality. I do things for kicks that would scare the pants off of most people. I skydive and bungee jump, and those are a couple of my more calm and serene hobbies. I've raced cars and motorcycles, and not always on racetracks in sanctioned events, if you catch my drift. I don't do things like that today, although I've looked over to see more than one person white as a ghost and hanging on for dear life when I'm behind the wheel of a car. They say I drive through Manhattan like it's the last lap of the Indy 500. I say I simply enjoy a dose of adrenaline now and then. That's who I am and who I've always been.

So adrenaline junky me walked into the largest Christian bookstore in the city, whipped out my credit card and asked the clerk to load me up with all the really fun, hardcore, exciting, adrenaline-pumping, Christian cool stuff in the store. After the clerk picked himself up off the floor and wiped the tears from his eyes from his extreme fit of laughter, he informed me that what I was looking for barely existed. He led me to a tiny little shelf with a handful of books and DVDs that came close, but not many of them did much for this guy who drives 100 miles per hour while talking on two cell phones and eating a sandwich. Sure, there were a few products that tried to be innovative and cutting-edge, but I was looking for the really *hardcore* stuff, the skydiving kind of stuff.

I walked out of the store disappointed and a little disillusioned. Rather than complain to the store clerk I decided to take it up with God. "Yo, God, what's the deal here?" I said. This was sort of my own Ebonics version of the Lord's Prayer. "I told You I would follow You anywhere and do anything You wanted, but You've got to hook me up. You know how You made me. I like stuff that gets my heart pounding, but there isn't any cool Christian stuff like that. Why?"

God answered my prayer as clearly as if an audible voice had called out from heaven. "Okay, Stephen," He said, which was followed by a long and dramatic God-like pause. Once He had me straining to hear what He might say next, He asked, "What are you going to do about it?" Remember, I started that day and every day asking God to take me wherever He wanted me to go and show me everything He wanted me to do for Him. During my trip to the biggest Christian bookstore in all of New York City, God challenged me to start thinking about how to create the hardcore, fun, exciting, adrenaline-pumping, Christian cool stuff that I was looking for.

Not long after that God took me to an event called Beach Fest in Fort Lauderdale which was put on by the Luis Palau Association. There I saw a team of Christian skateboarders perform and share their stories of how they came to Christ. Imagine, I go to this huge, Christian festival with 300,000 other people and my expectations are pretty low.

But in the middle of what I thought would be this dorky, cheesy Christian deal, I see these gnarly skateboarders. As I'm watching these guys do their stuff, and dude, the tricks they pulled off were sick, I said, "Hey God, why don't I do something with these guys," to which I heard God say, *Why do you think I brought you to Fort Lauderdale in the first place, Einstein?!*

That experience led to a DVD called *Livin' It* I made with Kevin Palau. Not long after the DVD hit the streets we started receiving invitations from churches and other groups who wanted the skaters and BMX bikers on *Livin' It* to come to their town to perform and share their stories. There was only one problem: I didn't do that. Then God nudged me again and the *Livin' It Live* tour was born. In 2005 we spent twenty-five weekends on the road, sharing with over 50,000 kids and their parents and their siblings, with over 5,000 kids coming to Christ.

I didn't realize it at the time, but while I wasn't looking God dropped me into full-time Christian ministry, thus fulfilling the second half of the prophecy given to Augusta. I never saw it coming. Here's the really wild thing: I have no idea where God will take me next and I can't wait to find out. That's what waking up with a smile means to me. It means giving God permission to disrupt my life and turn all my plans upside down. I'm not calling the shots, He is.

Hold on there, Stephen. Are you telling me you now live your life without any certainty as to what you are going to do or where you are going to go or how you are going to get there? Yep. There's a verse in the Bible that says, "God's Spirit beckons. There are things to do and places to go! This resurrection life you received from God is not a timid, grave-tending life. It's adventurously expectant, greeting God with a childlike 'What's next, [daddy-o]?'" (Romans 8:14-15, MSG). That's the life I'm experiencing with God. That's what keeps that stupid smile plastered on my face. This is the gnarliest thrill ride I've ever been on. And it's not even about me. On this ride my life now matters. God is touching lives because little Poindexter Stevie B finally got smart enough to say to God, "You take over. I'm just along for the ride." How can I keep from smiling?

BAD DAYS

Does waking with a smile mean I'm always happy and never have a bad day? Yeah, right. Following Jesus doesn't mean He fills your life with nothing but sunshine and roses. Bad stuff happens to me just like it happens to you and everyone else. When it does I wrestle with the same emotions every normal human being feels. Phone calls in the middle of the night telling me someone I love just died shake me and leave me in tears. I experience setbacks and heartaches and all the other garbage that comes with life.

So many people think that since I'm famous I never have to worry about anything. They don't know that my annual income is now only one-quarter of what it was before I became a Christian. I have those days when bills pile up and companies call looking for the money I owe them. I don't enjoy those days. Who does? But that's life.

However, and this is the one thing you really need to get from this chapter, bad news phone calls in the middle of the night and all the unpaid bills in the world have absolutely nothing to do with waking up with a smile. What is going on in my life on the outside is irrelevant compared to what is happening on the inside. And it's on the inside where the smile begins, because that's where I make a choice to surrender my will to God's will.

When bad things happen, when life takes an unexpected turn for the worse, when the worst life can dish out lands right on top of me, those are the days everything else I've said in this chapter gets put to the test. I can hear God say in the middle of it all, "Okay, Stephen, do you believe I am really in control?" Yeah, Lord, I do. "Do you really believe I know what I am doing?" Yeah, Lord, I believe it. "Then trust Me."

That's what I choose to do, and when I do, the smile remains even when I'm hurting. The smile God gives has nothing to do with emotional happiness. He gives a joy that does not depend on the circumstances going on around me. It comes when I choose to surrender everything to God even when I do not know what He is doing. Knowing He is in control sets me free to truly enjoy life, even when life isn't too enjoyable. That's what makes this experience I'm having with God so incredible.

As I travel and talk with people, I find almost everyone wants the freedom I just described, but something keeps blocking their path. They want freedom from worry, but they look for it in the wrong places. People are always moaning about their depressing lives and saying stuff like, "If I could just hit the Lotto, then I would be happy." That's the stupidest thing I've ever heard. People think that if they could just have Puff Daddy's life, or P Diddy, or Diddy, or whoever, people think if they could have some other life hanging out with hot babes rubbing suntan lotion on their backs on South Beach, then they would be happy.

I even meet a lot of Christians who buy into this load of junk. They talk about God, but they still spend all of their time and energy trying to squirrel away nuts that don't last. I've had them come up to me and squeal something like, *Oh my gosh, I can't believe you aren't pursuing your career in Hollywood like you did before you were saved. Couldn't you have tried to change it from the inside and still made all those movies* and by inference, all that money. The simple answer is no, I couldn't. In my opinion you can't make money and success in this world your priority and still live a life that pleases God.

Like I said at the beginning of this chapter, what you have has absolutely nothing to do with real, lasting joy. But people make themselves miserable by spending all their time whining about what they don't have and how life hasn't been fair and how if they would just catch a break once in a while, then they too could find true happiness. Not true. When you think that you have fallen for one of Satan's biggest lies.

You don't need more stuff and you don't need a hotter wife, you just need to get over yourself and surrender your will to God. Only then will you discover the joy I'm talking about.

Does this mean that I've perfected the art of depending on God and I never struggle with trying to live my life my way? What do you think?

Not long ago I got together with some old friends. I've known these guys from when we grew up together in Massapequa, long before I went to Hollywood. So we go hang out and I'm one of the only Christians in the group. If I had focused on what God wanted me to do in this situation I would have worked really hard to show them through my actions how much God has changed my life. Instead I was a loud, obnoxious jerk, just like I was back in the day. Then, right in the middle of the evening, I made a rude comment that made me cringe the second the words came out of my mouth. All I could think was, "Did I ever just blow it! I'm such an idiot."

Now here's the amazing part of the story. As soon as I confessed my sin to God, He forgave me. When I woke up the next morning, He was waiting for me with the same invitation He makes every morning, "Are you ready to go have some fun serving Me today?" Immediately this verse from the Bible came into my head: "Because of the Lord's great love we are not consumed, for his compassions never fail. They are new every morning; great is your faithfulness" (Lamentations 3:22-23).

My making a fool of myself and a mockery of my faith the night before didn't cancel out the love God has for me or the plan He has for my life because His mercy is made new every morning. You might be sick of hearing this by now, but once that knowledge hit me squarely between the eyes, I couldn't stop smiling. He's in control, even on those days I try to act like He's not.

THE BIG LIE

The day I finally understood I wasn't in control of my life and that I never really had been was one of the most liberating days of my life. But when I tell people about it they usually don't have a clue what I am talking about. Everyone likes to think they control their own destiny. Hey, man, I walked around for thirty-five years thinking I called the shots in my life. That's what we all want to think. *I am in control of my life. I have a choice. I have a free will. I can do whatever I want whenever I want to do it and drop dead if you don't like it.* I used to think this. And I was wrong.

My experience in Jesus has shown me that the free will you think you have outside of God is a lie from Satan. *Hey, Baldwin, don't push your religion on me!* Okay, I won't. But don't complain to me about your miserable life.

You don't have to believe me. After all, this is just my opinion. But since this is my book, I have even more to say on this subject. I believe, based on my understanding of the Bible and my experience with God, that Satan has devised a system in this world that he uses to keep people right where he wants them. He has fed the world a line of bull and we swallowed it whole. This big lie tells you that you have a choice; you have an autonomous, independent, free will that can choose to do anything you want, as long as that choice doesn't involve God.

Satan doesn't want you to think God is even an option. He slithers up to your ear and whispers things like, "You aren't going to let that guy run over you again, are you? You don't have to put up with that." Or, "Go ahead and have your way with your secretary. Why not? She's hot, and she wants it. You deserve it. It doesn't matter as long as your wife doesn't know, so go for it."

Every day as you live in this world system you face all sorts of multiple choice exams of what you want to do. The problem is, the guy who's issuing you the test is Satan. He is so good at what he does that he has convinced you he's just a facilitator of that class when he's really the freaking dean of the college. He wants to convince you that you are really the professor, that you're the one with all the knowledge and the options, and that you are the one calling the shots. In reality he wrote the curriculum; he laid the college foundation and laid the bricks for every building. He built the whole system that controls you like a puppet on a string, and you have no clue. You think you are in control, that you are in charge, and all the while you are doing a little jig as he pulls your strings.

I know, I know, Baldwin doesn't know what he's talking about. After all, I'm just an actor, a dumb jock, a lucky bum from Long Island who happened to become famous. Why should you listen to me? I could be completely wrong. But if I am, why is it that everyone I've ever met has some sort of bad habit they can't break, something they are ashamed of but powerless to do anything about? You know I'm telling you the truth. Every person has a dark side they try to keep under wraps, but it always comes out. Some dirty little secret or hidden fear will eventually come out.

If you are in control of your life like you claim, why don't you do something about it? You know the answer. You don't because you can't. It seems it can't be that simple, but it is.

The big lie Satan pushed off on the world is what keeps most people from experiencing the joy I've described in this chapter. I know because I've been there. You read my story of how I came to faith. I'm still the new guy when it comes to God. It wasn't long ago I scrambled around with the rest of the rats trying to grab my share of the hunk of cheese.

I don't think I am now better than the poor schmucks who are still trapped in the maze. I know better than that. I didn't wake up one morning and figure this all out for myself. God changed me, I didn't change myself. He showed me how He is in control and told me the only way I could be completely free is to surrender my will to His, so I did. He tells me in the Bible to present myself to Him like a sacrifice and to stop conforming to the world system. When I choose every morning to let Him have His way with my life, I am agreeing with God that I need to be different from the world and I'm asking Him to change me. I admit I am too weak and powerless to change myself. I wave the white flag and ask God to do for me what I could never do for myself.

You know what, dude, your whole Jesus thing is just your way of being a big wuss, a weak little pussycat who can't handle life in the real world. No, dude, your lack of willingness to attempt the Jesus way just shows you've been blinded by the king of all lies. I tried it your way. I tried to find happiness in the world system of take, take, take. It didn't work. But in choosing to surrender my will to the will of God, I found something that does. I wake up with a smile. Why would I ever want to turn back now?

Covenant

Main Entry: ¹cov·e·nant

Pronunciation: 'kəv-nənt, 'kə-və-

Function: *noun*

Etymology: Middle English, from Middle French, from present participle
of *covenir* to agree, from Latin *convenire*

1 : a usually formal, solemn, and binding agreement : COMPACT

2 a : a written agreement or promise usually under seal between two or
more parties especially for the performance of some action **b :** the
common-law action to recover damages for breach of such a contract

---

CHAPTER 7

She Never Has to Worry Anymore

I was on an airplane not long ago and the in-flight video in-
cluded a segment from an A&E special on Neil Simon, *the*
greatest American playwright of all time. He's won the Pulitzer
Prize and Tony Awards and found more financial success than
anyone in his field, ever. So this A&E special comes on and I
watch it.

In the middle of the special, the greatest American playwright of all time started talking about the failure of his first
marriage. I will never forget what he said. Neil Simon looks at
the camera and says, "And you know, in marriage, when things
just start falling apart, there is just nothing you can do about it."

With all due respect Mr. Simon, if you knew the awesome
power of God and His Holy Spirit you would understand how
wrong that statement is. I know because I've experienced that
power in my own marriage, and it is beyond words.

Now, I don't claim to be some kind of genius on marriage.
I'm just a guy this publishing company was crazy enough to
hand a book contract, but I can tell you what I've experienced.
Few people ever worked harder to make a mess of their marriage than I did mine. I crossed lines I never should have even

approached, much less crossed. Luckily (and I know it wasn't luck but God working in my life even before I knew Him) I married a patient, forgiving woman who put up with more than she should have. Why she did it I do not know, except to say that it was God. Pure and simple. Long before either Kennya or I came to Christ, God worked to keep our marriage together when so many Hollywood marriages fail miserably. If He did that without our permission, imagine how our marriage changed when we invited the Holy Spirit into every aspect of our married life.

That is why, with all due respect to Mr. Neil Simon, the greatest American playwright of all time, I find the statement "And you know, in marriage, when things just start falling apart, there is just nothing you can do about it," to be absolutely, 100 percent bogus. I say that because thousands of people out there who watched this interview probably think he is right. As a result, when things start going south in their own marriages, instead of working hard to fix them, they will simply throw up their hands, give up, and say, "Oh well. There's nothing I can do. After all, if a genius like Neil Simon can't make a marriage work, what chance do I have?"

If Kennya and I had adopted this attitude our marriage would have ended a long time ago. More than once things started falling apart in our marriage. I helped the process by engaging in behavior that should have made our marriage crash and burn. But not only did it not end, Kennya and I are happier, more committed, and more in love with one another today than at any time in our lives. If God can do that for my marriage with all the baggage I tossed into it, He can do the same for anyone.

A SPIRITUAL BATTLE

Okay, okay, I can hear you already. *Who do you think you are, Dr. Phil? What makes you an expert on marriage, you dumb actor?* I agree. Who do I think I am? I never studied interpersonal relationships in college. I don't have some advanced degree in psychology or sociology or counseling or anything else. So if you don't want to listen to what I have to say, fine. But if you have the guts to hear me out I know you will be glad you kept reading. This opinion isn't just something I thought up one day while hanging out on a movie set waiting to shoot my next scene. I lived this. I experienced the transforming power of the Holy Spirit in my marriage, and I had God open my eyes to the truth about the lies I used to swallow hook, line, and sinker.

That's right, truth. Yeah, I know I said this was only my opinion, but I also happen to think this little opinion of mine is based on the eternal truths of God's Word, the Bible. This is God's opinion as well, and His opinion is never wrong.

The first truth I learned after God threw on the lights in my understanding is this: The battle to save a marriage is a spiritual battle. There are invisible, spiritual forces at work in the lives of every human being on the planet even though most people have no idea there's a battle going on around them. As with any battle, there are casualties and the number keeps climbing every day. Between 1970 and 1996 the number of divorced people in America quadrupled from 4.3 million to 18.3 million.[1] The marriage rate has fallen nearly 30 percent since 1970 while the divorce rate has increased about 40 percent.[2] And how's this for a kicker. Statistics show the Bible Belt states have the highest divorce rates.[3]

I've traveled around the world and I've seen these same forces at work in every culture in every country. You can see them most clearly in the prevailing attitude about men and sex, an attitude that permeates every culture. Most people believe that men engage in sexual activity outside of marriage simply because they can't help themselves. That's just how we are. We're animals. Once a man gets a scent of pheromones, hormones fire up, that natural sex drive kicks in, and the male of the species just can't help himself. People around the world believe this lie, not just because we hear it in the media, but because Satan keeps feeding this pack of lies to us. More and more the same can now be said of women.

Not long ago I was talking to a very intelligent and successful guy and the conversation turned to travel. We compared notes about the places we'd been, while this guy's wife and seventeen-year-old daughter stood next to him listening to the whole conversation. At some point the guy asked me if I'd ever been to Thailand, and I said yes. Then he asked if I'd ever been to Bangkok, and I said yeah. He then let out a sly little laugh, and said, "Boy is that a great culture or WHAT?" His daughter shot him a look, but he pretended not to notice and said, "There's nothing quite like getting a massage in Bangkok, is there?"

His tone of voice and the stupid giggle he let out as he said this made it clear he really enjoyed the Thailand custom of every massage ending "happy," if you know what I mean. And he said this right in front of his wife and daughter. When he did, his daughter said, "Oh, yeah, that's a real nice thing to say in front of Mom."

I'll never forget his reaction. He said, "Oh come on. What's the big deal? Take it easy. It's just a custom, that's all. You know, when in Rome." I honestly think the guy believed what he said. He didn't see anything wrong with a massage having a "happy ending." After all, it was just sex. What was the big deal?

This is just one example of what I believe is the very accepted and unspoken perspective on how men behave that sociologically breeds this kind of misbehavior. This is more than an attitude toward sex. This unspoken perspective is a spirit. The presence of sin in the world, and the spiritual and moral blindness that comes with it unleash this spirit into the world. But it's not as if it has to work very hard. Like every other lie Satan tells, this attitude toward sex tells people exactly what they want to hear, especially men. Men want to think having a little action on the side is normal, natural, perfectly acceptable behavior.

Women feed this spirit by putting up with this kind of conduct in their men and even engaging in it themselves. Somewhere in the world right now two women are sitting down, drinking coffee, and one woman will say to the other, "I think my husband is into his secretary." I guarantee you there are friends out there who will tell this distraught wife, "Don't worry about it. It will be all right. It's okay. He's just a man. It's normal. They're animals, they have to hunt." I've heard this from society and the media and textbooks my entire life.

People just accept immoral behavior as normal. They regard the little flirtations and the roaming eyes as nothing more than "boys will be boys." Wives feed the monster by letting their husbands read magazines that, even if they aren't pornography, they might as well be. All of this opens the door to lust and enables the spiritual forces of darkness to have a field day.

Hey, lighten up man. This isn't such a big deal. If everyone is cool with it, what's the harm? Everyone isn't cool with the sexual climate of our culture today. Why do you think so many marriages end in divorce?

Many marriages don't have a chance from the very start because of one of our cherished American customs: the bachelor party. What a twisted way for most of American wives to start their marriages. "Oh, he's going to go have a bachelor party and I am never going to know what happened there." Why do women put themselves through this? When you do you are already starting your marriage with a question and a doubt. *But it's a tradition. It's just the way it is.* No, it's sick, and it doesn't have to be this way. Yet, the acceptance of the bachelor party mentality and the whole, *What happens in Vegas stays in Vegas* attitude are symptoms of a much larger, spiritual problem. That's the first truth God opened my eyes to in my own marriage.

MORE THAN A PROMISE

Magazines and the Internet are crawling with moronic marriage quizzes that are supposed to help you figure out your mate. Well I've got a quiz for you. If you lined up 100,000 people and asked them what their marriage vows really meant, I believe most would have no idea. For the majority of people, wedding vows are just part of the ceremony. That's why people find them so easy to break. "Love, honor, and cherish 'til death do us part . . . ," are just words the preacher told you to repeat. That's it. They are just so many sounds that spilled out of their mouths. Nothing more. Most people have no idea what these words mean or their ultimate purpose in marriage. I know I didn't for the first dozen years of my marriage.

Then one day a light flickered on. After my conversion, someone told us that marriage is like a pyramid with God at the top. The closer we get to Him the closer we will be to one another. So we tried it. Kennya and I started praying together and discussing the things God was teaching us in His Word. It worked. Putting God in the center of our marriage made a huge difference.

But that by itself wasn't enough. God showed me something more. One of the words the Bible uses over and over to describe the vows people make to one another is the word "covenant." It appears over three hundred times in the New International Version of the Bible. Whenever someone in the Bible entered into a legal contract with another person, they made a covenant with them. Back then, they didn't just shake hands. Part of making a covenant with another person was taking an animal and whacking it in half. Then the two people making the covenant, who would now be covered with blood from the animal, would step between the two halves of this dead ox or sheep and bind themselves before God to keep their word. People even did this when they sold an acre of land. Today, we just wave away an acre, but back then the whole process was part of this solemn ceremony which called God in as a witness.

I don't remember where I was or what I was doing at the time when this truth finally hit me. Wherever I was I started thinking about Kennya and all God had done in our relationship. Then I started thinking about those words the preacher told me to repeat as I slipped the wedding ring on her finger.

For the first time in my life I finally understood that when I made my marriage vows, I was making a covenant not only with Kennya, but also with God. I wasn't just telling her I would stick with her until death; I was binding myself before God to keep my word.

This was the second truth about marriage God taught me after my conversion. Marriage is a covenant. In the Bible, the people making a covenant would cut an animal in half as a way of telling God to do the same thing to them if they didn't do what they said they would do. When I stood in front of a church and repeated my wedding vows, I was telling God the very same thing. I promised him I would love, honor, and cherish Kennya. No, I didn't know that's what I was doing, but let me tell you, ignorance is no excuse.

Hey gang, once God turned on the lights of my understanding to the true nature of this wedding covenant, everything changed. The vows I made are sacred, and not in some touchy-feely Hallmark card way. I mean sacred as in a promise I made to Almighty God. Once I understood this truth, I was then able to let God change me and my marriage. I didn't do this because divorce is so messy and so expensive, and not because I wanted my children to grow up in a strong home, and not because of any of the other reasons people give for trying to strengthen their marriage.

My understanding of the divine nature of the marriage covenant means I now sought God's healing power in my marriage as an act of love for Him. Anything less wouldn't cut it, not in the understanding of the Bible God has given me. His Word tells me to love the Lord more than my wife. That's why my vow to Him comes first, and my efforts to be a better husband and father are acts of obedience to the God I love more than my wife or kids. This perspective set me free to really love them in a way I never could before.

I don't say all of this because I'm better at this than you. If I said I didn't struggle I would be lying. Thirty-five years of bad habits are hard to break, but the understanding God has given me has changed my perspective completely. Now I understand that if I let my eyes glue themselves to some woman's chest as she walks down the street, I'm not just betraying Kennya, I'm betraying my God. That's the negative. The positive is much stronger.

When I understand my vows are a sacred covenant I made with God, I then invite God to pour Himself into my marriage and bless us like we've never been blessed before. The results of that, my friend, are un-freaking-believable. Not only has God given us a spiritual intimacy I never imagined possible, not only has He transformed our friendship so that I only thought we were close before, He has also empowered the physical aspects of marriage and taken it to new, holy heights (I want to thank my writing partner for finding such a proper way of putting that).

I like to ask friends of mine, happy couples who seem to have a pretty good marriage, "How's your sex life?" They will say something like, *pretty good* or *okay* or *no complaints here*. Here's what I tell them: Imagine taking a healthy sex life and inviting the power of God into that exchange?

You can't talk like that! How dare you mix God and sex. Hey, listen, I'm not the one who did that. God did. Go read the book of Song of Solomon in the Bible. That book is steaming. It should have an R-rating. Keep the kids away from it because it may give them some ideas. Don't believe me? Read it for yourself.

The fact that one entire book of the Bible is dedicated to

romance and sexual intimacy between a husband and a wife shouldn't surprise anyone since *God invented sex in the first place!* How's that for a radical idea? God wants married couples to have a hot sex life. Why else would he tell Adam and Eve to "be fruitful and multiply"? What do you think he was telling them to do, go watch *Matlock* reruns? Come on. God intended couples to give themselves to one another completely in sex, as well as give themselves to Him.

Through the anointing of the Holy Spirit, the act of physical intimacy becomes a very unique form of prayer and an expression of gratitude to God. I won't go into any details about Kennya's and my personal experience, because that's none of your business, but let me simply say that I had no idea what love and sex were supposed to be before I came to Christ. And as I've said before, my life B.C. was pretty great.

THE DECISION TO LOVE

God taught me a third truth that radically altered my view of marriage. Back before Christ took over my life, I thought I had certain rights within my marriage. If I wanted to hit the clubs or go hang out with my boys until who knows when, what was the big deal? Like I said when I talked about going to the Playboy mansion in an earlier chapter, my philosophy was that as long as I wasn't misbehaving, I could do whatever I wanted. If it ticked Kennya off, too bad for her. She just had to get over it because this was just the way it was.

That wasn't even her biggest beef with me. Back then Kennya would tell me that I was disconnected from her and our girls. Even when I was physically present, mentally and emotionally I was somewhere else. I would be home but I would be on my computer, watching TV, talking on the phone, trying to do whatever I could to escape the pressure of my life.

After coming to Christ, Kennya and I found in the Bible where God compares the relationship He wants to have with people with the relationship between a husband and a wife. The Bible says Jesus is the bridegroom, and believers are His bride, see Revelation 19:7. This means that in a Christian marriage, the home is like a living picture of the love of Christ. Then I discovered a verse in the Bible, Ephesians 5:25, which told me I had to love my wife in the same way Jesus loves me. That, my friend, blew me away. It also altered my understanding of what love means.

Love can't just be an emotion, because you can't order someone to feel an emotion. Instead, the love Jesus tells me to show Kennya is a choice I make. It means that instead of pushing my weight around and doing what I want, I put her and her needs first. I can't even think about putting my career first, not if I'm going to love her like Jesus loves me. Could you imagine Jesus saying, "Yo, Stevie B, I know you need Me to do something about your sins, and I really intend to get around to dying on a cross, but I need to close this deal first. But, believe Me dude, I'll get to it. Eventually." If Jesus wouldn't do that to me, I can't do that to my wife.

Loving my wife like Jesus loves me doesn't come naturally. Thankfully the Bible tells me what I am supposed to do.

1 Corinthians 13 says:

Love is patient, love is kind. It does not envy, it does not boast, it is not proud. It is not rude, it is not self-seeking, it is not easily angered, it keeps no record of wrongs. Love does not delight in evil but rejoices in the truth. It always protects, always trusts, always hopes, always perseveres.

According to God, when you love someone, this is what you do. And this is what God expects Stephen Baldwin to do every day for his wife. I used to let my desire to serve myself set my agenda. That won't fly anymore. God not only expects more out of me, one day I will have to stand before Him and answer for how I treated my wife.

Loving my wife like Jesus loves me has changed my approach to everything, especially my career. It's not just that I put her before making movies. My commitment to her has changed the types of roles I now accept. During my career in Hollywood I made a lot of movies that had some pretty graphic scenes. Even though I wasn't really having sex with the women on screen, the way the scene played out in the picture put a huge strain on my marriage. Before you pass this off as no big deal, put yourself in my wife's shoes. I would take my wife to a premiere of one of my pictures, and she would have to sit there in the dark watching as her husband got naked with some hot chick. To say it made her uncomfortable would be an extreme understatement. After a while she stopped going to the premieres with me.

There is almost no way humanly possible to watch the person you love engage someone else intimately and not be bothered by it. That is just not normal. And yet, the Hollywood industry breeds this sort of ideology. *Hey, relax, it's just acting. It's no big deal. It's okay.* Well if it's okay, then why do so few Hollywood marriages make it?

You can count on one hand the number of high-profile celebrity marriages that survive, but those that haven't read like a who's who of the Hollywood elite. Paul Newman and Joanne Woodward's marriage has lasted fifty something years, but Drew Barrymore and Jeremy Thomas barely lasted one month. Her marriage to Tom Green only lasted five months. Statistics show male actors are twice as likely to end up in divorce court as the non-celebrities, while women are fifty percent more likely to have their marriages fail. Yet within the industry that's just an accepted behavior, and it has been since silent film superstar Rudolph Valentino's marriage to Jean Acker lasted all of six hours.

Of course, adopting the biblical philosophy of love and

marriage puts me at odds with business as usual in Hollywood. I've been on movie sets where one co-star is sleeping with another even though both are married to other people. Hardly anyone on the set acts like this is anything out of the ordinary. In fact, most of the time the crew jokes around about it. If news gets out about the little affair, all the better. The publicity will create more buzz for the movie. In Hollywood, for the most part, no one cares if a marriage crashes and burns. There are some people who believe that a failed marriage is a small price to pay if Brad's affair with Angelina can jack up the box office.

I refuse to live that way. God has changed me. Thankfully He did it before I crossed one line too many. Kennya never has to worry about me anymore. I'm sorry she ever did.

Heaven

Main Entry: **heav·en**

Pronunciation: ˈhe-vən

Function: *noun*

Etymology: Middle English *heven*, from Old English *heofon;* akin to Old High German *himil* heaven

1 : the expanse of space that seems to be over the earth like a dome : FIRMAMENT — usually used in plural

2 a *often capitalized* : the dwelling place of the Deity and the joyful abode of the blessed dead **b** : a spiritual state of everlasting communion with God

3 *capitalized* : GOD 1

4 : a place or condition of utmost happiness

By permission. From *Merriam-Webster's Collegiate® Dictionary, Eleventh Edition* ©2005 by Merriam-Webster Inc. (www.Merriam-Webster.com).

CHAPTER 8

My Heaven Is Now

One of the biggest perks of this experience I am having with God is the knowledge that it never has to end. I will enjoy this relationship with Him forever. When I buy the farm, my life will only get better, which sounds pretty frickin' crazy when you think about it. When I die my life only gets better? That doesn't make any sense, unless you have eternal life, which is what God gives you when you give your life to Him. Then, when this flesh and blood package that contains Stevie B quits ticking, my real life in the Spirit really gets rolling. Yes, I, Stephen Baldwin, being of sound mind and body, honestly believe that there is a heaven and that I will go there when I die.

But that's not what my experience with God is about right now.

I've been around people who constantly talk about heaven and hell and eternity and all of those churchy words. Don't get me wrong. I take the reality those words describe very seriously. Like, for instance, hell. I think it is pretty funny that some people believe war is hell. Well, guess what? War is not hell. Hell is hell, and I'm not sure how gnarly hell is going to be, but one thing I think some idiots are not taking into consideration is that it's FOREVER. And I'm not quite sure but I think that's probably going to suck. But I'm never going to find out, praise God.

However, when I hear a lot of Christians talk about heaven, to my ears it sounds like that's all they have going for them. "Well, when I die I will go to a better place, blah, blah, blah." And all I can say to these people is, Dude, what about right now?

Eternal life doesn't start when you die. It just relocates. God gave me a whole new life the second I asked Jesus Christ to save me. That's when my eternal life began. I don't have to wait until I die to start enjoying it. Jesus said He came so that I might have life to the full, and baby, that's what I want. When I made my covenant with God, I told Him I wanted the full load, nothing held back. If God has it, I want it. I'm not talking about getting more stuff. I've had stuff. I'm talking about life in the Spirit. And that's what I am experiencing now.

I didn't write this book so I could tell you about something really great that awaits you thirty, forty, fifty years down the road, or however long you have left on earth. I wanted to write this book so I could share with you the greatest experience I've ever had, an experience so much better, and so far beyond anything that has ever happened to me, that I still can't believe I'm living it.

Yes, I look forward to going to heaven someday. I sure don't want to live on this messed-up planet forever. To see Jesus face-to-face after loving Him from afar for so long is going to be awesome. But let me tell you, because of the experience I am having with God right now, in a very real sense, my heaven is now. And I'm not alone.

Not long ago I talked a good friend of ours into coming to one of my *Livin' It Live* events. Now keep in mind she is a pretty intense Jewish gal. She knew this was a Christian event, but I'd talked so much about *Livin' It* that she wanted to see for herself what it was all about. During the day she hung out at the skate park, watched the team do all their tricks and listened as they shared their testimonies. Later, she came with Kennya and me to a VIP event service with the *Livin' It* team and several people from the Palau organization.

That's where my friend, the intense Jew, found herself trapped in a room with around fifty evangelicals who were doing the whole Christian fellowship thing big-time. After a while one of the guys running the event got up and asked if anyone there would like to say something. I glanced over and saw my friend raise her hand. This Jewish woman who just happened to come to this event for the fun of it, got up and said, "I'm a Jew. I'm not even supposed to think the word Jesus, but I've got to tell you I am genuinely starting to understand that you people are experiencing something that I have not experienced through my faith."

THE PRESENCE

My friend has never experienced anything like this through her faith because this is an experience only Jesus can deliver. I sometimes describe this experience as skydiving without a parachute, but I need to explain what that really means.

My life before I came to Christ was also a free fall. I feel like I stood at the edge of an empty elevator shaft with the doors thrown open. If I leaned my head into the shaft and looked up, I could see the brightness of heaven. But when I looked down all I could see was black. That darkness was my soul. I just never realized how deep the darkness could be. But I didn't get that then.

As I stood peering down into the darkness, my natural thoughts told me the black of the shaft represented opportunity. I didn't need God. Instead, what I needed to do to really enjoy life was to back up about a hundred yards from the shaft, put on my track shoes, and run as fast as I could toward the shaft and dive in. Talk about skydiving without a parachute, this was it. As I tumbled deeper and deeper into myself, the world kept telling me that what I really wanted to do was go faster. If I could just pick up more speed then I would have it all. The success, the money, the fame, all of it made me want to go farther and farther down, not into some particular sin, but into myself.

I've already talked about how I came to realize that I didn't want to keep going in this direction. That's when I said a prayer asking God to save me. Do you know what happened? My life felt like a wind came up beneath me and lifted me out of the darkness and saved me from falling deeper into myself. Then the wind carried me back to the floor from where I had jumped. When my feet touched the floor I heard a voice say, "Now stay here buddy. Take the track shoes off. Relax. Stretch a little, and wait to hear from Me. And if you do what I tell you, you will get a chance to put the shoes back on and dive back into the shaft. Only instead of falling down into yourself, I will raise you up and let you fly into Me."

This is my new skydiving experience. This is my heaven now. The experience I enjoy today comes through this wind that carries me upward, this presence that is the Holy Spirit. I may have jumped out of the airplane without a parachute, but now I am soaring, not falling. There's more to this than just a thrill ride, although the thrill is pretty sick (for those of you out there who don't know skater lingo, sick is good; very, very good). Even though the thrill of this journey tops any adrenaline rush I've ever found, when I say I now experience heaven on earth I'm talking about a presence that carries me along every day through the Holy Spirit. As He lifts me up, everything changes, especially me.

PEACE

Back in the day, if a problem came up with a contract for a project I was working on or if a studio didn't pay me on time, I would blow up and start yelling "F this" and "F that." Now, when something happens that would normally make me angry, I find myself chuckling because I don't flip out. The peace of the Holy Spirit comes over me. Instead of launching into a string of profanity, I ask the Lord what He is up to in this situation.

I've got to be honest. As I stand back and look at this transformation, it seems really weird. Seeing myself NOT react with anger and profanity is so out of character with who I was before September 11, 2001, that I can hardly believe it myself. But it reminds me of what it says in Romans 12:2: "Do not conform any longer to the pattern of this world, but be transformed by the renewing of your mind. Then you will be able to test and approve what God's will is—his good, pleasing, and perfect will."

When I see this change in my reactions, I realize how different I really am. But I didn't change me. God did. Now I find it funny that my first response to some problem coming across my radar screen isn't anger or fear or I've got to drop everything and focus all of my energy on this problem or I better call my lawyer. I just don't think that way anymore. Instead I can sense the peace of the Holy Spirit sweep over me.

When this happens, I get a feeling words cannot describe. All my life I heard that cliché "Get high on life, not drugs." Even after going through a twelve-step program I never knew what that saying meant until I gave my life to the Lord. Jesus is life, and that truth was never so obvious to me than it is now. Without question, I am having an actual, factual, tangible experience that has touched me mentally, emotionally, and psychologically as a result of the spiritual step I was willing to take. In a time when true peace is so hard to find, I've found it, baby, and there ain't nothing like it.

This peace set me free from the worries of the world. Most days I don't even notice the things that keep most people awake at night. Thank God I have a great staff, that's all I have to say. Otherwise my bills would never get paid. I don't worry because I now have an absolute freedom from the weight of the world. I don't carry around the worries that dragged me down back when I thought I was in control of my world. I feel like I just walked into heaven's spa and every day I get the full package. This peace and freedom are the manicure, pedicure, seaweed scrub, and shiatsu with a nap at the end. That's right, guys, this deal ends with a better happy ending. Then I wake up to a seven course meal God made me.

That's how I feel almost every day. And again, this is spiritual. The Holy Spirit does all of this inside me no matter what is taking place on the outside.

Yeah, but what about all the spiritual experiences people of other faiths have, Stevie B? What about them? I'm not responsible for those other people and those other faiths. This book is my story of what God has done in me. If you are feeling the same peace and freedom and incredible experience I have, but you're doing it with Allah or Buddha or whatever, knock yourself out. If eternity doesn't matter to you, stick with whatever else is working for you. All those people are praying to something, but it ain't the one true God and it isn't the truth.

Here's my point. In Jesus I found the one thing that most people want but don't have: Peace. Yet when I throw in the word "Jesus" a lot of people stop listening. If that's you, I want to tell you: Stop doubting the potential of Jesus Christ because the world or the media or your personal spiritual guru told you this Christianity stuff doesn't work. It works better than your mind can imagine. But, you won't get the peace, you won't get the freedom, you won't get the experience until you are willing to give it a try God's way. Until you are willing to give this faith a chance you will never know whether or not it is true.

CONFIDENCE

I've always known something about my life that frightens people. Yeah, I know if you've seen my movies I can be pretty frightening. But this secret I've always known even frightens me. I've always had this overwhelming sense that I am supposed to achieve greatness with my life. *So much for Christians being hum-*

ble there, Baldwin. Yeah, I know how this sounds, but I don't mean it that way.

Since I was a little kid I've always felt like I have already seen my life and I know how it's supposed to turn out. This feeling that I was supposed to accomplish things with my life that went beyond my wildest imagination has been confirmed continuously year after year through all these things that happened to me that weren't supposed to happen to a nobody from nowhere. Once I came to faith, this feeling didn't go away. It only grew stronger. I wrote earlier how my life never made sense before Jesus stepped into the picture, and that's true here. It was like once I came to faith this lingering sense that had always lurked in my soul started to come into focus. It wasn't until I realized my life wasn't about me that the whole idea of greatness began to make sense.

All of this flows out of the presence of the Holy Spirit in my life that makes my heaven now. When I get up in the morning I don't look in the mirror and wonder what the heck I am doing on this planet. After reading God's word I understand who God made me to be and the purpose He had in making me in the first place. I wake up every day knowing that I have been given a position on the playing field of life, and the name of that position is Stephen Baldwin. All I've got to do is play that part. My coach is God, and He walks up to me with the ball at the beginning of this thing called faith and says, "Okay buddy, we've already won the game. Here is the ball. Do what I tell you and greater things will happen than that kooky little brain of yours can imagine."

"But Coach," I say. "How can You be sure we are going to win?"

God comes back with the same line, "Didn't you hear what I said? I didn't say we were going to win, but that we have already won. Don't worry." That's why I'm having so much fun in this game with God. Knowing He's already won the game lets me know that everything I do for Him cannot fail.

Here's an understatement for you: Running out on the field knowing God's already won the game fills me with confidence to attack life with all I've got. Does that mean I never get nervous or wonder whether I am wasting my time? Come on. I'm still human. Of course I have days where I look at God and say, "Okay Coach, I want You to assure me that if I make this effort and play this position for You that I won't be wasting my time. Prove to me that if I make this valiant effort on my part that I am going to end up on the winning team."

God doesn't slap me around for being an idiot. Instead he simply says, "Stephen, do you believe in Me?"

"Yes, of course," I say.

"Okay," God says, "here are a couple of miracles to show you that I am who I say I am. Once I prove that, will you accept the fact that I am the boss and I am the coach? And then will you shut your yap and play the position I assigned you?" Then I shake my head yes, shut my big mouth, put on my helmet, and run back onto the field.

I've found you don't get to put on the cleats, you don't get to hold the ball in your hands, you don't get to have this awesome radical experience until you become willing to play this game by the coach's rules. But once you do that, He fills you with a strength that comes from knowing that no matter what life throws at you, you can't lose. That's why I know greatness lies in my future. I don't know what God wants to do through me, but I know it will be something that will last forever. Donald Trump may put his name on every building he can find, but nothing he does will last for an eternity. You can't say that about Stevie B. I'm playing a game where the win counts for time without end. And I get to enjoy it today. Could life get any better?

PASSION

This presence also fills me with a passion, a fire, a purpose and a focus that makes me want to jump in this game and score as many touchdowns as I can for God. I want to make some noise for this Vince Lombardi. If I had my way, every play would be a kickoff and I would be Tony Dorsett, running every one of them back for a touchdown for Jesus. Okay, I just dated myself with the Tony D reference. You young guys are out there going "Who?" So make that Reggie Bush scoring a TD on every play. That's what this presence inside of me makes me want to do for my coach. And after I've scored a couple of hundred in the first half, I want to hand the ball to my coach and tell Him it's all for Him.

I get even more fired up when I step off the field and start roaming the sidelines looking up into the crowd. My biggest thrill comes from finding someone who isn't in the game, bouncing the ball up and down in my hands and saying to them, "Hey man, want to play?" Most of the time the person I ask will say something like, "I heard that game sucks" or "I heard there's no fun in that game" or the most popular response, "I heard that game isn't even real." I look at them with the excitement I have for this game called life and the fire of God blazing in my eyes, and I say to them, "You have no idea how real this game is until you step on the field. Why don't you give it a try?"

Every once in a while they do. My passion is watching them put on the pads, step into their cleats, strap on that helmet, and step on the field for the first time. Let me tell you, the moment their foot touches the playing field for the very first time, they get it. They're convinced and their lives are never the same. For me, this is my biggest thrill. My gift is sharing the experience of the game. This is my passion. This is what makes my heaven now.

Doesn't sound so exciting to me Stevie B. That's because you've never tried it. I feel like part of the role God has given me is that of a scout. I'm always on the lookout for new players. I love pacing up and down the sidelines, watching people and thinking to myself, I bet that guy would love to play. I'm not just looking for more converts. You've missed the point if that's what you think. I'm looking for people who are already looking for what I've found.

We are all searching and somewhere deep inside we all want to be in the game, but either due to fear, doubt, or whatever, we aren't willing to leave the comfort of the stands. I like to help people realize that their searching comes from God. The Holy Spirit, this presence in me that's changed my life, He's working on people who don't yet believe. When I look up in the stands the Spirit will bring my eyes together with that guy or that girl who's looking for God. They're ready. Something inside of them wonders about the game. Those questions about life are already rolling around inside their heads. They're ready. As soon as they see the ball in my hands and my eyes locking onto theirs, they're ready.

That's my passion, sharing with people my experience of playing the game of life with God. To me, you ain't living if you ain't in the game. And you won't ever get in the stadium until you become willing to try this thing. Don't bark at me about how wrong I am if you haven't picked up the ball. You see, I've been where you are. I've been on the other side. I won't ever go back.

Yeah, but haven't some people quit? Your game can't be so great if people walk away from it. Hey, I never said this life was easy. There is an opposing team that wants to kick your butt and grind your face in the mud until you put down the ball and run home crying. Every time one of Satan's defenders slams into me and knocks me down, I just remember the final score. Our side wins. How could I quit now?

LESS THAN PERFECT

Now of course, all of this means that I, Stephen Baldwin, experience so much peace, so much joy, so much excitement in my walk with Jesus every day that I never screw up as I live in this perpetual state of heaven on earth bliss. Yeah, right. I'm far from perfect. I make mistakes. I get too busy and let my priorities fall out of whack. I spend too much time on the cell phone when I should be spending time with my wife and daughters. I'm lucky my writing partner on this book didn't heave my cell phone off the George Washington Bridge. Once or twice I think he wanted to throw it off with me still attached to it. And I would have deserved it because there were times I didn't do all the stuff I talk about in this book. My heaven may be now, but that doesn't mean I live like a saint 24/7, 365 days a year. You'll hear more about this in a later chapter, so consider yourself warned.

Now, if I still struggle to live out the things I'm telling you in this chapter, does that mean I'm full of it and you should ignore everything I say? Not at all. Coming face-to-face with my imperfections is what makes everything else in this chapter work. The peace, the passion, the confidence, all of it would stop if my screwups got the best of me. One day when I was kicking myself again for doing something stupid, I had this little revelation. The fact that I am not now nor will I ever be perfect just makes me need God's Spirit even more.

This is the circle of life that is my experience of faith in Christ Jesus. And it makes perfect sense. From the day I was born until the day I die, there will never be a moment when I can say that I know how to live life perfectly. God already knows this. He knows I was born a sinner and that I will never completely get over that habit. But, here's the part that blew my mind—God already took care of this little problem. The only perfection I know of is God; yet, through Jesus, the Bible says I now share God's perfection.

You saying you're perfect, Baldwin? No, I'm not perfect. But Jesus is, and He shares his perfection with me. I told you this was mind-blowing. I don't completely understand how it all works. If I could I guess I would start to think I had God all figured out, which I don't. This gets back to the "been there, done that, tried it Stevie B's way and it didn't work." God wants me to recognize how little I understand and realize my absolute need for Him. Only then will I come to God on his terms and not my own.

Just because I don't completely understand how God pulls this off doesn't mean it isn't real. The bottom line for me is this: I now live with such an incredibly magnified sense of security, peace, trust, and joy through this walk of faith that I know it is real. This isn't some psychological reaction from an addictive personality. Instead, the peace and the presence of the Holy Spirit that I feel come over me when I need it the most.

It shows up when I find myself on the precipice of an angry moment toward my wife whom I love so much. The Spirit intervenes and gives me thirty seconds of grace emotionally, which allows me to think rather than react. He forces me to ask myself, "Do I really want to tell her everything that she's done wrong that's ticked me off? Or do I want to trust that God knows how to work through all of this?" This grace allows me to see in her all the wonderful things she is, and all she has been for the past twenty years we've been together.

I guarantee you that the power to step back from the situation and diffuse it rather than make a huge deal out of it comes from God, not me. If I did it my way I would flip out and prove to her beyond a shadow of a doubt that she is dead wrong and I am right. By his grace I recognize my job isn't to win arguments. God tells me to seek Him and His will, even when Kennya and I disagree over something. He put me to the test on this just last night. My wife made some comment about something and in my mind I rattled off six reasons in less than ten seconds why she was wrong. But you know what? It doesn't matter. I know she isn't perfect. And she knows I'm not either.

That's why we both need Jesus. Recognizing that need every day, then acting on it by seeking God with all my heart, is what brings heaven down to earth. If I could do this on my own I wouldn't cry out to Him every day. I wouldn't depend on the presence of His Spirit to pick me up and raise me to new heights.

Instead, I would lean on myself, do it Stephen's way, and fall merrily into the elevator shaft of myself. God loves me too much to let that happen. He shoves my imperfections right in my face, to make me turn to Him and experience the joy He wants to give.

Yeah, it will be great to go to heaven someday and not go through this daily struggle. But as long as God keeps answering my passionate screams for help and picking me up through His Holy Spirit, then, my heaven is now.

Discern

Main Entry: **dis·cern**

Pronunciation: di-ˈsərn, -ˈzərn

Function: *verb*

Etymology: Middle English, from Middle French *discerner*, from Latin *discernere* to separate, distinguish between, from *dis-* apart + *cernere* to sift — more at DIS-, CERTAIN

transitive senses

1 a : to detect with the eyes **b :** to detect with senses other than vision

2 : to recognize or identify as separate and distinct **: DISCRIMINATE**

3 : to come to know or recognize mentally

intransitive senses **:** to see or understand the difference

- **dis·cern·er** *noun*
- **dis·cern·ible** *also* **dis·cern·able** /-ˈsər-nə-bəl, -ˈzər-/ *adjective*
- **dis·cern·ibly** /-blē/ *adverb*

CHAPTER 9

Jedi Mind Trick

Stephen Baldwin's lost his freaking mind. I know that's what you've got to be thinking after all this talk of God greeting me every morning and my claiming that my life today is heaven on earth. Even the way I arrived at this faith probably makes you question my sanity. After all, the whole country watched 9-11 come down. Very few people took it as a sign from heaven that they needed to turn their lives over to God. But I did, because that's exactly what God wanted me to do. *That's a bit of a reach there, Stevie B.* Yeah, maybe, except I know it's not. God spoke to me. He first spoke through our housekeeper, then He spoke through my wife's conversion, and finally He spoke through the events of 9-11.

That's freaking nuts, Stevie boy. Are you seriously suggesting God talks to people today and that He spoke to you? If so it sounds like you lost a few too many brain cells before you checked yourself into that twelve-step program. I probably did lose too many brain cells, and it's not like I had any to spare, but that's not the point. Listen, I don't expect this talk of God and the way He worked in my life to make sense to most people. In fact, according to the Bible, my story will sound crazy to most of you. If it doesn't there are only two possibilities: Either you are nuts yourself, or the Spirit of God is now speaking to you. I can't help you with the first possibility, but if you are now experiencing the second, hold on. You are about to get swept away on a wild ride.

Okay, now we know you've lost your mind. And, of course, you are right. I lost my mind a few years ago, literally. But don't worry. I got a new one. When God saved me He didn't just forgive my sin and punch my ticket to heaven. According to the Bible, He gave me a spiritual brain transplant.

I needed to lose my mind because the way I used to think was out of whack. Everything I thought, from the way I understood the world to my perceptions of reality, were all off by 180 degrees. Romans 1:21 says that everyone who doesn't know Jesus has a mind that is dark and confused. That was me. In the words of the Bible, my mind was closed and my heart was hard. I was a fool who lived a lie.

And guess what? If you don't know Jesus, the Bible says you are in the same boat. But don't worry. There is hope. I told you God performed a spiritual brain transplant on me. He says I now have the mind of Christ in me (1 Corinthians 2:16). Isn't that scary? Stephen Baldwin, the nutty Baldwin brother, now has the mind of Christ controlling his thoughts. You only thought I was dangerous before.

If all this sounds really wild, it should because it is. The more I read what the Bible says about the human mind before and after someone accepts Jesus as their Savior, the more I am convinced this isn't just amazing; it is a flipping Jedi mind trick.

The whole thing is like that scene in the original *Star Wars* movie where Luke Skywalker and Obi-Wan Kenobi cruise into Mos Eisley spaceport in Luke's hover-car. Luke is all worried that the stormtroopers will nab him. So when some stormtroopers stop them and ask to see their identification Luke starts to freak out, until Obi-Wan waves his hand at the troopers and says, "You don't need to see his identification." The stormtrooper repeats everything Obi-Wan tells him and lets them go free. That's what I have discovered God does through His Word and through His Spirit.

I know it must sound like I've spent a little too much time on the Mos Eisley spaceport myself, if you know what I mean. Believe me, once I understood what God was doing, I realized it isn't a bunch of baloney, it is freaking brilliant.

Here's the deal: The reason people who do not yet have this experience with Jesus have so much trouble understanding the Bible or anything else concerning God is because God has waved His hand in front of their face and prevented them from understanding it. This isn't something I made up. God said it in His Book. Listen to what it says:

> No, we speak of God's secret wisdom, *a wisdom that has been hidden* and that God destined for our glory before time began. None of the rulers of this age understood it, for if they had, they would not have crucified the Lord of glory.
>
> (1 Corinthians 2:7–8, emphasis added)

God has a secret wisdom which He has hidden from the world. Without this secret wisdom, you cannot understand anything God says or anything He does. The Bible says, "The man without the Spirit does not accept the things that come from the Spirit of God, for they are foolishness to him, and he cannot understand them, because they are spiritually discerned" (1 Corinthians 2:14). Here is God's Jedi mind trick: *The only way you can get the understanding, the only way you can get the experience, is to be willing to believe it without waiting for proof.*

I told you this was brilliant. God won't give you the understanding until you are willing to believe it. Once you are willing, He throws the lights on and lets you in on His secrets which have been hidden since before time began. That's His Jedi mind trick.

Does this sound crazy? Good. It should. Like I said, it isn't crazy, it is brilliant. But what else would you expect since God is the One who came up with it?

Are you saying God purposefully keeps people from understanding His truth unless they are willing to believe it with no questions asked? No, I'm not saying that. God is. I just happen to believe it when He does. But hey, that's just me. Listen to what Jesus said and decide yourself. He told His disciples:

"You have been permitted to understand the secrets of the Kingdom of God. But I am using these stories *to conceal everything from outsiders*, so that the Scriptures might be fulfilled:

> *'They see what I do,*
> *but they don't really see;*
> *they hear what I say,*
> *but they don't understand.'"*
> (Luke 8:10 NLT, italics added).

God has set up a spiritual system that, until He waves His hand in front of your face and says "I am right here," you won't ever see Him. But, He promises that if you will believe Him, then you will come to a true understanding of both God and reality. Until that time you may look, but you won't see. You may listen, but you won't really hear anything. All this stuff about God and Jesus and the Holy Spirit will be nothing but chaos and noise.

Like I said, it is only after you become willing to believe that you will get the understanding you seek. Of course, that's just my opinion based on what God's Word says. You do with it whatever you want.

DUPED

If you find all this a little hard to swallow, you are in good company. I didn't understand any of it myself until I became willing to believe it, and the reason goes beyond the fact that God had hidden this secret from me. The Almighty isn't the only one pulling a Jedi mind trick. Satan is as well. God has devised a spiritual system whereby you won't see Him until He reveals Himself to you, but Satan has also come up with a system of his own. He concocted a system that dominates the world, and this system feeds you with so many lies that you won't notice the truth even when it hits you in the face.

Don't tell me you believe in a literal devil, Stevie B. I'm not the smartest guy in the world. Heck, I slid through high school with a C average and it took me four years just to make it through Algebra 1. But I am smart enough to know that Satan is alive and well today. I've seen too much in my life to think otherwise, and I'm not talking about "godless" Hollywood. I've see the hold Satan's lies have on people, and they don't even realize what he has done to them. These are people who think they have it made, people who think they are really living because they have piles of cash in the bank or people line up to see their movies, and they think that's enough.

But that's not the scary part. If you lined up 100 billionaires and 100 movie stars and polled them asking if they would give it all away for heaven or hold on to it and burn in hell for eternity, I am willing to bet 50 percent of them would choose hell and hang on to what they have now. That's how bad they've been Jedi-mind-tricked by Satan. He's made people think that all they need is what they can lay their hands on now. Most of all, he's fed them a line of bull that says they don't need God, that all they need is themselves. No wonder they can't see God when He stands right in front of them.

You may not believe Satan has the power to do that to you, and if that's you, then the joke's on you. The Bible says that when the devil tempted Jesus in the wilderness, he showed Him all of the kingdoms of the earth in an instant. Then he made Jesus this offer, "I will give it all to you if you will bow down and worship me" (Matthew 4:9). No one can give away something they don't own, which means Satan controls this world in the natural realm.

Again, this is only my opinion, but it is also what God says in the Bible. Satan has all kinds of power, and he is able to control the minds of anyone whose mind isn't controlled by God. If you haven't accepted Jesus, 2 Timothy 2:26 says Satan has taken you captive to do his will.

When Obi-Wan pulled his Jedi mind trick, he used his power to get people to do what he wanted for his own advantage. That's what Satan does. You can see it in the way people act, in the horrifying selfishness and arrogance that marks human beings. You can also see signs of his mind tricks when you hear people cop excuses like, "Hey man, it's not my fault I am a racist, it's the way I was raised." Or, "It's not my fault I'm a child molester, society made me this way." Or, "It's not my fault I keep sleeping around, the culture made me do it." All these lies are nothing but Satan waving his hand and whispering in your ear. He's got you under his control, man. At least, that's how it looks through the eyes of Stevie B.

I can already hear the howls from those of you out there that are too smart and too sophisticated to believe in something as hokey as the devil. I feel for you, because Satan has pulled his greatest Jedi mind trick on you. Kevin Spacey's character in *The Usual Suspects* said it best, "The greatest trick the devil ever pulled was convincing the world he didn't exist." And you fell for it. He's waving his hand in front of your face, keeping you under his thumb, and all the while convincing you that he doesn't exist. You think you are in control of your own life when you're just a puppet with his hand up your back.

Yeah, but I'm the dumb schmuck here. I'm the one who doesn't know what he's talking about. Except I do. I've been on your side of the game, but I chose the Jedi mind trick of life and was set free. I once bought into Satan's lie that said this life is all there is so you might as well go for it. Man, I lived for the adrenaline rush, I lived for the thrill, and here's the sad part: I never knew my priorities and passions were so out of line with reality.

Satan had Jedi-mind-tricked me into living for today. That's the ugliest part of his game, because today doesn't last.

No one knows how long they will live on this earth, but even if you live long enough to have Willard Scott stand out in front of his house and show your mug on the Smuckers Jelly label wishing you a happy one hundredth birthday, once this life is done, that's it. Game over. And then what do you have? Nothing. Your entire existence will have been wasted away on junk that doesn't last, all because you let Satan keep waving his hand in front of your face saying, "It's all about you, baby. It's all about you."

That's why the things of God sound so foolish to people who don't know Jesus. The devil has you in his hip pocket and you don't even know it.

TOO SMART

Satan's little Jedi mind trick isn't the only thing that keeps you from seeing the truth God keeps waving in front of your face. People make Satan's work really easy because of pride. Human beings think they are too smart for God. Now I know there are a lot of brilliant people in the natural realm. There are geniuses out there unlocking the mysteries of nature and curing diseases and counting cards in Vegas trying to win a million bucks. I like to stand around these people and have a good time playing dumb.

Here's what I've figured out with the little pea-sized brain God dropped in my melon. You might find a cure for cancer, and you might design a car that can get a couple of hundred miles to the gallon, and you might design a telescope that can see the edge of the universe, but if after unlocking the greatest mysteries of the physical universe you conclude that everything that exists is just the end result of some long string of coincidences, you are an idiot. And you are an idiot because you let your so-called brilliance keep you from seeing the most obvious truth in the world, and that truth is that God is real and you need Him if you are really going to live. But people are too smart to need God.

We've grown way past that, Stevie B. Those cavemen hiding from thunderstorms, they needed God. We know what causes thunderstorms, so we don't need to believe in those ancient superstitions. Yeah. Whatever. Only a fool would think that because they have figured out how storms form that they don't need the One Who throws those storms around any way He wants. But hey, that's only my opinion.

Human pride doesn't just tell us we've grown past needing God. It also feeds us the line of bull that we can be anything we want to be, and we don't need God to do it. We keep telling ourselves that the world is our oyster, that opportunity is what it's all about. You can be anything you set your mind to, that's what we pound into the heads of our kids. You want to be Michael Jordan? Go for it. You want to be the next Bill Gates? What could possibly stand in your way? Dude, you can go to the moon if you want it bad enough. That's the line of crap we keep feeding ourselves. God? Who needs God? All you need is drive and determination and you can do anything.

This line of thinking leaves us all scurrying around like a bunch of insane squirrels hiding nuts and all the while we miss God telling us that He can give us a wealth and a joy and a peace and a purpose that goes beyond Michael Jordan and Bill Gates. It's not just the devil that's Jedi-mind-tricking us. We're doing it to ourselves.

A NEW HOPE

Satan Jedi-mind-tricks you to steal your soul. God does it to open your eyes to the truth and to give you life. The second you open yourself up to His truth and choose to believe it without waiting for proof, He waves His hand in front of your face and opens your mind to His eternal, hidden secrets. I know this is true because I've lived through the experience of coming into

God's reality. Let me tell you, it goes far beyond anything I ever imagined. Here's what God promises. He says, "No eye has seen, no ear has heard, no mind has conceived what God has prepared for those who love him" (1 Corinthians 2:9).

That is just mind-blowing. God is saying He has stuff prepared for you that your mind can't even conceive of, that's how far beyond your little imagination God wants to take you. I don't know about you, but I read that and I go, "Sign me up." I want the biggest roller coaster on the planet and its name is the Holy Spirit. If God has stuff in store for me that is more than I can even imagine, I'm ready. Let's do it.

But again, there's a catch. You can't have the experience, you can't have the understanding, until you are willing to believe. As long as you hang back and wait for all your questions to be answered you will never get it. But once you take the plunge, once you say, "Okay God, let's do it. I believe," everything changes. The Bible says God makes you a new creation. He gives you a new heart and a new mind. All His eternal mysteries are now yours to know and understand. Old ways of thinking are made new as you are set free from the spirit of the world. In its place you receive a fresh perspective where you can see and understand the things of the spiritual realm.

Yeah, I know. It still sounds like Baldwin's gone nuts. But I'd rather be a nut whose eyes are opened to the true nature of reality, than go through life oh so smart, but oh so blind.

Coincidence

Main Entry: **co·in·ci·dence**

Pronunciation: kō-'in(t)-sə-dən(t)s, -sə-ˌden(t)s

Function: *noun*

1 : the act or condition of coinciding : **CORRESPONDENCE**

2 : the occurrence of events that happen at the same time by accident but seem to have some connection; *also* : any of these occurrences

---

CHAPTER 10

Prayer? What . . . Are You a Wuss?

I like playing tough guys in movies. It's fun. I enjoy being the hard-nose who would just as soon punch you as look at you. Characters like Michael McManus in *The Usual Suspects*, Bo Dietl in *One Tough Cop*, and Tuff Hedeman in *8 Seconds* are just more fun to play. The tough guy, the stud guy, that's the attitude I like to play in the movies.

Oh by the way, I especially want any punk out there who might ever think of dating one of my daughters to understand this is part of who I am. Any one of you who thinks he has the cajonès to knock on my door and ask for one of my girls any time in the next twenty years better be ready to sit down and watch a special highlight reel I've prepared just for you. After watching me beat up and blow away one pile of scum after another, I don't think you will want to do anything to my little girls that might make me mad. And I don't care if my girls won't be old enough to date for a few more years. Consider yourselves warned, punks.

Sorry to digress, but you get the point. Stephen Baldwin has never had a problem being the macho, tough, guy's guy. I played football with my bros and wrestled through high school. I like to jump out of airplanes, race cars and motorcycles, and take the kind of risks that make most men wet their pants. I've ridden bulls, yes, you read that correctly, real live bulls. I've ridden motorcycles faster than a human being should down Sunset Boulevard, and done about anything an adrenaline junky like me can find to do. The more dangerous a situation becomes, the slower everything seems to move for me and the more in control I feel. I won't say nothing scares me, but, for the most part, I've always known how to take care of myself.

Then Mr. Tough Guy finds Jesus, or more accurately, He finds me. I surrender my life to Him, but I even do that with my same arrogant bravado. Praying the Sinner's Prayer wasn't enough for me. I had to go and threaten God, telling Him I would wage war against Him if I found out He wasn't real. That's the Stevie B prayer of salvation. Tough. Hard-nosed. Billy Graham with biceps, that's how I saw myself.

So you can imagine my surprise when I started learning about the importance of prayer in this new life I'd been given. Getting down on my knees, bowing my head, and closing my eyes didn't exactly fit into who I was. The whole posture of prayer looked like, well it looked like something for wussies.

There I said it. I, Stephen Baldwin, thought only some big ole weak wuss would do the whole prayer thing. I thought it was pretty much a waste of time before I came to faith. Sure, I prayed from time to time and I will talk more about that later, but for the most part, my perception of prayer was skewed. I thought it showed weakness and dependence and all of the things me and every other real guy out there are not.

DISCOVERING THE POWER

Everything changed in my understanding of prayer when I started reading the Bible. There I discovered how powerful this simple act of talking with God can be. Back in the Old Testament in 2 Kings 18-19 there's a true story about a king of Judah named Hezekiah. His country is small and so is his army. One day he wakes up and discovers the biggest, baddest country in the world at that time, Assyria, had sent its army to surround his capital city, Jerusalem. These Assyrians were seriously bad. They'd wiped out every army they'd faced and turned most of them into slaves. They didn't just take prisoners. No, that would be too nice for these goons. When they conquered a country they would line up any able-bodied person they could drag back to Assyria and they would jab a large fish hook through their jaws and chain them together like a string of bass.

So the king of Assyria, a guy named Sennacherib, surrounds Jerusalem with a couple of hundred thousand troops and sends a letter demanding Hezekiah's surrender. Instead Hezekiah falls on his face and lays this letter before God. He prays and shows God how His name, the name of the holy Lord of Israel, has been insulted by a bunch of idol worshipping pagans. Then Hezekiah pleads for God to do something to rescue them. That night an angel from God kills 185,000 Assyrian troops in their *sleep*! Big and bad Sennacherib wakes up surrounded by corpses. He takes a look around and hightails it back to where he came from. He never threatened Jerusalem again. In fact, he never threatened anyone again. That night marked the end of his empire. The world's greatest superpower was destroyed by the prayers of one man.

Dude, that ain't no wussie stuff. That's the power of God! The Bible is filled with stories like this. Now I could dismiss all these stories as a bunch of myths some guys threw together in a book, but if I didn't believe the stories about prayers being answered in the Bible, how could I believe what it said about Jesus? I know by experience Jesus is real, which means the rest of the book has to be real as well.

This made me think there had to be something to this prayer thing. I already knew prayer could change lives. My wife prayed for me every day for twelve months solid and look what happened. To this day people still find it hard to believe that she never preached to me or shoved Jesus in my face. She just prayed. That's it. I'm no expert, but I believe this shows prayer is real and its power is awesome.

I still wasn't completely convinced, and I knew I didn't like the posture of prayer I'd watched for a year. But prayer is like everything else in this experience of faith. If you wait for rock solid, iron clad, beyond a reasonable doubt proof until you try it, you never will. God does not reveal the power and the potential of prayer until you become willing to believe He can do what only He can do.

So to all you macho guys who think all this talk of prayer is for the weak, you are wrong. I had to finally get down on my knees, close my eyes, and pray. But I couldn't shout out one of those cheesy Hollywood prayers and expect to get results. You know the ones I mean, "God, if You are really there, and if You aren't too busy . . ." The Bible says that anyone who comes to God must believe that He exists and that He rewards those who earnestly seek Him (Hebrews 11:6). That last part means you have to believe God answers prayer before you start praying. If you don't, He won't. But if you are willing to believe that God can and will listen to your prayer and act, then you are in business. Again, you don't get the experience until you are willing to try it God's way. If this sounds crazy, try it anyway.

That's what I had to do. I had to believe and act without any guarantees. So I did. And guess what? It works.

FACEDOWN

But . . . I still wasn't comfortable with the prayer positions I saw other people use, especially my wife. When she prays she doesn't just bow her head. She lays down and plants her face in the carpet. I asked her one day if she thought that was really necessary. I will never forget her answer. She told me, "Sweetheart, I can't explain it. There is an experience I have in prayer when I assume this position that is unlike any form of prayer I have ever encountered."

Her answer wasn't enough for me. I'm an experience junky, so I pressed for more details. She replied, "There is something about physically humbling myself before the Lord that makes a difference." I'm telling you, chills swept over me when she said that. She doesn't lay down with her face on the ground to help her concentrate. Her body language tells God she's surrendering everything to Him.

That's when I got it. God doesn't buy any of my arrogant, macho, mind games. Three times the Bible says God opposes the proud, but gives grace to the humble. It even says He mocks proud people. When I heard that, I realized I had to leave my tough-guy nonsense at the door if I wanted to have any serious talks with God.

But here's the beauty of the equation. When I humble myself completely before God as I approach Him in prayer, I find true power. That's right. When I become a wuss on a human level I find strength on a true spiritual level. That's what I find so freakin' hilarious. In a world and a society where men grab so much power, people miss the greatest power in the universe because they don't want to admit their weakness.

So hey, all you tough guys who are just like I used to be. Do you want real power? Do you want a Porsche Turbo? Get on your knees and start praying. But don't ask for a Porsche Turbo. Ask for God's will in your life, and a Spirit will come into your life that will take you on a ride far more exciting than any car ever could. And trust me, I had the 2001 Porsche Twin Turbo. That car would do zero to sixty in three seconds, but it was nothing but a little kid pedal car compared to the wild ride the Spirit will take you on.

Do you have to plant your face on the ground to pray? No. It's not like God tells you, "Sorry, wrong number," if you fail to assume the proper position. I get down on my knees at least two or three times a week. Other times I pray while lying in bed or sitting in a chair. The posture of my body doesn't mean nearly as much as the posture of my heart. Whether I lay on the ground or talk to God while walking down the streets of New York, the important thing is to make sure my heart humbles itself before God and surrenders completely to His will.

ASK AND BELIEVE

The other key is you have to believe. Without faith it is impossible to please God. That's not my opinion. The Book says it. The book of James says when you ask God for something, you must believe and not doubt because, "he who doubts is like a wave of the sea, blown and tossed by the wind. That man should not think that he will receive anything from the Lord; he is a double-minded man, unstable in all he does" (James 1:6-8). Jesus Himself said, "If you believe, you will receive whatever you ask for in prayer" (Matthew 21:22). Those aren't my words, Jesus said it. Some people find them controversial. Go figure. To me, Jesus meant what He said. If I believe that the Lord will hear and answer my prayer, He will. But it wasn't until I became willing to believe in the supernatural realm and that there is no such thing as a coincidence that I started seeing results from my prayers.

And yeah, God has answered my prayers. And no, I'm not confusing a coincidence with divine intervention. A coincidence cannot explain how four days after Hurricane Katrina I went before God for three days of very serious prayer. I wanted to do something that would make a genuine difference in the lives of the evacuees sitting around the Astrodome, and I wanted whatever I did to involve the *Livin' It* skate team. So I went to God. I told Him, "Lord, I don't know what your will may be here, but this is what is weighing on my heart." For three days I bombarded heaven with the same prayer, asking God to open a door for us to do something in Houston.

Then my cell phone rang. Rick Weigele, the director of the *Livin' It* skate tour, a division of the Luis Palau ministry in Portland, Oregon, had just received a call from the head guy of the

Astrodome. He asked if it would be possible for the *Livin' It* team to relocate to Houston!

Anyone who just read that and said to themselves that this was just an odd coincidence is a dumb-dumb. There is no way something like this would just happen in the natural. God opened this door in response to prayer, by myself and many others who hit their knees in response to a horrible natural disaster. But it was not a coincidence.

This story turned out great. I and a bunch of other people prayed. God answered. Good things happened. However, when I look back on all of this from a natural, human perspective I realize there is a humble quality to being a man of faith. Only a wuss sits back, does nothing but pray, and waits for God Who's off in God knows where. A real man takes the bull by the horns and makes things happen. He grabs the phone and starts making phone calls. After all, I'm a celebrity. Perhaps a phone call from me with a good ole, "Hey, do you know who I am?" could make things happen. If I needed to, I could get my brothers in on the act. Who could say "no" to the combined forces of the Baldwin family dynasty? Even if they could, *I know the President of the United States.* If a real man knew the leader of the most powerful nation on earth, he'd work those connections and get the job done. I think a well-timed call from W would probably get those Texas boys off their butts and make them throw open doors to some hardcore skater dudes who want to help out.

That's what a tough guy would do. That's what a man's man would do. Instead I took the wuss's way out. Tough guys might get things done here on earth, but when God steps into the picture, look out. If given the choice I would rather get the One Who created the universe involved instead of the leader of the free world.

THE PURPOSE OF PRAYER

Trying to get God to do something is not the purpose of prayer. Anne Graham Lotz is the one who opened my eyes to what prayer is really about. In case you don't recognize the name, Anne is Ruth and Billy Graham's daughter. Yeah, that Billy Graham. I heard her speak on a verse in Revelation 2 that says, "You have forsaken your first love" (Revelation 2:4). But she didn't talk about other people who'd forgotten their first love. She talked about herself.

As she spoke I said to myself, Wow, here is Billy Graham's daughter, a woman who was raised in the Ethernet pipeline of Christ in America. Yet she is telling me that the daughter of the greatest evangelist of all time, a girl who was raised in a Christian home, forgot that the most important thing in her life is supposed to be to love God. She went on to say that faith in Jesus is all about honoring God by pursuing Him in love.

A light came on for me that night. I realized that the only way to understand the experience of faith in Jesus Christ is to experience His love. This can only happen spiritually. I believe that connection, that flow of love between God and me and vice versa, occurs through prayer. Therefore, the real purpose of prayer is not to tell God all of my problems or to try to twist His arm to do something I really, really want Him to do. The primary purpose of prayer is to express my love for God and to experience His love in return. I go to Him just to love on Him and feel His love over me. That is what prayer is all about. I never knew any of this until that night when Anne Graham Lotz opened my eyes.

All of this gets back to not only the purpose of prayer, but the purpose of my existence. God made me to be a creature who would love his creator more than anything else in the world. The Bible says I am supposed to love God with all my heart, soul, mind, and strength. Jesus went on to say I am to love Him more than I love my parents or my wife or even my children.

Knowing all of this in my head is one thing, but actually doing it takes my experience with Christ to a whole new level. When I think about the lengths to which I go to demonstrate my love to my wife and children, and then I compare this to what I do to show my love for God, I find my life is seriously out of balance. The first time I ever threw these two things on a scale I found that I spent 99.9 percent of my time in the natural showing love to my family, and only about 0.1 percent on God. I still struggle to put these numbers where they should be, but I am trying. I've learned that when I love God like I should, I am able to love my wife and children in a way I never could otherwise.

Loving God is what prayer is all about. I don't start my prayers with requests. I've learned prayer is never about getting God to do what I want, anyway. To me, prayer is about offering up my heart to God and asking Him to show me where He wants me to go and what He wants me to do. I begin by telling Him how much I love Him, and I try to keep His love in front of every request I make. More than anything, I want God to do whatever will put a smile on His face, not mine. Sure, I have requests I bring to Him. But I have come to understand that God knows what I need far better than I do. My job is just to trust Him, love Him, and let Him be God. I think that's the greatest gift I've received from my faith, the knowledge that He is God and I am just His creation. I'm supposed to love Him and do what He wants. If I choose not to do that, then I'm not connected to Him. And if I'm not connected to Him, then there is really no reason to live.

Maybe you knew all this already. I didn't until God threw a switch in my head. I meet a lot of people who have never heard any of this. In conversations both with people I know and complete strangers, I will ask them what they think might be the purpose of their existence. I get the gamut of stereotypical answers, things like "to make a difference" and "to love people" but most of the answers convey the same idea: The majority of people have no idea why they are alive. Being the shy guy I am, I go ahead and tell them why they are on this planet. I tell people God created you so that you might live your life in a way that demonstrates how much you love God. That is God's first priority and purpose for making sure you were born. He wants you to spend your whole life reaching your arms out to Him and telling Him thank you for bringing you into the world and giving you the opportunity to experience His love.

You should see the looks on people's faces when I tell them this. I would say seven or eight times out of ten they start crying because they never even thought about this. A little bit of guilt also lies underneath their tears, and they don't even realize it's guilt. Deep down most people know they were made to love God, but somewhere along the line they let Satan's lies drown out this truth that screams from their souls. That's where prayer comes in. Through prayer you express your love for God and experience the real reason you are alive.

HOW TO PRAY

In case you haven't caught on yet, I'm not trying to pass myself off as some expert. I'm just a guy who's figuring all this out as I go along on this journey of faith. Being the novice that I am I thought I had exhausted my knowledge of prayer already, and then I realized I didn't answer the one question people ask me on this subject more than any other. *Hey Steve*, they ask, *how do you pray, anyway?*

How do you pray? What a question. You might as well ask me to explain how to breathe or how to keep your heart beating. I don't know. You just do it. You pray by praying. How's that for a profundity? And how's that for using a big, hard to pronounce word?

But seriously, I don't know how else to explain it. You learn to pray by praying. Before I came to Christ I had some experience with prayer because of the twelve-step program I went through. I knew there was a God, and I communicated with Him on an intellectual level. The eleventh step of the twelve says, "Sought through prayer and meditation to improve our conscious contact with God *as we understand Him*, praying only for knowledge of His will for us and the power to carry it out." Since I take these twelve steps very seriously, I did step eleven as best I could with the limited understanding that I had. But, I did this on a purely intellectual level. I prayed in my head. It was only after I came to Christ that I learned to pray with my heart. Once the connection between my head and my heart was made, then I learned the true nature of prayer.

I don't say that to in any way diminish the way God used a twelve-step program in my life. Looking back, I believe He used the twelve steps as a way of preparing me for this experience I'm having now. In my opinion, and again, this is only my opinion, that was the goal of the two Christian men who started the movement. They knew guys like me weren't ready for the whole load of the Gospel, so they came up with these twelve steps. By the time I went through them all, I was ready for the next thing God had for me. The transition didn't take place overnight. I'm a slow learner. I needed several years for the truth to sink through my hard head. But eventually it did.

What I know about prayer today is built on what I learned about prayer then. Remember, back when I first learned about prayer in a twelve-step program I didn't have Jesus. And buddy, Jesus makes all the difference. It wasn't until I came to Christ that the whole dang thing made sense. Now I pray with my mind, my soul and my spirit.

And again, I learned to pray by praying. I've discovered prayer is like a muscle. You gotta hit the weights, guys, and exercise this thing. It's like golf. Why do guys hit buckets and buckets of golf balls? They do it to get better. The same goes with prayer. When I first started praying I wasn't too good at it. But the more I prayed, the more natural it became.

When I talk about getting good at prayer I'm not talking

about having my prayers sound eloquent to other people. Hey man, when I pray I'm not talking to you, so I don't care what you think of how I sound. Getting better at prayer means not getting all twisted inside with worry over some stupid something that I can't control anyway. Instead I take it to God.

So if I take my problems to God instead of trying to figure out a way to fix them myself, does that mean I'm weak? It sure does. I wouldn't have it any other way because God says in 2 Corinthians 12:9 His power is made perfect in my weakness.

Believe

Main Entry: **be·lieve**

Pronunciation: bə-'lēv

Function: *verb*

Inflected Form(s): **be·lieved**; **be·liev·ing**

Etymology: Middle English *beleven*, from Old English *belēfan*, from *be-* + *lȳfan*, *lēfan* to allow, believe; akin to Old High German *gilouben* to believe, Old English *lēof* dear — more at LOVE

intransitive senses

1 a : to have a firm religious faith **b :** to accept as true, genuine, or real <ideals we *believe* in> <*believes* in ghosts>

2 : to have a firm conviction as to the goodness, efficacy, or ability of something <*believe* in exercise>

3 : to hold an opinion : THINK <I *believe* so>

transitive senses

1 a : to consider to be true or honest <*believe* the reports> <you wouldn't *believe* how long it took> **b :** to accept the word or evidence of <I *believe* you> <couldn't *believe* my ears>

2 : to hold as an opinion : SUPPOSE <I *believe* it will rain soon>

- **be·liev·er** *noun*

- **not believe :** to be astounded at <I could*n't believe* my luck>

CHAPTER 11

B.I.B.L.E.: Basic Instruction Before Leaving Earth

A lot of people think of the Bible as this big, boring, hard to read book. In my experience with God I have found the opposite to be the case. I have come to a place in this journey where reading the Bible is fun. You read that right. I actually used the words "Bible" and "fun" in the same sentence. *What else do you do for fun, Stevie B, watch paint dry? Do you go out in the yard and watch the grass grow when you really want to cut loose? What a wild man you are.* I know it has to sound that way. Believe me; I'm as surprised as you are. Never in my wildest dreams did I think I would ever find reading the Bible to be something I look forward to doing every day. Informative, yes. Interesting, sure. Important, of course. But fun? What a surprise.

My early experiences with the Bible weren't like this. From time to time I would hear a story on the news related to the Bible or I would see a picture of Jesus on the front of *Newsweek* and I would think to myself, "I wonder what that's all about." So I'd pick up a Bible and read a little. I never read much because, honestly, I could never get into it. Sure, it had some good stories, but all the "thees" and "thous" were too much for me.

Kennya's conversion sparked my curiosity which made me try reading it more seriously. I wanted to find out for myself what made this Jesus thing so appealing to her. Even then I had trouble understanding what I read. On a purely intellectual level I got it. God made the world. People screwed up. Jesus died on a cross. Three days later He rose again. Okay, that's the story line, I get it. But I never really connected with the book in the way I saw Kennya connect. These weren't just stories to her. They had something more. I wasn't sure what that something was.

After I gave my life to Jesus I realized there is a huge difference between just reading the Bible and opening myself up to believing it. Like everything else in this experience, you don't get the understanding until you are willing to try it God's way. And God's way means believing without waiting for iron-clad, rock-solid proof. This has to be about the thousandth time I've said this so far and you just passed the halfway point of the book. Get ready. I'm going to keep saying it. You don't get the understanding, you don't get the experience, until you become willing to believe. And that is especially true of the Bible.

TRUTH

When I talk about believing without waiting for iron-clad proof, I'm not talking about sticking your hands over your eyes and believing a bunch of fairy tales that can't possibly be true. I've discovered the Bible is truth. I think that may be the reason why so many people have a problem with it. It tells the truth without pulling any punches, especially when it talks about people.

I didn't like reading what the Bible said about me. The Book said my heart was "most deceitful and desperately wicked" (Jeremiah 17:9), and that it was so much worse than I thought that my mind couldn't even begin to comprehend how bad it is. Hey, I knew I wasn't perfect, but this was a little much. It told me I couldn't fix myself no matter how hard I tried.

I didn't like hearing that, but it rang true deep inside me. I knew I couldn't quit smoking and I couldn't quit using profanity and I couldn't quit doing a lot of things I didn't like about myself. If I had hit bottom maybe I would have found this easier to take. But I hadn't. My life was good. I was a good guy. Yet there were things about myself that I didn't like and I really couldn't do anything about them. The Bible told me why this was so.

Did I like hearing it tell me what was wrong with me? No. Was it right? Yes. I thought this Book was supposed to make me feel better about myself, like one of those *Chicken Soup* books on steroids. Instead, parts of it made me feel lousy. But the truth was I needed to feel bad. Really bad. The Book did me a favor by being straight with me about what was going on inside my soul.

THE REAL JESUS

The Book also rang true when I read what it said about Jesus. I always thought of Jesus as some mushy-gushy wimpy sort of guy. But then I started reading the Bible and came face-to-face with the real Jesus. Instead of the nicey-nice Jesus with the English accent Who walked around spreading peace and love like some ancient flower child, I found a radical Who said:

> Don't imagine that I came to bring peace to the earth! No, I came to bring a sword. I have come to set a man against his father, and a daughter against her mother, and a daughter-in-law against her mother-in-law. Your enemies will be right in your own household!
>
> (MATTHEW 10:34–35 NLT)

The first time I read that verse I literally had to sit down and pray. It took my breath away. Here I'd always imagined Jesus was the sweet, cuddly, loving dude, and suddenly I find out He makes Conan the Barbarian look like Conan the wuss. He didn't come with a guitar singing "Kum Ba Yah." Jesus brought a sword to the earth and He is still swinging it.

After I found this verse I went out and had a sword tattooed on my arm. That was one of the most powerful statements I'd ever read in my life. Jesus was saying that life isn't going to be a bowl of cherries. Believing in Him means making sacrifices, even if that means walking away from love and relationships of your own family. That's heavy stuff. Sure, Jesus showed people what God's love looked like, but He said His message would divide people.

That sure looks a lot like what I see going down in the world today. Jesus also said arrogant little human beings would never be able to solve the world's big problems like poverty and wars on their own. I think the past 2,000 years of history have shown He knew what He was talking about. Go ahead and delude yourselves thinking you can cure all of society's ills along with fixing the environment. People have been trying for 2,000 years to get it right, and they've only screwed up things more, just like Jesus said. I think that proves Him right and the skeptics wrong. But of course, that's only my opinion.

But that wasn't the only part of the Bible that rang true to me about Jesus. When He came to this earth in the flesh He knew what waited for Him at the end of His life. He came to die a violent death that He didn't deserve. Before He was even born He accepted His fate without complaint. As much as I try to comprehend it, my natural mind cannot understand how this guy comes to earth knowing in advance that He will take on Himself the punishment for the sin of every human being who has ever or will ever live. Mel Gibson caught a lot of flack for the graphic violence in his film *The Passion of the Christ*. Read the Book. Mel *toned down* what the Bible says Jesus actually went through.

Jesus wasn't some wuss in a toga. He was God made flesh. If He had wanted to, He could have unleashed an army of hundreds of thousands of angels, and all of them would do anything He told them to do. During His lifetime He *raised the dead*!

How do you think that would play out on CNN today? I can tell you how it would play out. Someone who can raise the dead or stop a hurricane dead in its tracks just by speaking a word would make everyone out there in CNN land mess their pants. He would me. Yet instead of using His power for His own gain, He died for me and you. That's the most radical thing I've ever heard in my life.

When I read what the Bible said about Jesus, I knew I was reading truth. Like I said, believing the Bible doesn't mean believing a bunch of fairy tales that couldn't possibly be real. It rings true because the Book is truth. *Doesn't the Bible say people used to live 7, 8, even 900 years? That sounds like a fairy tale to me, Baldwin.* I'll admit, I don't know how that was possible. The Bible says Noah was 950 years old when he died. Is that possible? I don't know. No one can live that long today.

But here's the beauty of the whole thing: I don't have to figure it all out. God's done so much in my life, and He's proven so many other things in the Bible, that when I read where people lived nearly a thousand years right after God created the world, I'm willing to take it on faith. I can't explain it, but I figure God can. I also think God knew what He was doing by putting a lot of the really hard to believe stuff in the very beginning of the Book. It's almost like He was saying, *Here's some stuff that will blow your mind. If you can keep reading after this, then hang on. I'm gonna show you some stuff that will change your life.*

BASIC

None of this is really rocket science. Believe me, if I can understand the Bible, anyone can. But most people open the Book with a couple of strikes against them. They go into it thinking it is a lot harder than it really is. It is almost as though people think they aren't supposed to be able to understand it. Maybe they tried reading a King James Bible when they were a kid and struggled, and they never tried again.

Hey, guess what? There are a lot of new translations out there that are much easier to read. The guys writing the Bible spoke Hebrew and Greek, which is why we need someone to translate it into English for us. Some people dig the King James Version of the Bible, to which I say, hey, if it works for you, go for it. Me, I need something a little more on my level. I like the New International Version. I even have a Bible with footnotes that explain the back story and the history. People like me need all the help we can get.

The Bible isn't supposed to be hard to understand, but I'll tell you one thing that doesn't make the Bible any easier for people to get into, and that's these dummies that go on television waving a Bible around asking for your money. They give the Bible a bad rap by saying the Book says for you to send them some of your hard-earned cash. Whoa. That's dangerous, brother. These dudes are messing with God when they use His Book to line their own pockets. I'm praying for these guys, I really am. A lot of these guys look good, with their tans, and their Botox, and plucked eyebrows, and dyed hair, all in the name of Jesus, of course. They like to spend all that money flying around the world to exotic places and living like movie stars. I just have one thing to say to those guys: From your dark tan I understand you like warm weather. Well bubba, I hope so, 'cause it's gonna be real hot where you're going.

To everyone else I say this: Don't let some Botoxed phony keep you from experiencing God through reading His Word. Don't let that happen. I'm not exaggerating when I say reading the Bible has literally changed my life. Everything I need to know about God is found in the Book, baby. He wrote this thing for people like me. It is as though God used people like Moses and Paul to FedEx *the* most important book in the world to me.

If I told you the God who made the entire universe in six days had something to say to you, wouldn't you want to hear it? Well, He does. And it's called the Bible. This Book is the truth of God on a level that even dummy me can get. It's basic. The most basic truth you can find. I think if people would start seeing this Book as basic truth their lives would be a lot easier. It worked for me.

FROM DUTY TO FUN

That still doesn't explain the statement I made in the very beginning of this chapter where I said reading the Bible is fun. Reading that sentence for myself I keep thinking, how lame does this sound? I feel like the brownnose girl in fourth grade who says, "Homework is fun," or that nerd in high school that enjoys Algebra. "Reading the Bible is fun!" I sound like such a dork. Sorry. I can't help it, because it's true.

Here's what got me hooked on the Bible. I started reading it right after I gave control of my life to Jesus. People told me I needed to read it, so I did. I even heard one guy say that he and a group of his friends get together every morning with the slogan, "No Bible, no breakfast." And they mean it. They don't eat anything until after they've read the Bible. That's how important the Bible is to this faith experience. Okay. I get that.

So I started reading some of the Bible every day. It didn't take me long to discover this Book was not what I expected. I started reading stuff that absolutely blew my mind. One of the verses that I found amazing was 2 Corinthians 10:3-5. It says:

> For though we live in the world, we do not wage war as the world does. The weapons we fight with are not the weapons of the world. On the contrary, they have divine power to demolish strongholds. We demolish arguments and every pretension that sets itself up against the knowledge of God, and we take captive every thought to make it obedient to Christ.

This is one of the most radical things I've ever read. For one, it says there is a war going on, and it's not talking about the

Marines storming a beach. According to the Bible, a spiritual war is going on all around us. That's heavy. And the weapons of this conflict are not like the weapons of the world. These are divine weapons, the weapons of *God Himself*! This verse then tells me I get to use these weapons to demolish arguments and take every thought captive that sets itself up against the knowledge of God. We're talking about changing the way people think!

If you grew up around church and the Bible and all of this is pretty ho-hum to you, let me tell you, there's nothing ho-hum in these words to me. This is powerful and scary and hardcore. I put 2 Corinthians 10:3-5 in the *Livin' It* DVD, but I had it flash on the screen too fast for the kids watching it to be able to read the whole thing at once. They're going to have to back up and reread it a couple of times to get it. That's the plan. Imagine some little punk skater, he watches this video and sees these guys who are legit in their abilities talking about Jesus while music plays in the background that connects.

And then what do they hear this video tell them? It says we are human, but we don't use human plans or methods. No, we use *God's* mighty weapons to kick down the devil's strongholds and demolish every argument that keeps people from God.

Now for a kid who likes to play violent video games, he's going to read this and go, *Whoa, that's hardcore. Where do I sign up?*

These verses in 2 Corinthians aren't the only references to the invisible spiritual battle that's going on. Ephesians 6:12 says, "For our struggle is not against flesh and blood, but against the rulers, against the authorities, against the powers of this dark world and against spiritual forces of evil in the heavenly realms." That sounds like something out of a movie, but it's better because it is real. That's another verse I like to share with kids. I want these little skater kids who watch the video to realize God wants to make them spiritual warriors who can demolish anything that sets itself up against God. That's what makes all this so fun for me.

When I first found these verses I didn't just read them and think, "Oh, that's interesting, now on with the rest of my day." No. The Bible changed the way I see and understand reality around me. It opened my eyes to the truth. I tell you, I felt like Neo in *The Matrix* when he swallowed the red pill. The pill opened his eyes to the truth and ushered him into a battle most people were sleeping right through. The Bible is my red pill. If that ain't fun, I don't know what is. When I pick up my Bible now I cannot wait for God to open my eyes to something new. Every day I tell Him, "Show me more. I want more."

And yes, I believe the knowledge He has given me already has dropped me into the middle of a battle most people don't even know is going on. I hear all this talk about Red States and Blue States and culture wars. Brother, let me tell you, none of that even scratches the surface of the real battle that's raging. In Matthew 11:12 Jesus says, "From the days of John the Baptist until now, the kingdom of heaven has been forcefully advancing, and forceful men lay hold of it."

That's where the battle is taking place. It isn't about politics, but about the kingdom of God advancing and the forces of Satan trying to stop it. But they can't, because these weapons in the spiritual battle demolish anything the devil can throw at us.

I get excited talking about it. I don't want to sit on the sidelines and watch all this happen. I want to get in the middle of it. That's why I share verses like these with kids I meet in skater culture. I want to be a soldier for Christ, and I want these kids to join me. This is the essence of the hardcore movement of faith. We're battling the devil, brother, and according to the Book, we can't lose.

So how can reading the Bible be fun? In light of what you just read, how can it not be?

The Bible talks about more than spiritual warfare. The more I read this Book, the more alive it becomes. I read things in here just when I need them most. In the last chapter I talked about prayer. How do you think I learned to pray? Through the Word. I would struggle trying to figure this whole thing out, then I would read about somebody in the Bible praying, and lights would come on.

The stories in the Bible are powerful because the people are real. I read about people doing some powerful stuff, and it makes me go, "Wow! That's awesome. I want to experience God like that." Shadrach, Meshach, and Abednego stood up for God even though it meant being thrown in a fiery furnace. Their story challenges me to surrender everything to God every day, even if that means dying for Him. I read about Peter and John praying for sick people and those people immediately getting well. That's the kind of faith I want to have when I pray. That's how the Bible comes alive. It opens my eyes to reality and pushes me to want more and more of God.

God also uses His Word to challenge the way I understand the events taking place around me. During the last week of August 2005, the worst natural disaster up to that point in U.S. history hit New Orleans. As if Hurricane Katrina wasn't bad enough, the handful of people who went on a crime spree in New Orleans took the catastrophe to an even higher level of bad. Throw in how helpless the government on every level appeared to be in those first few days after the storm, and you had the biggest natural catastrophe any of us ever saw.

So while all of this is happening, in the middle of the first week of Katrina when CNN showed one horrible scene after another and the mayor of New Orleans said tens of thousands could be dead, I got up one morning and started reading my Bible. For a couple of weeks before Katrina I'd been reading through the book of Mark. I stuck with the same schedule, and opened my Bible to Mark 13 on the day after Katrina hit. Since I'd read Mark 12 the day before, this was where I was supposed to read today. And in the middle of the worst natural disaster up to that moment in U.S. history I opened my Bible only to hear Jesus talking about the signs of the end of the world and His second coming. On television I watched catastrophe on a biblical scale take place, and in my Bible I read about an even greater catastrophe that will come soon. I have to tell you, the timing blew my mind.

Are you saying Hurricane Katrina is a sign the world is about to end, Stevie B? No, that's not what I am saying. Only God knows those things. But reading about the future wrath and judgment God has in store for the earth helped put the scenes of lawlessness and disaster from Katrina in perspective. If the unthinkable can happen and a major U.S. city can nearly be destroyed with over $100 billion in damages in a matter of days from a supersize thunderstorm that grew out in the Gulf of Mexico, what does that say about the probability of the events described in Mark 13 taking place?

Like I said in my testimony chapter, when the impossible happens, anything is now possible. And if anything is now possible, Jesus may come back at any moment, which means the apocalyptic events the Bible says will take place immediately before His return are also now possible. That's the kind of changed perspective the Bible gave me in the middle of the worst natural disaster in U.S. history.

And you found this somehow comforting? Yeah, I did. The stuff I read in the Bible reminded me that God is in control. It also reminded me that this world is not my ultimate home. Some day this world will end and we will leave this place.

That's where this basic instruction book from God comes in. It is basic instruction before leaving earth. This Book contains everything you need to know to be ready for whatever the future brings. And the Book even tells us what that ultimately will be.

Yeah, the Book is fun for me now. It is fun because it changed my life and it comes alive for me every day. I'm not special. I'm not some rocket scientist who unlocked the hidden secrets of the Bible. There's no real mystery to it. It's all right there in black and white for anyone to read. There's just one catch. You have to be willing to believe it before you will experience the understanding it will give. For me, that was an easy deal to make.

Passion

Main Entry: **pas·sion**

Pronunciation: ˈpa-shən

Function: *noun*

Etymology: Middle English, from Old French, from Late Latin *passion-*, *passio* suffering, being acted upon, from Latin *pati* to suffer — more at PATIENT

1 *often capitalized* **a :** the sufferings of Christ between the night of the Last Supper and his death **b :** an oratorio based on a gospel narrative of the Passion

2 *obsolete* **:** SUFFERING

3 : the state or capacity of being acted on by external agents or forces

4 a (1) **:** EMOTION <his ruling *passion* is greed> (2) *plural* **:** the emotions as distinguished from reason **b :** intense, driving, or overmastering feeling or conviction **c :** an outbreak of anger

5 a : ardent affection **:** LOVE **b :** a strong liking or desire for or devotion to some activity, object, or concept **c :** sexual desire **d :** an object of desire or deep interest

- **pas·sion·less** /-ləs/ *adjective*

synonyms PASSION, FERVOR, ARDOR, ENTHUSIASM, ZEAL

CHAPTER 12

Get Thee to the Driving Range

I've got a question for all you golfers out there.

Two-inch ball.
Four-inch hole.
Four hundred yards.
Four swings or less.

What are you, nuts?

Though I can't blame you. I lived in Tucson for eight years, and for a while I was out there three or four days a week, twelve months a year, chasing that little white ball. I know the hold golf gets on you. Watching the pros on television makes the game look so simple. The two-inch ball, that four-inch cup, those four hundred yards, and the pros usually take fewer than four swings to get it there. Nothing to it.

But of course there is a whole lot more to it. The game drives you nuts. You spend a lot of your time hunting down the ball and once you find it you have to whack your way out of a bad lie. Of course, the worst lies come at the end of the round. Any game that features foot wedges and mulligans is the perfect liar's game. Even then most people's scores stink.

About the time you're ready to throw your clubs in the lake it happens. You're standing 170 yards out, slight wind at your back. You pull out your five iron, line up the shot, and whack it, only this time you nail the sweet spot. The ball starts out a little left, and then fades back. It bounces onto the green, catches the slant, and rolls about a foot from the hole. Every golfer on earth says the same thing after a shot like that: "Now that will keep you coming back." I've said it. And it did keep me coming back.

You golfers know what I'm talking about. You can play like crap for two or three months, but one brilliant shot wipes every bad experience from your memory. That one great shot doesn't just get you back, it gets you hooked. Hooked on the drug that is golf. That one swing of the club plants an idea in your head that begins with the fateful words, *If I can do that once . . .*

So you don't just come back to the golf course to play another round. You start going to the driving range swinging away at one bucket of balls after another. Then there's a new set of irons. Then a new set of woods. At some point you pay for lessons and maybe a computer program to analyze your swing.

Of course your scores drop a bit, but not as much as they should after dropping that kind of cash. So you keep hitting the driving range and going out to the course day after day. Every time you shank one you convince yourself that the bad shots are the exception, not the rule. After all, you remember *that* shot. Somewhere along the way you will probably hit another almost as good. That only makes the addiction worse. Now you really become convinced that every shot ought to look like Tiger Woods hit it.

That's why I have to ask all you golfers out there: Two-inch ball. Four-inch hole. Four hundred yards. Four swings. What are you, nuts?

Wadda ya have against golf, Baldwin? Nothing. Nothing at all.

But it struck me one day how much golf is like the Christian life. The only way you will ever get any good at golf is to pour yourself into it. You've got to spend a ton of time and a ton of money to keep from embarrassing yourself in front of the guys on the first tee. Golf requires commitment. You only get out of it what you are willing to put in to it.

Which makes me wonder why guys who say they love the Lord will spend hour upon hour at the driving range, but hardly spend any time reading the Bible, praying, or pursuing the indescribable experience God wants to give them. I don't get that. If you are willing to invest yourself in a game like golf, why wouldn't you exert at least the same amount of time and energy in this experience with God?

FEEDING THE ADDICTION

I see one huge difference between golf and faith: You can get good at faith. I believe that faith in Jesus Christ is shooting par golf or better every day. Walking with Jesus beats the thrill of the greatest shot you've ever hit. And you can have that thrill every day, if you are willing to do what it takes to reach it.

That's the problem for most people. They aren't willing to do what it takes. I hear the whining. People tell me all the time that they don't have time for prayer and they don't have time to spend in the Word and they don't have time to get involved in some kind of ministry that will make a difference in some kid's life. Then they tell the biggest lie this side of the golf course, but they are lying to themselves, not me. They say they would love to do the whole prayer, and Bible, and ministry thing if their schedule would just allow it. What a load of crap.

When you want to do something bad enough, you will do anything you can to make it happen. Don't believe me? Go down to the local driving range. Guys will go to any lengths necessary to get better at golf. Me, being the psycho, over-the-top kind of guy that I am, took improving my game to a whole new Stevie B level. But, since I was a celebrity, I hardly had to pay for it. Ha. How's that for unfair? I didn't go down to the local pro shop for clubs. Where would be the fun in that? My pal John Daly took me to the freakin' Ping headquarters in Carlsbad, California. The experts there did a three-camera, superslow-motion computer analysis of my swing and customized a set of clubs around my natural swing based on the data the computer churned out. So what if the computer told me I sucked and should give up the game? It didn't, really, but it probably should have because I did. I took a dozen or so lessons from the pro at the La Paloma Country Club in Tucson, not that they did any good. And I played a lot. When I wasn't shooting some movie in California, I was playing golf at one of the local clubs. I didn't have to play the munis' like every other poor schmuck. I played the best courses in Tucson. Like every other idiot golfer in the world, I would drag my lazy butt out of bed at 5:00 a.m. to make a 6:10 tee time. Today if I try to get up to pray at 5:00 I'm drooling on the pillow by 5:05. But for golf I would get up and stay up.

Here's the hilarious part. In spite of the lessons and the high dollar equipment and playing on some of the finest courses in the country and getting tips from my friends on the PGA tour, my best honest score ever (i.e., Mulligan free) was an 88. That was the only time in my life I ever broke 90.

I should have known going in that I would never be any good at golf because golf, like most games, has a lot of the things I never really liked: rules. I'm not just talking about the officially sanctioned rules of golf written on stone tablets by the finger of God that Old Tom Whoever carried down from a mountain in Scotland, although I never really cared for them either.

No, I'm talking about the commonsense rules of things you should or should not do to keep from sucking at the game. I never paid any attention to those either. To me, I didn't see a problem with trying to hit a ball out of the rough and through the trees while the wind is blowing 75 miles per hour during a lightning storm. The Stevie B approach to golf looks at the situation and says, "Hmmmm, this looks like about a three club bump to me. So if I just ricochet the ball off the trees and around the tornado and across the chasm opening in the ground from the earthquake, I should make it to the green." That's just the kind of guy I am.

Somewhere between the custom club fitting and writing another snowman on my scorecard at 6:30 one Thursday morning, I figured out that I would never be any good at golf. That's when I decided I might as well have fun with it. Not long after coming to Jesus I figured out the opposite was true of faith. I knew I would be good at it, and it better be fun.

What, Stevie B, are you claiming to be some super saint who lives the whole faith thing better than anyone else? No way. Anyone can get good at faith. All you have to do is try. The formula for getting better isn't hard to master. If you want to get better at golf you head to the driving range and start hitting balls. If you want to get better at prayer, you just get up in the morning and hit your knees. Then after a while you get up and start reading the Bible. After that, you go take a shower, get dressed, walk out the door, and start doing whatever you just discovered in the Bible that you need to start doing.

This isn't some secret formula. Like I said in the last chapter, this is all pretty basic. If I can get a handle on it, anyone can. However, I've learned that the secret to success in my faith experience is the same as the secret to success in golf: practice, practice, practice. I never knew anyone who mastered golf by playing once or twice a month and never touching a club in between rounds. It doesn't happen. The occasional weekend hacker may hit a good shot once in a while, the kind of shot that will keep him coming back, but no one can master the game that way. That's why serious golfers go to such great lengths to get better at hitting a two-inch ball into a four-inch cup from four hundred yards in four strokes or less.

Why, then, wouldn't a serious Christian invest the same time and energy to excel at Christianity? I want to challenge those believers out there reading this to evaluate your schedule and find an hour each day for prayer. That's right. One solid, uninterrupted hour in the Word and praying to the Lord. Dedicate yourself to discipleship in the same way most golfers dedicate themselves to the game. If you can get up at 5:00 to make an early tee time, couldn't you find some time during your day for God?

And for those of you who play golf, putting God before a game will probably end up improving your golf scores. Trust me; I know there are a lot of you guys out there whose golf game needs prayer.

I'm serious. I think if you would commit yourself to your faith with the same energy the average golfer devotes to playing a game, I believe the Lord will give you examples of that one great shot in your spiritual life. I think miracles will happen. But, and here I go again, you don't get the experience without doing this God's way. You've got to get to the driving range of faith and hit fifty, a hundred, a thousand balls. That means hitting your knees in prayer, spending time in the Book, growing as a disciple, asking someone to hold you accountable, the whole package of life as a Jesus follower.

If you want the experience bad enough, you will do whatever it takes to get it. And believe me, if you put in the effort, God will not disappoint you. That's not just my opinion. That's a fact.

DISTRACTIONS

Writing that last part was easy, but you know, I ain't stupid. I can see what's going on in the lives of most people, even those who claim to love God. The Christian life they are experiencing falls far short of what they could have. What's the problem? I think the answer is very much like the reason why so many people never get good at golf.

You play golf on two levels. First is the physical ability. This is what you work on while you're at the driving range. You learn the mechanics. You develop the muscle memory. You work on the game.

However, a lot of people can hit one great shot after another on the range, but once they get on the course, they still suck. They screw up the second level of golf: the head. Great golfers have incredible powers of concentration. When they stand over a shot, they block out everything going on around them. All they see is that ball and that cup and the four hundred yards between them. That four hundred yards might be covered with lakes or sand or gator filled swamps, but it doesn't matter. Nothing distracts them.

That's where I see a lot of people blow it when it comes to the faith experience. Their lives are filled with too many distractions. I don't even have to tell you what those distractions are because they've hit you as well. The enemy has played such a head game on everybody in the world that almost everyone's priorities are all out of whack. That's where I see the most misery in life. We allow the world to pull us onto its treadmill of money and cars and stuff and all that crap that doesn't last.

Especially money. This is just my opinion, but I think most evangelical Christians are just as hung up on money as the people in the world they are supposedly trying to save. In spite of all the talk about God coming first, they still want the big house and the nice car and everything else the world says is important.

Listen, I've had money. I used to make what most people would consider to be a lot of money. Since coming to faith my income has dropped by 75 percent, but do you know what? It doesn't matter. I will say it again, the amount of money I make DOESN'T MATTER because God will take care of me. Jesus tells me to put Him first and He will take care of the rest. He's obviously NOT talking about making people rich. If faith made you rich in the things of the world, my income would have gone up, not down. No, Jesus means He will provide what I need to live in this world when instead of living for this world, I live for His kingdom.

But that doesn't stop people who claim to believe the Bible from getting so hung up on money that they can't think about anything else. That's especially true when they start talking about retirement. I'm tired of hearing people, even Christian people, talk about their hedge funds and their retirement accounts that it makes me want to puke. If I hear one more person tell me they plan to really get busy for God someday but first they have to sock away enough money to retire at fifty, I may have to throw them in a headlock and shake some holy sense into them.

Listen, when it comes to serving God, there is no retirement age. Moses was eighty flipping years old when God sent him to save the children of Israel. Eighty! Do you think he was worried what that might do to his 401k or 501b? I don't think so. Sure, you need money to operate on this planet. I get that. But the Bible tells me everything belongs to God anyway. So what are you worried about? All this money talk is just a distraction designed by the devil to keep you from doing what actually matters.

Money isn't the only distraction. If anything, it's just the easiest to see. Well, maybe money and sports. The subject of this chapter is a huge distraction. Some people get so hung up on playing golf that they don't have time for anything else. And I've heard the whole, "when I'm on the course I commune with nature" load of bull. People who fish use that line as well to justify spending their entire Sunday on a boat on the lake instead of worshipping God at church. Watching sports is just as pointless on an eternal scale. I enjoy going down to Yankee Stadium for a ball game as much as the next guy, but when baseball or football or anything else gets in the way of doing things that yield eternal fruit, there's a problem.

IDOLS

I hope I'm making sense here. I know I'm the new guy around here. I didn't grow up in church and I've only been a Christian a few years. But in my short time as part of this family I've seen some things that really bug me. I don't understand a lot of what I see going on because it doesn't line up with the way the Book says things should be. In my opinion, many people who claim to know God are missing out on the experience that could be theirs. They settle for less, and I think the problem goes beyond a lack of discipline in their spiritual lives, and it goes beyond out of whack priorities brought on by constant distractions.

In my humble opinion there are a lot of so-called Christians out there who are serving idols instead of God. *What a stupid thing to say, Baldwin. I don't know anyone who prays to a little wooden statue, especially not any Christians.* Okay, fair enough. They may not have idols made of wood. No, the idols I see are worse. They're made of flesh and blood and range in age from newborn to eighteen, nineteen or even older. People don't realize it, but their own kids can become idols.

Before you slam the book shut thinking I don't know what I'm talking about, think about this: Anything that keeps you from seeking God is not only a distraction, if it receives the affection God deserves, it becomes an idol. Watch how parents allow their children to take over their lives. The same thing can happen with your spouse. If you love your husband or wife more than you love God, there's a problem.

I know. Nutty Baldwin has gone off the deep end again. Think whatever you want, but here's Jesus' opinion. He said, "Anyone who loves his father or mother more than me is not worthy of me; anyone who loves his son or daughter more than me is not worthy of me" (Matthew 10:37).

Most people sort of pass over those verses and never take them seriously. Why would Jesus say this if He didn't mean it? Here's what I think He means. I think Jesus is telling me that my faith must be so hardcore that if I had to choose between my children and what I believe, I would choose the latter. If I had to choose between the lives of my family and loyalty to Jesus Christ, there is no choice. Jesus comes first. When I tell people this, they think I'm absolutely nuts. I've had people tell me, Christian people mind you, that they would never, ever in their lives love God more than they love their children. I tell them they've got it backward. You've got to love God more or you can't be His disciple.

Is doing this easy for me? Not always. I look at the beautiful woman God gave me as a wife and I love her more than words can describe. But I have to constantly tell the Lord, "O God, forgive me if I ever get to a place where I love Kennya or my daughters more than You."

It's tough. I know there are people out there who, like me, married way over their heads. You have this great relationship with this incredible human being, but you have to be careful. If your spouse comes before seeking the Lord, your husband or wife is an idol. If you spend more time looking for ways to please your family than you do thinking about how you can please the Lord, they've become an idol.

But I thought God wanted me to love and care for my family. He does. But you always have to keep Him first. When you learn to love God more than your wife and kids, your love for them will be better than it ever could have been otherwise.

SETTLING

There's one final thing that I believe keeps people from hitting the driving range of faith and taking their experience with God to a whole new level. Their mediocre brand of Christianity gets in the way. And I'm not slamming any denomination or church, although, if you go to a church that doesn't preach and believe the Bible, you need to find one that does. Instead I'm talking about the guy who goes to church every Sunday, keeps his nose clean, reports all his income on his 1040, and is generally an upstanding member of society. But this guy misses out because he thinks that's all there is to the Jesus experience. Do some good works. Don't use bad language. Don't beat the wife or kids. Be so syrupy sweet and nicey-nice that you make me want to throw up. This guy misses out because he bought in to the lie that there's nothing more. Then this guy checks into the world system and goes to work, brings home a paycheck, and does the whole safe, little American thing. Dude, wake up.

But this guy's not completely at fault. There are a lot of people out there claiming to be Christian teachers who cherry-pick the parts of the Bible they like. God's love is good; God's wrath is bad. Jesus the loving Savior is good; Jesus the radical is bad. Going to church every Sunday is good; going out on the streets and telling the homeless about Jesus and treating them like human beings instead of human garbage—that might be getting carried away.

This is the worst distraction and the worst idol of them all, the idol of self-righteousness. That's like Tiger Woods saying that making the cut in half the tournaments he enters is good enough. Tiger plays to win, and that should be your approach to the Christian life.

Come on, people. Wake up and smell the Spirit. God has this exciting experience just waiting for you. Like I said at the beginning of this chapter, the Holy Spirit wants to give you an experience that is like hitting that perfect golf shot every day. It all starts with hitting your knees every day, spending time in His Word, opening your life to anything God wants to do, and not letting anything get in your way. If you believed this could all be yours, why wouldn't you go for it?

Go

Main Entry: ^{1}**go**

Pronunciation: 'gō

Function: *verb*

Inflected Form(s): **went/**'went/; **gone/**'gȯn *also* 'gän/; **go·ing/**'gō-iŋ, 'gȯ(-)iŋ; "*going to*" *in sense 13 is often* 'gōə-nə *or* 'gȯ-nə *or* 'gə-nə/; **goes** /'gōz/

Etymology: Middle English *gon*, from Old English *gān;* akin to Old High German *gān* to go, Greek *kichanein* to reach, attain

intransitive senses

1 : to move on a course : **PROCEED** <*go* slow> <*went* by train> — compare STOP

2 : to move out of or away from a place expressed or implied : **LEAVE, DEPART** <*went* from school to the party> <*going* away for vacation>

3 a : to take a certain course or follow a certain procedure <reports *go* through channels to the president> **b :** to pass by means of a process like journeying <the message *went* by wire> **c :** to proceed without delay and often in a thoughtless or reckless manner — used especially to intensify a complementary verb <why did you *go* and spoil it> <*go* jump in a lake> **d** (1) **:** to extend from point to point or in a certain direction <the road *goes* to the lake> (2) **:** to give access : **LEAD** <that door *goes* to the cellar>

CHAPTER 13

_____

GO

I was up in Halifax, Nova Scotia, working on a movie with
Tom Selleck, and I was running behind, which I often do. I
rushed out of some breakfast joint, cell phone pressed to my ear,
and shot across the street. In the middle of the street I nearly ran
over this young guy coming from the opposite direction. As we
sidestepped one another, I said excuse me and tried to rush on.
But he recognized me and said, "Hey, Stephen, how are you
doing?" I did my best to be polite but brief. "Yeah, man, nice to
meet you, but I gotta go," I said and kept walking. This guy turns
around and starts walking with me and says, "I met you at one of
your skate events in Scottsdale, Arizona."

At this point I felt that familiar tap on the shoulder by the
Holy Spirit. What are the odds that while crossing the street in
Halifax, Nova Scotia, I would just happen to run into this guy
who I'd met but didn't remember, just a few months earlier in
Arizona? It's only 3,346 miles from Halifax to Scottsdale. Call
me crazy, but this didn't strike me as a coincidence. I prayed a
quick little prayer, "Okay, Lord, what are You doing now? And,
oh by the way, I'm late."

So I stopped just long enough to find out this young, good

looking, rock and roller Christian living in Halifax is an architect who grew up skating. I said something like, "Yeah, bro, that's awesome," handed him my business card and told him to get in touch with me. Then I darted on down the street. While dialing another number on my cell phone I said to God, "Lord, if You really did set up that meeting just now, do it again when I'm not late for the studio."

Three days later my wife came to see me. I took a little time off to see the town and do a little shopping together, and guess who we run into? That's right. Kennya and I walked out of a store on Main Street and I ran into this guy again. Answered prayer. Okay God, I get the hint. I guess I've got to deal with this guy. We start talking and the guy tells me about how he and his wife love the Lord and how they love what I am doing with the *Livin' It* skate ministry. My focus on reaching youth resonates with this guy, and he thought the skateboarding was really awesome since he is an old skater himself. Then he goes on to tell me how he and his wife keep praying, asking God to show them some way He can use them. The two of them are willing, he tells me, but they don't know what God might want them to do.

After he tells me his whole story I look at him—and this could have come from me but I think it was the Lord since He set up this meeting to begin with—I look at this guy and I say to him, "If you love skateboarding and you want to make a difference for the kingdom, then do something about it."

His eyes got big and he said, "You know, Stephen, you're right." He may have wanted to leave it at that, but I kept going. I told him that he could be the guy that starts something that could grow into the greatest outreach Canada has ever seen. Since he is an architect, I told him he could perhaps design a skate park where the Gospel would be shared.

By this point I was on a roll. I challenged him to start contacting the richest guys in Halifax and the richest Christians in Canada and challenge them to invest in changing the lives of potentially tens of thousands of kids. "You should build a 50,000 foot warehouse, the largest indoor skate park Canada has ever seen," I told him, "where whoever wants to can come and skate for free. But at some point the music stops and you share the information these kids need to really live." Yeah, I like to think big. "But don't say to yourself, gosh, golly, gee, I wonder if I should try to do something," I said. "Do it. Tell yourself, I'm going to do this."

Now I don't know if my idea for this guy to build the biggest indoor skate park in the history of Canada is exactly what he ought to do. But I do know this: This kid and every other Christian out there needs to do something. When you get to the end of your life, you don't want to stand before God and have to say, "Gee, God, I really wanted to do something, but I didn't have time. But my lawn looked really good. And did you notice the size of my retirement account?" Don't waste your life on stuff that doesn't matter. God has called you to do something, and while the specifics of that something might be a little fuzzy, the heart of what God wants you to do is not a mystery.

LAST WORDS

Now for me to tell some guy I just met on the streets of Halifax, Nova Scotia, how he needed to start contacting billionaires to raise money to build the biggest skate ministry in the history of Canada is hilarious. This came from me, a guy who, when he was told twelve years earlier that a man in a Brazilian church had prophesied that he would become a Christian and have a ministry of his own, laughed until he nearly wet his pants. And here I was challenging some young architect to devote the rest of his life to reaching kids.

Either I was totally out of my gourd, or the Lord had ignited a passion in me that I could not control even if I wanted to. Now I know I am out of my gourd, that much is a given, but that's not the reason I would stand on Main Street in downtown Halifax and spin a vision for a ministry to a guy whose only thought up until that moment was, *Weird, I just met Stephen Baldwin.*

If you thought in reading the story of my meeting with the guy on the streets of Halifax that I was primarily concerned with talking him into building a building, you missed my point. Nor was I trying to get him to do in Canada what I am doing in the United States with the *Livin' It* skate ministry. I firmly believe that if you got rid of all the church-type buildings and stopped doing every sort of activity associated with the Christian movement globally, Christianity would not only survive but thrive as long as you did one thing.

Understand, Christianity is all about Christ. C-H-R-I-S-T. Not skate parks and not church buildings and not building houses for the poor. The whole movement is all about Jesus Christ. And the last thing Jesus told His followers to do before He hightailed it back to heaven was to go and make disciples.

Simply put, if you have experienced God's love and you know Jesus personally, God tells you to get out on the street and share that experience with people who have not yet had it. This is called evangelism, and it should be the number one focus of every church, every ministry, every individual believer on the face of the planet. With all that is wrong with the world, it just seems to me that if more Christians would make this their number one priority, everything else associated with the movement would be far more effective.

This was all I was trying to get across to the guy in Halifax. I challenged him to go and do the last thing Jesus told him to do. Maybe it's my movie background, but I happen to think a person's last words are pretty important. I see them as the ending of a great movie or the crescendo of a great speech. Everything that comes before builds up to those final words.

So, to me, on a commonsense level, it seems that when we talk about the Son of God, Who He was and what He did and why He did it, that if the last thing Homey said was to GO, we probably ought to listen. It doesn't take a nuclear physicist to figure out the Savior meant what he said. He said GO. He didn't say create Habitat for Humanity, although it is a wonderful organization that I've worked with myself. He didn't say raise money to build His kingdom. He didn't say pray. He didn't say any of those things. That doesn't mean those things aren't important. But the last and obviously most important thing He told His followers to do was to go and make disciples of all the nations.

So I would like to make a suggestion to all the believers in America: Wake up. Snap out of it. Get up off your lazy butts. And go and make disciples of all the nations. If you don't like what I just said, God bless you. But it ain't rocket science. Read the Bible. You know I'm right. Say what you want about the complexities of discerning God's will for each individual, but I'm telling you that if you aren't out there actively telling people about Jesus in the hope that they will come to faith in Him, you are not obeying God.

If I've ticked you off by saying that, too bad. I hope it does. Statistics show that about 90 percent of you have basically treated Jesus' last words like you would a flipping fortune cookie. You read it, thought, *oh how nice*, and threw it on your plate and never thought about it again.

That, more than anything is what I wanted to get across to the guy on the streets of Halifax. If I met you right now on the streets of New York, and you told me you were a Christian and you told me you were trying to figure out God's plan for your life, I would tell you the same thing. God's plan is for you to GO. It's as simple as that. We can build all the churches we want. We can write all the books we want. We can sing all the songs we want. But until globally the body of Jesus Christ and its believers go out into the nations and start making believers and disciples, in my opinion, all of this other activity is just so much noise.

I believe the first thing every pastor in every church in America should say to its congregation every Sunday morning is, "You need to tell people about Jesus." Let me say that again. The first thing that every pastor in every church in America should tell its congregation is, "When you leave here today, and until I see you again, the first thing you should be concerned about is telling others about Jesus." This is where it all begins.

Once you clearly understand the go, then you can figure out who God wants you to go to. Me, He wants me to go to the youth culture in this country. I believe a lot of what is wrong in America today is a result of the fact that we are not evangelizing the youth culture of America.

We can build camps, we can have parks, we can do this, we can do that, we can do whatever we think is good for them and will better their lives and yada yada yada ya! But, if they don't know about Jesus, then none of that other stuff matters. It misses the point.

In my opinion and based on what I've been through and the awesome power of my conversion experience, God has called me to go and make disciples of the youth of America. That is what I am going to try to do, and if you try to stop me I am going to break your face. Sorry about that last part. But I am excited.

How do I know God wants me to reach the youth in America? He told me. It just took me a little while to hear what He was saying.

THE CALLING

I already told the story of the day shortly after my conversion when I kicked in the door of the largest Christian bookstore in New York City and asked to see all the Christian cool stuff. I didn't find much. However, I did leave the store with a CD by a guy I'd never heard of, a guy named Kirk Franklin. The cover caught my eye because it had this kind of hip looking, young, black guy in a pose that I thought was not common. It made me say to myself, "This looks like maybe, possibly, it could be cool, and it's on the Christian shelf, so what the heck." I bought it. I am not exaggerating when I say that I listened to that CD every day for the next six months. I was digging Kirk Franklin. This guy was loud. He's proud. He's doing his thing. And it's all in the name of Jesus. I knew I needed to connect with this guy and figure out a way we could work together on a project.

About a month after I bought this CD, my sister, Beth, called me from Syracuse and told me about some guy named Luis Palau who was coming to town to do a festival. She knew about my conversion, and since this was a Christian organization, she figured I would be interested in attending. I was already planning a trip up that way to visit Mom, so Beth thought I could kill two birds with one stone. Me, I wasn't interested. I'd never heard of Luis Palau. I didn't know what the heck a Christian festival even was, and I had no interest in going. That didn't stop my sister from asking me if I wanted tickets every time I talked to her for the next three or four months. My answer was always the same, *Whatever*.

Finally, I go to Syracuse and visit my mom and my sister, Beth. When I see Beth she says to me, "I've been trying for several months to get you to make a commitment to go to this Palau festival. It's tomorrow. Here are some tickets, and here's the brochure explaining the whole thing." I'm thinking to myself what a pain in the butt my sister is, but I take the brochure and tickets and say a very heartfelt, yeah, thanks a lot. Whatever.

Imagine my surprise, then, when I look down at the brochure and the first words I see are: Performing tomorrow, Kirk Franklin. Beth then starts in and says something like, "I'm sick and tired of trying to convince you to go to this thing. I got you the tickets. You can do whatever you want with them. Throw them away for all I care." I looked up from the brochure and said something like, "Uh, thanks. Yeah. I think I will go."

I have to tell you, I was tripping inside. What are the odds that I would ignore my sister for four months while she was trying to get me to an event featuring this singer that I'd been listening to for six months? This was my first post-conversion experience with a genuine act of God. A chill ran down my spine.

I couldn't wait to go the next day and find out what God was up to. I told Him, "Okay, is this how this could work in the future? Just as You orchestrated my life up to now, will You continue to reveal certain potentials that, if I just trust You, You will lead me to them?" God didn't say anything, but I knew the answer.

What happened the next day wasn't nearly as important as the string of events God orchestrated as a result of the connections I made. I met Kirk Franklin, and I also met Luis Palau along with his son, Kevin, and other members of the Palau team. They invited me to attend their next big event, a thing called Beachfest Fort Lauderdale later that summer.

The Syracuse event was good, but they told me Beachfest would be even bigger and better. It was. Over 300,000 people attended the event. I didn't know there were that many Christians in America who cared about something this loud and gnarly. As all of this is happening, the Holy Spirit keeps whispering in my ear. I knew God wanted me to connect with this Palau guy somehow.

At Beachfest I first observed a Christian skateboard team perform. That launched the idea to make the *Livin' It* DVD in partnership with Kevin Palau. I told Kevin if the Palau organization would put up the money for me to create the video with them, I would help get it out there and promote it.

I didn't want to reinvent the wheel on this thing. Skate videos succeed primarily because they are skate videos. Kids buy them to watch the tricks, and that's what I wanted to do. Yes, I wanted to include God and the guys' stories of how they found Him somewhere on the DVD, but I primarily saw this as a way of making something cool, hip, and cutting edge for the Christian market. Nothing more.

I also thought we might sell between 15 and 20,000 of them. Thus far we've distributed five times that amount and counting without any kind of national distribution deal. It's the hand of God. There's no other explanation.

So what does all of this have to do with Jesus' command to go make disciples, and God calling me to direct my obedience of that command toward the youth culture of America?

During the editing process of the first *Livin' It* DVD, one of the Palau people, a guy named Dave Redelfs, came to me and told me twelve churches had already asked about flying me and the skate team to their towns to do a skate demo and share Jesus with kids. Dave asked, "Would you be willing to do this?" I thought for a moment and then told him sure. I wanted to get the video out there. It was new, it was edgy, it was hardcore, and the kids would really get into it.

A live skate tour would help get the word out and share the Gospel message in a new, innovative way. Sure, I told him, I would go. And then Dave said to me, "That's great Stephen. Now we've been doing evangelism here at Palau for forty years. Based on our experience, we have a feeling a lot more invitations are going to come rolling in." All this was cool with me. Then he said, "In order for us to organize all of this activity for these first twelve cities, and for these events to run as smoothly as we want things to run in our organization, in this thing that will become your *Livin' It* ministry then . . ."

That's when I cut him off. I said, "Hey, Dave, wait a minute. Dude, chill. Do me a favor. I love the Lord and I want to get this DVD out there, but don't ever refer to this whole reality as *my ministry*. I'm just not that guy. No offense to you or Luis, but if my name in Hollywood ever gets associated with the word 'ministry' that is unequivocally career suicide. So, don't go there. Is that okay?"

Dave just looks at me while I'm making my little speech and then says to me, "Are you done?"

"Yeah."

"Can I ask you a few questions?" he asks.

I say, "Sure. Fire away."

"Did you give your life to the Lord?"

"Sure."

"Did you make this video?"

I say, "Yeah."

"Are you going to go to twelve cities and talk about all that?"

And I said, "Yeah."

"Is it all about Jesus Christ and the Gospel?"

"Yeah, man, yeah," I said, "what's your point, dude?"

He says, "Well, there, *dude*, you are kind of new to this whole thing. But around here we call that kind of a situation A MINISTRY!"

That moment was literally the most powerful moment of my entire life. More than my wedding. More than the birth of my kids. In that moment a chill ran down my back because my very next thought that came to my head was, this confirms the second half of the prophecy. I remember going, Whoa. While I stood there trying to soak all this in, Dave said to me, "Stephen, you thought you were just making a DVD. But clearly, this is a path the Lord has set up for you if you choose to accept it." I made a promise to the Lord in my covenant where I told Him I would do anything He asked. He asked. What choice did I have but to obey?

Here's the thing that hit me in that moment. The reason God spoke through a guy whose name I may never know in a church in Brazil, and the reason God sent a Brazilian house-keeper into my home, and the reason God orchestrated all of the events of my life including putting me together with the Palau organization wasn't to make skate videos. And it wasn't to take a team of skaters on a national tour every summer. And it wasn't to make Christian cool stuff. Jesus told me to go and make disciples. And now I knew who He wanted me to go to.

Was obeying this command and embracing this ministry career suicide? You tell me. The day I had that conversation with Dave Redelfs my head was already filled with questions about my future in films. Between what I was reading in the Bible and the conversations I'd had with my wife about the kinds of roles I should now take, I thought I was pretty well screwed when it came to Hollywood. I honestly didn't know how I would make a living. Most movies contain so much gratuitous sex and violence that I knew I couldn't go about business as usual anymore.

But after this conversation when God threw the lights on for me, I realized that wasn't even the point any more. Jesus told me to go. The Holy Spirit showed me where. I knew what I needed to do next.

FAMILY TIES

Going out to tell people about Jesus just isn't something you do with your mouth. And the people you are supposed to tell aren't just strangers out there who don't really know you. The hardest people to go to are the people who know you best and the way you tell them about Jesus has to go beyond words.

Everywhere I go some Christian will come up to me and ask something like, *So Stephen, are you telling those pagan brothers of yours about Jesus?* Here's my answer: It doesn't matter. *What do you mean it doesn't matter? Doesn't that contradict what you just said? These are your brothers, your own flesh and blood. How can telling your brothers the most important truth in the world not matter!?* I'm not saying it doesn't matter whether or not I am talking to my brothers about God. I'm saying the constant questions don't matter.

Here's why. If someone comes up to me and tells me they are praying for my brothers, I respect that. Please continue to pray for them. Pray for me, too, while you are at it. I don't know anyone who would turn down prayer. What I don't get are the people who come up and act all psycho and overzealous and make it sound like my converting my brothers is the single most important issue facing America today. I've even had people say, "If you'd only tell Alec about Jesus and then he became president and blah, blah, blah." Okay, I get it. You don't like my brother's politics. By the time you finish reading this book you may not like mine either. So what does that have to do with my telling my brothers how they can have the same experience I'm having with Jesus?

A lot of people ask me these questions with a tone in their voice that implies I am the one responsible for getting my brothers into heaven, as if I better focus all of my time and energy on making sure the Baldwin brothers all become born again. I've even had people imply that the whole world would come to faith if all the Baldwins went out preaching the Good News of Jesus. I don't think that would happen, but you never know. The Lord works in mysterious ways.

So here's my answer for all those people who want to know if I am actively sharing my faith with my family: Trust in the Lord. Doesn't that answer hack off a good Christian? But I mean it. Trust in the Lord. If you aren't sure what I am saying, go back and reread chapter four. I became a Christian because my wife prayed for me every day and lived out her faith in front of me. She focused all her energy on pleasing the Lord and didn't worry about me. Not once did she shove Jesus in my face.

I believe it was Saint Francis of Assisi who said we should preach the word at all times and when necessary, use words. What's he saying? Shut up and live it. That's a key part of how we are supposed to go and tell people about Jesus. My wife used that approach with me and look what happened. When it comes to my brothers I figure God wants me to do the same thing. You want to do something for the Baldwins? Pray. Specifically, pray for my example to my family and to the other people in my life. If God doesn't shine through the way I live my life, what would be the point of me ever saying anything about Him to my brothers or anyone else?

By the way, people also want to know how my coming to faith affected my relationship with my brothers. They don't ask about my sisters, probably because they don't realize I have any. In all, there are six of us Baldwin children, four boys and two girls. I am the youngest of the six, which I believe explains a lot about why I am the way I am.

Anyway, people want to know if anything has changed with my brothers since I became a Christian. The question usually comes in a form like, *So, Stephen, has your stand for Christ gotten in the way of your relationship with your politically left brothers who are serving Satan in Hollywood?* Ha. That's the funniest thing I've ever heard.

The short answer to that question is this: The love we have as a family is stronger than any of our personal views about politics or anything else. My brothers and sisters have been very supportive of the change in my life. Very supportive. We have a mutual respect for one another, and I will not violate that by throwing Jesus in their faces. I don't think I am supposed to. If you disagree with that statement, reread the first chapter.

My family supports my newfound faith, but that doesn't mean they've supported everything I've done since my conversion. They didn't do backflips when I went to the Republican convention in 2004. I think they were more shocked by that than anything, not so much because of me going to the *Republican* convention but because of how little I've cared about politics. Alec always said I was the least political person on the planet. He didn't think I even knew how many justices were on the Supreme Court, much less what any of them stood for. Since becoming a Christian I have become more politically involved. I vote and speak out on issues now based on what I perceive to be the moral implications involved, not because of blind loyalty to any party.

After all, when I made my covenant with Christ I didn't make a covenant with the Republicans or the Democrats.

But when it comes to my family, politics never get in the way of our love for one another. We're family. We always have been. And we always will be.

HARD TO IGNORE

I try not to throw my faith in my family's faces, but sometimes that happens anyway. One of my brothers told me that three or four times a month he will be stopped on the street by someone asking if he was one of the Baldwin brothers. This happens all the time to all four of us. Then, my brother told me, these people will ask if he will do them a favor. He will say sure as he automatically reaches into his pocket for a pen for the autograph request that always follows that question. But instead of asking for autographs my brother tells me people will say, "Please tell your brother Stephen, praise the Lord for what he's doing for the kingdom."

One of my brothers was also involved in a play that led to him receiving a letter from someone who saw the production months earlier. This particular play contained a line that some people found objectionable because of how it referred to God. My brother got a letter that read, "Dear Mr. Baldwin, my name is so and so. My wife and I attended your production but we didn't stay for the second act because we didn't agree with the content. We tried to get a refund on our tickets, but the theater would not reimburse us. We also contacted the show's producers, but they wouldn't either. We were hoping you would personally reimburse us. It is a strange request, but we thought you, if anyone, would understand why we found this play objectionable. If for any reason you need further explanation, ask your brother Stephen."

My brother didn't send them any money, nor should he. Yet I find it interesting that this Christian couple who found this play offensive told my brother to talk to me about why they would feel this way. Episodes like this now happen all the time. Do they get my brothers closer to God? That depends. But the one thing these episodes hopefully do is allow me to set an example to my brothers through both my public and private expressions of faith.

I don't have to tell my family how much I've changed. Hopefully they can see it. And if they can't, my talking about it won't do any good. Obeying the last words of Jesus doesn't just mean talking about God with my lips. I have to do it with my life as well. It sounds like a cliché, but I know this is true: I may be the only Bible my family ever reads. Because of this, I better live my life in such a way that this Bible is always open for them to read.

I wake up every day knowing this has to be my first priority if I want to make any kind of difference in the youth culture in America or in the lives of those I love the most. Again, I want to challenge you, if obeying the final words of Jesus Christ is not your top priority, something in your life needs to change and fast. God doesn't just tell people like Stephen Baldwin and Luis Palau to go make disciples. He laid this command on every single person who claims to love Jesus. What are you waiting on?

Heart

Main Entry: ¹**heart**

Pronunciation: 'härt

Function: *noun*

Etymology: Middle English *hert*, from Old English *heorte*; akin to Old High German *herza* heart, Latin *cord-*, *cor*, Greek *kardia*

1 a : a hollow muscular organ of vertebrate animals that by its rhythmic contraction acts as a force pump maintaining the circulation of the blood **b :** a structure in an invertebrate animal functionally analogous to the vertebrate heart **c :** BREAST, BOSOM **d :** something resembling a heart in shape; *specifically* **:** a stylized representation of a heart

2 a : PERSONALITY, DISPOSITION <a cold *heart*> **b** *obsolete* **:** INTELLECT

3 : the emotional or moral as distinguished from the intellectual nature: as **a :** generous disposition **:** COMPASSION <a leader with *heart*> **b :** LOVE, AFFECTIONS <won her *heart*> **c :** COURAGE, ARDOR <never lost *heart*>

4 : one's innermost character, feelings, or inclinations <knew it in his *heart*> <a man after my own *heart*>

5 a : the central or innermost part **:** CENTER **b :** the essential or most vital part of something **c :** the younger central compact part of a leafy rosette (as a head of lettuce)

CHAPTER 14

Heart

I will never forget back in high school how intense it was when I was a member of the wrestling team. In case you are unfamiliar with wrestling outside of the fake WWE garbage on television, real wrestling is the single most intense individual sport on the planet. Tennis, golf, track, none of them compare to six minutes of mano a mano, using every ounce of strength in your body to pin the other guy's shoulders to the mat while he tries to do the same to you. No one on your team can bail you out. If you don't have it that day, baby, you're toast. And there were days I didn't have it. The other guy would throw me to the mat, do a couple of moves, and be right on the verge of pinning me.

Even with all the noise in the gym from the crowd going nuts and everyone in the place screaming at me, I could always hear the voice of my coach. When I had one shoulder on the mat and my opponent was grinding as hard as he could to pin the other one, my coach would yell one word as loud as he could: Heart! That's all he had to say. Heart. With that one word he asked me if somewhere, somehow, I could conjure up the strength, and the will, and the pride to do what I had to do to get off the mat, turn the match around, and win.

It usually worked. We Baldwins were and still are today intense competitors. Our dad was a coach and my brothers and I have an intense desire to win no matter what. For him, it all came down to the heart. I firmly believe that's why we've succeeded as we have in Hollywood. Growing up we didn't know how to fail. We didn't have the heart for it. So when I heard my coach screaming "Heart!" it was for me more than a motivational ploy. His words struck who I was. Did I have the heart to will myself up from the brink of defeat, reverse this jerk, and win the match? Even if I didn't win, I would pour out my heart trying.

THE POWER OF THE HEART

My high school wrestling coach could not know then what the scientific community has only now begun to uncover about the power of the heart. Proverbs 23:7 says that the way we think of ourselves in our hearts defines who we really are. Research has now discovered how true that statement really is.

A research think tank called the Institute of HeartMath found that the physical heart in your chest you probably thought of only as a blood pumping muscle exercises considerable influence over who you are and how you act. The heart influences the rest of the body in ways that go beyond its physical functions. Researchers have discovered what is called cardioelectromagnetic communication between the heart and the rest of the body. They found the heart's electromagnetic energy is sixty times greater than that produced by the brain, and the magnetic field it produces is 5,000 times stronger.[1] They've also found the heart has what they called cellular memory.

Basically this means the heart has its own "brain" with its own memories. It remembers all of the emotional experiences of our lives.

Now here's the really wild part. Studies conducted on heart transplant patients have found that the heart's "memories" are often transferred to the recipient. I know this sounds like something out of a movie, and since I make movies you may think I've confused a script I read somewhere with the real world, but believe me, I haven't. Solid science backs this up.

One documented case involved a forty-seven-year-old foundry worker, a white dude and a real Archie Bunker type. The guy nearly flipped out when his doctor told him he'd received a heart from a seventeen-year-old black male. He didn't like the idea of a black man's heart inside his chest, but since death sounded like an even worse idea, he took it.

After his surgery the white foundry worker made jokes about how he would probably start listening to rap music. He didn't. Instead the guy fell in love with classical music. He hated it before his surgery, now he couldn't get enough of it. This isn't as strange as it might seem once you learn that the donor loved classical music. In fact, he died clutching his violin case after a car hit him while he was on his way to a lesson. The heart recipient's wife also told how her husband has now starting building relationships with black co-workers, something he would never do before.[2]

Of course this could all be a coincidence. So could the story of the college professor who received the heart of a police officer killed in the line of duty. The professor made a full recovery, although he started having strange dreams a few weeks after the surgery. In the dreams he would see a bright flash of light, followed by a burning sensation in his face. Just before the flash of light he would see Jesus' face. As it turns out the police officer died from a gunshot wound to the face. They never caught the guy who did it. Witnesses said the killer had long hair, deep eyes, a beard and a calm look on his face. Most said he looked like Jesus.[3]

And then there's the story of an eight-year-old girl who received the heart of a ten-year-old murder victim. Not long after receiving the heart, the little girl started having nightmares about the man who killed the donor. When the dreams wouldn't go away, the girl's mother took her to a psychiatrist. After several sessions the doctor decided there had to be something to the girl's dreams. They called the police, and using the description of the man from the girl's nightmares, *they caught the murderer!* Is that a freakin' miracle or what? The little girl didn't just nail the man's looks. She also told investigators the time of the murder, the place, the weapon, and what the dead girl said to the man right before he killed her.[4]

HEART IN THE BIBLE

So what, Stevie B? It sounds like you swallowed a science book. Why should we care? Here's why: These discoveries confirm what the Bible and Jesus have said for the past 2,000 years. According to the Bible, the heart determines the direction and destiny of every human being. In Genesis 6:5 the Bible says the hearts of the human race were filled with evil thoughts. As a result God's heart was broken, and He started over by wiping out the entire human race with a flood. And yes, I believe a flood really did cover the earth and the human race survived because of a big ole boat Noah built.

In Exodus 7:13 the Bible says Pharaoh's heart was hard which led to the destruction of Egypt. Deuteronomy 4:39 tells us to seek the Lord with our whole heart and Deuteronomy 6:4 says to love the Lord your God with all your heart. David was a man after God's own heart, so the Lord made him king of Israel (1 Samuel 13:14). Proverbs 4:23 says to guard your heart. Jesus said the pure in heart are blessed (Matthew 5:8) and that wherever we put our treasure, our heart will be there as well (Matthew 6:21).

In all, Jesus mentioned the heart twenty-eight times, while the word appears in the Bible as a whole—are you ready for this—570 times.

Okay, okay, okay, Stephen. We get it. The heart matters. Geez. So what? I'm not just saying the heart matters. I'm saying your heart is the ONLY THING THAT MATTERS. Americans are obsessed with lowering their cholesterol and looking good and staying in shape and all of that. We will do anything to look as young as we can as long as we can. Beyond their looks, what is the main thing people want to keep fit? The heart.

I have discovered that there is a spiritual heart disease that is even more deadly because it messes up your health now and your eternity later. But, I believe if people would simply plug into the greatest power in the world, and let God purify their hearts, they would not be able to comprehend how unbelievable the change in their lives would be.

I know from experience. Of all the changes that God made in the life of Stevie B, the biggest, most amazing change of all was this: He gave me a new heart. The same old blood pump may beat in my chest, but the core of who I am is now brand-new. God did for me what He promised in Ezekiel 11:19-20, "I will give them an undivided heart and put a new spirit in them; I will remove from them their heart of stone and give them a heart of flesh. Then they will follow my decrees and be careful to keep my laws. They will be my people, and I will be their God." But that's not all.

Before this change of heart, I operated on a level where my brain dictated the course of my life. When I encountered information, I filtered it through my brain and decided what I would do in response. Now, my new heart guides my life as it is touched and led by the Spirit of God. I now filter all the information I encounter through my heart and then to my head.

You're losing me, Stevie. What's the difference between thinking with your brain and being led by your heart? That sounds like a bunch of mushy-gushy, touchy-feely nonsense where you let your emotions take over your life. That sounds pretty dangerous to me. Listen, when I say I now allow my heart to lead me, I'm not talking about letting my feelings rule my life. What I have discovered is that for God to touch my life and lead me in His will, my heart must be sensitive to His Holy Spirit.

The Spirit works through the heart, rather than bombarding the brain with arguments and logic. Proverbs 3:5-6 puts it this way, "Trust in the LORD with all your heart and lean not on your own understanding; in all your ways acknowledge him, and he will make your paths straight." There is a direct connection between trusting in the Lord with your *heart*, and Him leading you in the direction He wants to take your life. The verse doesn't say to trust God with all your brain, but with all your *heart*. It isn't about feelings, but about the instinctive, intuitive nature of the heart that God is able to speak to and guide you through.

I now understand there is a huge difference between following Stephen's will that comes from my brain, and following God's will that flows through my heart. You can only imagine how radically different my life is now. Prior to becoming a Christian, everything I accomplished, I achieved through my own intellect, talent, and will. God kept trying to get through to me. I wrote earlier how I always had a nagging question ringing in my ears, wondering what the real purpose was behind my success. Something inside me knew something bigger and greater than making movies had to be going on. Deep in my heart I knew God had to be involved, but I didn't understand the hows or the whys. Nor did I try to find the answers. Those questions came from my heart, but I didn't listen to my heart. My head was in charge.

But now, one of the greatest blessings in the experience of my faith is the power and presence of the Holy Spirit Who now guides me as He touches my heart. When things in life happen to me, good or bad, when decisions in my life have to be made, good or bad, there is a grace, there is a pause that occurs within me waiting intuitively for my heart to send a message to my head about how to proceed and what decision to make. That is the place where the Spirit works and God guides me in His will.

Do you see the difference? God didn't just get rid of some of my bad habits. Nor have I had a religious experience. As a result of the inner workings of the Holy Spirit of God, not only has my life changed, but the mechanics that determine every decision I make and my approach to life are completely different. What was once dead inside of me is alive and in charge.

WHY THE HEART MUST BE MADE NEW

Okay, okay, okay. Slow down there Stevie boy. What do you mean what was once dead inside of you is now alive? How can the heart be dead and you still be alive? That's the point. Can't you see it? I wasn't alive before. My heart was dead spiritually, which meant I was as well. The Bible says that before Jesus "you were dead in your transgressions and sins, in which you used to live when you followed the ways of this world and of the ruler of the kingdom of the air, the spirit who is now at work in those who are disobedient. All of us also lived among them at one time, gratifying the cravings of our sinful nature and following its desires and thoughts" (Ephesians 2:1-3). Learning this was a real revelation for me. It helped me understand that the way I was before wasn't my fault.

The problem was the heart I was born with. The Bible says the heart "is deceitful above all things and beyond cure. Who can understand it?" (Jeremiah 17:9). This means the heart with which I was born contained a nature that innately pursued sin.

Basically, sin is the default position of the human heart. The Bible isn't just saying the heart innately pursues bad stuff, like getting stoned or sleeping around. That's only a result of an even bigger problem. And that problem is selfishness. Just look at little kids. "Mommy give me this, Daddy buy me some candy, let me do this, buy me that, gimme, gimme, gimme." That's the human animal. It's all about serving ourselves. There aren't a lot of Mother Teresas running around out there who spend their entire lives serving others. Deep down we're still that little kid with the gimmes. That's just who we are. That's the nature of our hearts.

God speaks to that dead heart. He throws commands at us

telling us to seek Him with a whole heart (Deuteronomy 4:39), love Him with our hearts (Mark 12:30), and to be pure in heart (Matthew 5:8). There's only one problem: I had a dead heart. I couldn't do any of this on my own. But, when I became willing to open my heart to God, He removed the sin that filled it, and filled it up with His Spirit and with a knowledge and understanding of the experience I'm having now.

My heart was busted, and God not only fixed it, He replaced it. It fascinates me that there are so many millions and millions and millions of people out there that will dedicate so much time and energy into doing what they have to do to maintain or improve the condition of their heart on a physical level, when what they don't realize is that it is more than just a muscle that pumps blood. That's just its function in the natural. There is a whole other infinite level of purpose and power that our hearts serve. You can experience this if you simply become willing to open your heart for God to come in and remake it.

My heart's fine, Stevie B. Leave me alone. You don't get it. The spiritual condition of your heart affects every part of who you are and what you do. Jesus said, "For out of the heart come evil thoughts, murder, adultery, sexual immorality, theft, false testimony, slander" (Matthew 15:19).

Dude, listen. I had some stuff in my life I didn't like but I couldn't get rid of, physical addictions like to cigarettes. I couldn't quit smoking. I could not, absolutely could not keep myself from using bad language. It was a part of who I was to say the "F" word whenever I wanted. I said it didn't matter, but intuitively deep down inside me I didn't like it. I didn't like that I had to once in a while have a cigarette. I didn't like that every day I had to express myself in such a way that I had to use vulgarity to be hip or cool or accepted. I couldn't stop because all of this flowed out of my heart. My problem wasn't willpower. My problem was the condition of my heart.

Listen, I'm not claiming to be some expert on all this. But I have been blessed with an ability to see things simply. To my simple mind it seems to me that if the Bible has been saying for a long time that my life is the way it is because of the condition of my heart, then it makes sense to me that I could consider pursuing change in my life by becoming willing to allow God to change my heart in a supernatural way that my brain could never possibly comprehend.

This is what I have said before. I didn't just pray a prayer to be born again because I wanted to go to heaven. I slowly but surely over time throughout my life had enough experiences that were both positive and negative that made me curious as to whether God was real.

I then questioned so strongly the potential of his power and truth that I spiritually, in my mind, reached into my own chest and pulled out my own heart and held it before God. I said, See this. I heard that this is the key. And with my own blood running down my forearms, spiritually, I said, God take this from me and do with it what You will. Because that's what I am told according to your Book is what I have to do in order to have the total experience that your book suggests. So that's what I did, and that's when this change took place.

DAILY OFFERING

What does all this mean? It means the work God does on your life is an inside job. I learned this truth back when I first went through a twelve-step program. We had a saying back then that says you cannot become someone who understands what it takes to become victorious over addictions until you start to explore emotionally what is happening within you. It wasn't until I came to Jesus that I could perceive the full power of that statement. Back then I would take one day at a time and focus on staying sober. Now, I focus one day at a time on living for God. But I don't try to muster up a bunch of willpower. Instead, I rip my heart out again and offer it fresh to God each day. My prayer is always, Lord, do with my heart what You will. And God, if You want my opinion about what I would like for You to do with it, here it is: Humble it. Make it quiet. Make it peaceful. Bless me by giving me a heart that only needs You and your Spirit and all that comes with it, the love and the joy and the peace and the satisfaction. If my heart can be filled with that, and nothing else, then I don't need anything else.

I've learned that the pursuit of that desire is my purpose for being born. There is a greater experience in this life than just the physical. And to everyone who reads that and says, *I don't believe it, I don't agree with it*, you are missing out. If the world has convinced you that what I am sharing with you isn't worth your time, or is unrealistic, then you are a victim of the lies that rule the world. Because I know beyond a shadow of a doubt that the reason I was born was to have the experience that I am having now.

As I have said, you name it and I have been there, done that. I have already existed within a world and a reality that less than one percent of the world's population ever experiences. From the money to the fame to the glory to the prestige. Been there, done that. The only sense of gratitude and satisfaction that has even come remotely close to the experience that I am having in my journey of faith has been the love that I have had from my wife and my children. Even that has not been as great as the experience that I have had with Jesus.

Does that mean I never mess up and I now live a life of spiritual perfection? Keep reading. The next chapter answers that question. Yet I've found that not even my failures can mess up what God has done in my life through my heart. And all of this comes down to one thing: Heart. My life has changed because God gave me a new heart where His Spirit now dwells.

Flesh

Main Entry: ¹**flesh**

Pronunciation: 'flesh

Function: *noun*

Etymology: Middle English, from Old English *flǣsc;* akin to Old High German *fleisk* flesh and perhaps to Old Norse *flēan* to flay — more at FLAY

1 a : the soft parts of the body of an animal and especially of a vertebrate; *especially* : the parts composed chiefly of skeletal muscle as distinguished from visceral structures, bone, and integuments **b :** sleek well-fatted condition of body **c :** SKIN

2 a : edible parts of an animal **b :** flesh of a mammal or fowl eaten as food

3 a : the physical nature of human beings <the spirit indeed is willing, but the *flesh* is weak — Matthew 26:41 (Authorized Version)> **b :** HUMAN NATURE

4 a : human beings : MANKIND **b :** living beings **c :** STOCK, KINDRED

5 : a fleshy plant part used as food; *also* : the fleshy part of a fruit

6 *Christian Science* : an illusion that matter has sensation

7 : SUBSTANCE <insights buried in the *flesh* of the narrative — Jan Carew>

- **in the flesh :** in person and alive

CHAPTER 15

Flesh

For we know that the law is spiritual; but I am made out of flesh, sold into sin's power. For I do not understand what I am doing, because I do not practice what I want to do, but I do what I hate. And if I do what I do not want to do, I agree with the law that it is good. So now I am no longer the one doing it, but it is sin living in me. For I know that nothing good lives in me, that is, in my flesh. For the desire to do what is good is with me, but there is no ability to do it. For I do not do the good that I want to do, but I practice the evil that I do not want to do. Now if I do what I do not want, I am no longer the one doing it, but it is the sin that lives in me. So I discover this principle: when I want to do good, evil is with me. For in my inner self I joyfully agree with God's law. But I see a different law in the parts of my body, waging war against the law of my mind and taking me prisoner to the law of sin in the parts of my body. What a wretched man I am! Who will rescue me from this body of death? I thank God through Jesus Christ our

Lord! So then, with my mind I myself am a slave to
the law of God, but with my flesh, to the law of sin.
(Romans 7:14–25 HCSB)

"I am made out of flesh." That statement is freaking brilliant.
Even though I am now a believer in Jesus Christ, even though I
am now having this incredible experience with God through the
Holy Spirit, even though God has given me a new heart and made
an unbelievable change in my life, I am still made out of flesh.
Which means, believe it or not, I still screw up.

I'm not just saying I'm not perfect. I'm telling you I still have
inside me the capacity to do all the bone-headed, self-centered,
make your hair curl if I talked about them things I did before I
came to Christ. Some people got their hands slapped for reaching into the cookie jar. I strapped an M-80 firecracker to the
cookie jar and blew it up so I could get all the cookies at once.
That kid is still in me and all of my good intentions, all of my de-
terminations, all of my good thoughts, can't do a thing about it.

So to all of you people who say to me, *Hey, Stevie B, I would
try that God thing but I know I can't live up to it*, I say, join the club.
Honestly, there's not one of us on this side of the Jesus experience who can live up to what God expects. Go back and read that
Bible passage at the beginning of this chapter. The guy who
wrote it says he can't live up to God's standards, either, and he
wrote thirteen books in the Bible. If a guy that God used to write
the Word of God can't live up to God's expectations, what makes
you think any of us can? And if none of us can, stop using this as
a lame excuse to keep you from opening your life to God.

*Yeah, but Stephen, if no one can live up to what God expects, what's
the point in trying?* Dude. Listen. Let me let you in on a little secret: God already knows there ain't a one of us who can do what
He tells us to do. He doesn't have a problem with that. Does that
mean I can go back to doing all the stuff I used to do and God
will be fine with it? No. God meant all that stuff in His Book

about how He expects us to live even though He knows we can't do it on our own. But, He says He will do all this for us. Philippians 2:13 says, "For it is God who works in you to will and to act according to his good purpose." Did you catch that? I can't do this, so God works in me to give me both the willingness and the ability to do what He wants me to do. That's a pretty sweet deal.

THE POWER OF FLESH

God works inside me, but I'm still flesh, which means I have to rely on Him 24/7. Here's what I mean. I am a red-blooded heterosexual American male. Back in the day, when I would see a woman walking down the sidewalk with some really nice, er, boots, my natural human reaction was not only to notice, but once I checked the front of her boots, I would turn around after she passed to make sure the heels were as nice as the toes.

But now I am a Christian as well as a married man. I don't have any business checking out any boots that are not on my wife's feet. And I sure as heck don't have any business checking to see if the heels are as nice as the toes. So the next time I'm walking down the street and some really shiny boots come my way, I tell myself not to look. Don't look, Stephen. Keep your eyes straight. Look away. Look anywhere. Just DON'T KEEP STARING AT THOSE BOOTS. Which of course I am doing. Maybe not every time, but when I tell myself not to do something I fail at least as often as I succeed. Why? Why can't I keep myself from checking out any good-looking female who comes within a quarter mile of me? Because I am flesh.

Does that mean I still look today? No, and not because my wife puts blinders on me every time I leave the house. My eyes are now free from both the bondage of cleavage and from my brain screaming "don't look" eight thousand times a day. Now when I face this situation I just laugh at myself and the way I used to be. I know now that I have a choice. I am free. I am no longer under the bondage of sin because God's Spirit has delivered me. That's what the passage at the beginning of this chapter is talking about.

Do I still feel tempted? Yes, because I am flesh. But the realization of my own weakness immediately makes me go to God for strength and deliverance rather than telling myself to avert my eyes.

That's the difference between walking in the flesh and walking in the Spirit. When I'm in the Spirit, if Jennifer Lopez said hi to me on the street, I would respond with a "How are you?" and keep going. Back in the day, in the back of my mind I would be going, "Wow, how can I swing this one," but now I'm praying for the woman as I'm talking to her. That's the difference between who I was and who I am. And the difference is God's Spirit. I am never going to be perfect, but it is in my acceptance of my lack of power that the Lord fills me with His strength. I know I can't do this on my own without it. But I didn't come to that place of understanding until I became willing to give Him the power.

SOMETIMES THE FLESH COMES OUT ON TOP

I met up with an old friend in New York recently for dinner and afterward we went to the Rolling Stones concert at Madison Square Garden. Now this guy is an old buddy from way back. Mind you, he is going through some personal struggles which means on this particular night he was cutting himself some slack. He's having a few beers and talking old war stories about all the chicks we used to chase. He knows my situation. He knows I don't drink and he knows I'm a Christian, and he's cool with that. But he has had a few beers and he's feeling them. And you know what? I allowed myself spiritually to get sucked right into the vacuum of this guy's lack of discipline. I said to myself, *Play it cool. Be cool. Don't be a geek. Don't be a nerd. You don't want him to get turned off from your faith by being too blah blah blah blah blah.*

And sure enough I am sitting at a table with four or five guys, telling fart jokes and, you know, doing the kind of things guys do when there aren't any women around.

One of the guys is flirting with the waitress; she's flirting back, looking for a better tip. After a while I allowed myself to get comfortable enough that I let my guard down. Before long I turned around and I blurted out a pretty graphically lude, crass comment, the kind of thing that was just business as usual when this old friend and I used to hang out.

The nanosecond after the words left my lips I cringed and thought to myself, *Well that wasn't so smart.* And then immediately I thought, *Okay you slipped up. That was wrong. You just contradicted yourself and about ninety-five percent of what's been coming out of your mouth for the last twenty-four months. But, you didn't realize it, you didn't mean it. If I could back up the DVD of life right now I would have done it differently. No big deal, don't do it again.* Now I had all of those thoughts in about three seconds, maybe less. I was pretty quick to forgive myself.

But something that was almost unforgivable was the husband and wife at the table next to us. They heard what I said. When the husband caught my comment, his neck craned, and he turned his head to see who'd said it. I caught all of this out of the corner of my eye, and immediately felt like a phony. I remembered why I am not supposed to say things like that. In my mind I could hear myself saying something like, "You know, Stephen, this is the type of behavior that gives Christians a really bad name."

After the guy at the next table looked back at us, he turned to his wife and asked if she was finished with her meal. Within thirty seconds of me the idiot opening my fat mouth, this couple gets up and leaves. You know what dude? I screwed up bad. Even though I forgave myself for letting the flesh take over, I still got pretty bent out of shape for about ten minutes as the reel to reel in my mind kept playing back what I did. *You are an idiot. You've* been reading the Bible and praying every day in the hope that a moment like this would never come. What did you just do? I wouldn't be surprised if the guy shows up at a book signing and spits in my face. And if you are that guy and you are reading this, please do come to a signing so that I can ask your forgiveness in person. I know I am only flesh. I know I'm never going to be perfect. It is no excuse. But it is the truth.

Here's what's so frustrating about this whole episode to me. A few hours before the Stones concert I asked God, "Lord, do You want me to go to this thing?" I can't say I heard God say yes, but I also didn't hear Him say no. Looking back, I don't think the environment where I placed myself was the real problem. The problem was I hadn't prepared myself spiritually for that environment. I knew going in that getting together with these old friends meant there was going to be drinking, there was going to be bad language, and once we got to the concert the smell of weed would be everywhere. None of that took me by surprise.

Some might say I should have stayed completely away and not put myself in that kind of place. Fair enough. You can think that if you want. However, I knew if I was ever going to reach these friends, I would have to spend time with them, and that might place me in an environment like this. No, what got me into trouble was my failure to prepare myself like I should have as a follower of Jesus Christ. I should have spent the hour before I left in prayer. But I didn't because I thought, "Hey, it's okay. I'm strong enough to handle this without compromising anything." Like the Bible says, my spirit was willing but my flesh was weak.

Later on that night after I got home I started thinking to myself, What if it was that couple's honeymoon? What if it was their anniversary? What if I ruined their evening? Then I started thinking about what I would do if I was that guy. Boy, I would have really been in the flesh. I would have probably kicked my own butt.

So, I prayed about it that night. Again, I asked the Lord to forgive me, went to bed, and woke up the next day. When I awoke the next morning the first thought that came to my mind was, *I guess so far so good, I am awake. The Lord didn't kill me in my sleep for that sin.* Then I kind of looked around the room and like a little kid I said, "Lord am I in trouble?" Really. I said this. "Lord, am I in trouble for last night?" And a feeling came over me, and I really mean this, a sensation swept over me as if I heard the Lord's voice with almost a parental chuckle. He said to me, "You know what Stevie B, there have been enough deposits put in your holy bank account that I am going to let this one slide." That statement may not be entirely scripturally accurate, but that's the message I sensed from God. He wasn't going to strike me dead. Instead, He forgave me. An overwhelming feeling of grace came over me, which was soon followed by an even more overwhelming feeling of thankfulness and gratitude.

THE POWER OF FORGIVENESS

This was such a powerful moment for me. Yes, I'd blown it. Yes, I offended two people and discredited my witness in front of some old friends. Yes, I brought shame on my Lord. But, He forgave me. As a result there was no longer the vicious cycle and pattern of my past. I didn't have the guilt and the shame and the anger and my day starting off on the wrong foot because of something that transpired the night before. There was no harboring resentment toward myself because of this or that. All of that was gone. It had been removed.

I try to remember this when I correct my own children. There are moments when I call my daughter over when she has misbehaved, and I say to her, "You know what, I'm just letting you know that I'm going to let this one go in the hope that you will correct the problem that you've been showing on your own." That is the feeling that I got the first time in my life I felt a genuine sense of the Lord's forgiveness through His Holy Spirit.

When it comes to this battle with the flesh, there is nothing more powerful than forgiveness. I know who I used to be. So does God. So does my wife. Behavior like I showed at the restaurant was mild compared to who I was before.

Back in the day I prided myself for being a sexual Neanderthal. I always thought men just went out in the woods, found what they wanted, hit it with a club, threw it over their shoulder and drug it back in the cave. I always thought this desire to hunt and the desire to be hunted was a huge part of the dynamic between males and females. And that's what I did. That's how I acted. I figured this was just a part of being male.

When I came to Christ I had to bring this past behavior to Him and confess it as sin. I also confessed it to my wife. You can never comprehend the awesome power of forgiveness until you experience it. I went to my wife, told her I had sinned against her, told her I behaved in ways that were unacceptable, and confessed the lies I'd told.

After all of that she looked me in the eyes and said, "I forgive you because at that time you didn't know Jesus." That is more powerful to me than any force of nature. Kennya and I have conversations that send shudders through me. I had to tell her things that had the potential to be nuclear bombs in our relationship, and she defused them all with three little words. "I forgive you."

Forgiveness sets you free from the power of the flesh. The flesh doesn't just get you with temptations. It sinks its hooks into you through guilt. You can hear it constantly in your ear, reminding you of everything you did wrong, telling you that you're nothing but a phony, filling your head with the lie that you might as well give up because you will never be able to pull this off. Forgiveness shoots guilt in the head. It sets you free from failures in the past so you can focus on doing what needs to be done both now and in the future.

I still have a long way to go. That's obvious. I need God's Spirit to make me constantly aware of how critical my attitudes and my choices are. At the same time, God doesn't want me to live in some kind of stream of perpetual paranoia. Instead He wants me to live my life trusting in the Lord's spirit and not let my guard down. On a commonsense level I know that if for whatever reason I go and spend each afternoon hanging out in a barbershop, eventually I am going to get a haircut. Success doesn't come from trying harder in the flesh. The ultimate goal is to come to the place where I recognize that the flesh is the set-up. God created me to understand that I need Him. I can deny that and do things my way, which I did for a long time, or I can surrender to His authority and trust in the sovereignty of that reality. That's the only way.

WHAT WOULD JESUS DO?

A few years ago everybody ran around wearing these W.W.J.D. bracelets. The idea was to look at them and ask yourself what Jesus would do before you did anything. That's not a bad thing. I'm supposed to try to be like Jesus if I'm a Christian. But here's the thing: I'm never going to be like Jesus and He knew that before I was born.

Nights like my experience in the restaurant before the Stones concert remind me of that little fact of life. But here's what I discovered on this journey. What Jesus wants me to do is make the attempt. He wants me to come to Him and say, Lord, I want to be like You. He wants me to ask Him to remake my character. The Bible says we're supposed to crucify that old fleshy nature. Colossians 3:5 and 8 says, "Put to death, therefore, whatever belongs to your earthly nature: sexual immorality, impurity, lust, evil desires and greed, which is idolatry . . . But now you must rid yourselves of all such things as these: anger, rage, malice, slander, and filthy language from your lips." I can't do this on my own; God has to do it for me. That's where dependence comes in.

In the place of all the garbage He empties from my life, I'm to ask God to fill me with humility, patience, love, and forgiveness. Why? Because that's how Jesus lived. You see, asking my-self "What would Jesus do?" just reminds me of how little I can do on my own. It makes me go back to God again and again, pleading with Him to do this for me. I'm going to screw it up myself. I'm going to mess up on my own. But if I will go to Him every day and pray and read the Word, and do my best to at-tempt, not achieve, but *attempt* to do my best, God will take care of the rest. He doesn't want us to wake up and be perfect. He just wants us to be willing to try.

Earlier in this chapter I talked about how powerful it is to ex-perience forgiveness. But having others forgive you is only the beginning. In this battle with the flesh, in my attempts to get into the "What Would Jesus Do" thing, I've found the most im-portant thing I can do is forgive myself and others.

Instead of beating myself up over my inconsistencies, I have to forgive and move on. Even more important, I have to show the same grace to other people. In my opinion, I believe people can get over a Christian who makes an idiot of himself in a restaurant once every four years. And I think they can overlook the occasional slip of the tongue with bad language. But, when someone claims to have experienced God's forgiveness, and then they hold grudges against other people and refuse to forgive, to me that makes this whole Jesus message sound like nothing but noise.

In all of Christianity we can preach, we can evangelize, we can write books, we can build churches, we can do whatever we want. But if the world does not hear through our words and see through our actions Jesus' message of forgiveness, we're wasting our time.

If you would be willing to forgive your wife for not doing this or that, or your children for not doing what you told them, or the guy who cut you off on the freeway, or your boss for being a jerk, they would all know your Jesus is real. If we could learn to walk in forgiveness then we would have achieved the closest possible understanding of who Jesus was, what He did, and why He did it.

Yeah, I'm only flesh. That means I can't live up to God's standard. I'm going to screw up and I'm going to disappoint God. Not only that, everyone else in the world is only flesh, which means none of us can live up to the standards we set for one another. But God can take care of that, both through His power working in me through His Spirit, and His forgiveness washing over me when I blow it. With that one-two combination there's no way I can fail. I may only be flesh, but when I put this flesh in the hands of God, that's not a problem.

Time

Main Entry: **¹time**

Pronunciation: 'tīm

Function: *noun*

Etymology: Middle English, from Old English *tīma;* akin to Old Norse *tīmi* time, Old English *tīd* — more at TIDE

1 a : the measured or measurable period during which an action, process, or condition exists or continues **: DURATION b :** a nonspatial continuum that is measured in terms of events which succeed one another from past through present to future **c : LEISURE** <*time* for reading>

2 : the point or period when something occurs **: OCCASION**

3 a : an appointed, fixed, or customary moment or hour for something to happen, begin, or end <arrived ahead of *time*> **b :** an opportune or suitable moment <decided it was *time* to retire> — often used in the phrase *about time* <about *time* for a change>

4 a : an historical period **: AGE b :** a division of geologic chronology **c :** conditions at present or at some specified period — usually used in plural <*times* are hard> <move with the *times*> **d :** the present time <issues of the *time*>

5 : finite as contrasted with infinite duration

CHAPTER 16

Kairos

Imagine today is September 10, 2001, just another day in this little slice of paradise on earth that we call the concrete jungles of Manhattan. You're whoever from wherever and for whatever reason you are walking down the street in New York City. You may be a Wall Street guy or a tourist or a native like me who drove into the city for the day. Whatever. As you walk down the street minding your own business, somebody comes up to you and says, "Can I ask you a question? You see, I had the strangest dream last night and I can't get it out of my head. It was more of a nightmare than a dream, and it seemed so real that I woke up this morning thinking it had really happened."

You don't usually talk to nutcases on the street, but since this is a chance to talk to a genuine New York City nutcase, you say, *Sure, go ahead.* The guy says, "In my dream I watched two planes take off about thirty minutes apart from Boston heading to Los Angeles. But instead of heading to L.A., they make a sharp left turn toward New York. In my dream I watched as the first plane flew right into one of the towers of the World Trade Center. I'm standing on the street in my dream, and I watch this huge explosion and smoke billowing out of the tower. All around me everyone is panicking and people in the building that was hit by the plane start jumping out of windows to their deaths.

"Just when it seems things can't get any worse, the second plane slams into the second tower. Not long after that, the second tower collapses killing everyone inside. And not long after that the first tower does the same. As I woke up from my dream a huge cloud of smoke, dust, and terror hung over New York and the rest of the country. Now I can't shake that image from my head. I just had to come to the city today to make sure the towers were still standing and everything was okay."

After the guy finishes spilling all the details to his crazy dream, he turns to you and says, "Do you think anything like that could ever happen?" I'm curious to know how many of you reading this book right now would have said "yes" to this guy's question.

Be completely honest. How many of you on September 10, 2001, would say that you thought events like this guy saw in his dream could actually take place in twenty-first-century America? I think most of us wouldn't have been surprised by a terrorist group trying to pull off some kind of attack. After all, a group tried to bring down the World Trade Center with a car bomb in 1993.

How's this for scary weird: one of the witnesses said it felt like an airplane had hit the building in that attack. But the first World Trade Center bombing didn't come close to bringing the buildings down. Five people died, not thousands. So, prior to 9-11 we might have thought some terrorist group might try to attack the twin towers, but, most of us thought the worst that could happen would be something like what happened at the Pentagon on 9-11. The attack there was horrible, but only one portion of the building was destroyed. One hundred twenty-five people died, which was tragic, but that number was small enough to fit into the view of reality we had of the world prior to 9-11. Never in our worst nightmares did anyone think that twelve terrorists could bring down both of the twin towers and kill nearly

3,000 people. Not in America. Not in New York City. Not using our own planes against us.

NEW REALITY

For Stephen Baldwin, September 11th was clearly the demonstration of the impossible becoming reality. What I *knew* could not happen, did. I've already shared how that opened my eyes to see that *anything* really is possible. Prior to that day I always thought of myself as quite the imaginative fellow. I told people, "Hey now, come on, where is your sense of imagination? Don't you believe that in this life anything is possible? Don't you think in life you can do what you want and be who you want to be and the sky is the limit?"

I thought the human capacity to achieve something positive was unlimited. But if someone asked me if I thought two planes from Boston could hit and bring down the twin towers prior to September 11th, my answer would have been no.

That day, 9-11, left me with a new perspective where now the possibilities were endless. In my mind I now accept the fact that nightmares can become reality at any time. That epiphany changed the way I live my life. Don't get me wrong. I didn't freak out. Instead I very simply, very calmly said to myself that if the world could change in an instant, then the way I think about the world needed to change.

Not only did the impossible happen on 9-11, the day marked a turning point in history. From the moment the first plane hit the North Tower, life would never, ever be the same again. I personally never could have imagined how different the world was going to be after 9-11.

The Greeks had a word to describe moments in time like this: the word "kairos." The word means "time" but that's only the beginning. The Greeks had another word to describe the passing of minutes and hours through the day, the word "chronos." They used kairos to describe critical points of time, the turning points of history. The Bible uses the word when it says that at just the right time God sent His Son to earth (Galatians 4:4). That, gang, was the ultimate kairos moment.

I still ponder all of 9-11 in absolute amazement. I just don't understand how anyone could live through it and not seriously reevaluate their existence. How could anyone go back to business as usual? I am sure that 9-11 caused many people to have life changing experiences. People came to faith. People stopped and took a long, hard look at how they lived and why. Statistics show that nationally, church attendance increased drastically after the attacks, but only for about a year. That's what I don't get. Maybe it's just me. How does something like that happen in America and people get over it in a month or a year or even a decade? It's like they forget what happened.

I see people on lines at security checkpoints at airports who roll their eyes and sigh before they have to take their shoes off and step through a metal detector. Don't get me wrong. There were at least half a dozen times not long after 9-11 that I thought, *don't we have any technology better than this?* And there were even a few times when I was late for a flight that I sighed and rolled my eyes. But then within a few minutes I remembered how lucky I am. It wasn't until after 9-11 that I at thirty-five years old really understood and felt in my heart how lucky I am to have the freedoms I've had as an American.

I will never forget walking through an airport a few months after 9-11 and seeing soldiers with M-16s. One of the people walking through the airport near me turned to me and said, "Now America will know how the rest of the world has lived." Obviously he meant that other countries have had these kinds of security measures for decades. But that comment really touched me. I thought to myself afterward, *Wow, this guy is right. It was only a couple of weeks ago they raised the terror threat level here in New York, which meant police officers in full anti-terrorist gear carrying machine guns walked the streets and patrolled the subways.*

How can we pretend life can ever be anything close to normal when events like this happen all too frequently? And if life will never be normal again, how do we keep from wondering what the point of this existence is to begin with? Those are the questions that kairos moments leave us asking ourselves.

OTHER KAIROS MOMENTS

September 11th changed the world. It was, for me and many other people, an incredible kairos moment that altered my understanding of the world forever. Here's the really weird part. Since 9-11 we've witnessed other kairos moments that in some ways were even bigger. On December 26, 2004, the ground under the Indian Ocean shifted which spawned a wave that killed hundreds of thousands of people and caused hundreds of billions of dollars in damages. Life will never, ever, be the same in Indonesia, India, Sri Lanka or any of the other countries hit by the worst tsunami in recorded history.

On the last weekend of August 2005, a storm rolled onto Louisiana, Mississippi and Alabama from the Gulf of Mexico. Initial damage reports were bad, but they were nothing compared to what happened the second day of the storm. Levies around New Orleans gave way and flooded the city. By the time Hurricane Katrina was over, it was the single worst natural disaster in American history.

As if the storm wasn't bad enough, people made a bad situation even worse. Looters ravaged the city, and reports came in of robberies, assaults, and rapes taking place within the shelters set up to protect people from the storm. And if that wasn't bad enough, the damage to the city was so bad that rescuers couldn't get to the people fast enough. Watching CNN was like watching the scary parts of the Bible coming true.

I've got to ask, how can you go back to your normal, everyday life after Katrina? I will never forget one woman they showed on the news after the hurricane. She was walking down a street with two Wal-Mart bags in her hands. It was, she said, all she had left in the world. If everything you own, everything you think is important in life, can be blown away by a single storm, how can you *not* re-evaluate your life and question what you live for?

People wonder why God allows something like Hurricane Katrina. Turn it around and look at it from His point of view. It's not like Katrina should have taken anyone by surprise. In 2004 four major hurricanes hit Florida alone. New Orleans knew their time would come. Government leaders on every level knew it was just a matter of time before a major hurricane hit the area. But here's the crazy thing: No one did anything about it.

Officials knew for years that the levies couldn't take anything stronger than a Category 3 storm. I heard Bill O'Reilly ask one guy who was supposed to be part of the advance planning for storms, "You mean to say that the plan for the state of Louisiana was when a Category 4 or 5 hurricane was coming in they were just going to set there and let people die? I mean why weren't the levies ready, why weren't the pumps ready? What's the deal?" No one was ready because even though everyone knew a storm like this was possible, no one believed it would ever really hit. That's what kairos moments do. They rip the scab off the wound of human pride and denial and remind us that anything really is possible and that we should live our lives that way.

The reason I bring all this up isn't to open some can of negative worms or try to bum you out. I guess it is really just to share my point of view and I'm not even sure what that is. But I know this: Everything happens for a reason. Yeah, yeah, yeah, that's one of those things I used to say, too, like *anything is possible*. There's a difference between saying it and believing it, and I believe kairos moments come for a divine reason.

I came away from 9-11 saying to myself, *I don't know what it is, but I have a feeling God is involved here.* As I've wandered down this road of faith, having given my heart to Jesus, I've come to realize that God is always involved. I'm not saying God sent 9-11 and the tsunami and Katrina to punish the world or give us a taste of His wrath. Do I think it's possible? That's a question you will need to take up with God. However, I have learned that I need to open myself up to a new perception of discovery. When things happen, instead of looking at the surface events like the wind and the flooding of Katrina, I need to ask what God could be up to through these events.

For Stephen Baldwin, being the kook that I am, now, in this new realm of possibility, I'm having an awesome time. Things keep getting weirder. Weather patterns are changing. The unimaginable is pretty much the lead story on the news every day. Just about everybody I know is wondering where this whole deal called life is going. Me, I'm not worried. Why? I no longer rely on myself for the outcome.

Somehow emotionally I'm at peace as a result of something that has transpired that I cannot explain. But what I do know is this: If I get in a car accident my air bag is going to pop out and probably save me. I don't know all of the intricate techno details as to what it takes to make that happen. The guy who sold me the car said the air bags will protect me, and that's good enough for me. In the same way, I've read God's Book and I know He is in control. Now, instead of worrying about what the future may hold, I find I need to constantly watch and listen for what God wants to teach me.

GOD AND KAIROS

When I look back on my life, I realize God has tried to open my eyes to this truth for a very long time. Long before 9-11 I had my own mini-kairos moments of experiences I walked away from even though I knew I shouldn't have been able to.

There was the time a drug dealer in an abandoned building on the Lower East Side of Manhattan said to me, "Bro, don't let the drugs control you." That was a personal kairos moment because the next thought I had was, "Wow, what have I become that the guy who profits from this mess I'm making of myself is telling me I need to go home?"

My wife going five stops past the stop she was supposed to take on the day we met was another personal kairos moment. Making a skate video that went on to become a reality and completed the second half of a prophetic word spoken over my life more than ten years earlier is a kairos moment. I can't explain all of that, but maybe that's the point. God sends these moments to get my attention and redirect the course of my life forever.

I believe God does the same thing with the big kairos moments that affect entire nations and sometimes the whole world. The world changed over sixty years ago with the end of World War II and the dropping of the first atomic bombs. Then Russia got the bomb and everyone was afraid we would blow up the planet. There's a word for moments like these.

So what did God do in the middle of this kairos moment? He dropped down guys like Billy Graham. No one ever saw anything like Billy Graham before. He went all over the planet and millions of people came out to hear him. That's what God does. He allows these kairos moments to hit to get our attention, then to make sure we get His point, He sends someone to speak up for Him.

I believe God does the same thing today. There's no denying the world has changed. I heard the city of New York is planning to put 500 video cameras in the city's mass transit system. That's like living in lockdown. We now live in a terrorist society. Everyone is afraid. Everyone wonders what bad thing will happen next. So what is God doing about it? He's raising up a new apostolic movement in the world.

Now before any of you good Christians freak over my using the word "apostolic," just settle down. The word apostle is a Greek word that means "someone who is sent with a message." And no, I can't read Greek, but my writing partner can. He made sure I got this right. So if the word apostle means someone who is sent out with a message and if God is sending out a new breed of messengers today who will preach His message in a radical, relevant way, that, in my opinion, qualifies as a new apostolic movement.

Just like God sent Billy Graham sixty something years ago, He's sending out an army of new Billy Grahams today. None of them will probably ever become a household name, but believe me brother, they're coming.

So who are these new apostles, God's new breed of messengers? They're an army of young men and women that are going to go out and tell people about Jesus in a new hardcore original way just like the original apostles did.

In the Bible the apostles trained others and taught them what it meant to be a hardcore, sold-out follower of Jesus. That's what the hardcore movement is doing. This is a new breed of rock and rollers for Christ, people God saved from addictions, crime, you know, erratic behavior that most people would think make these new radicals the last people God would ever pick. Sort of reminds me of the original apostles.

In the past a new radical for Jesus Christ was Billy Graham, guys who still wore ties and looked respectable. But now you have the bass player from Korn and tattooed nutcases like me, Stevie B going out. That's how I respond to the kairos moments I see busting out all around me. I want to be a part of what God is doing to get the word out.

The days of business as usual are over. Look around. Pay attention. It's coming. Another kairos moment will arrive sooner than you think. If you pay attention you will realize life should never be the same afterward. Now, what will you do about it?

Radical

Main Entry: ¹**rad·i·cal**
Pronunciation: 'ra-di-kəl
Function: *adjective*
Etymology: Middle English, from Late Latin *radicalis*, from Latin *radic-*, *radix* root — more at ROOT
1 : of, relating to, or proceeding from a root: as **a** (1) : of or growing from the root of a plant <*radical* tubers> (2) : growing from the base of a stem, from a rootlike stem, or from a stem that does not rise above the ground <*radical* leaves> **b** : of, relating to, or constituting a linguistic root **c** : of or relating to a mathematical root **d** : designed to remove the root of a disease or all diseased tissue <*radical* surgery>
2 : of or relating to the origin : FUNDAMENTAL
3 a : marked by a considerable departure from the usual or traditional : EXTREME **b** : tending or disposed to make extreme changes in existing views, habits, conditions, or institutions **c** : of, relating to, or constituting a political group associated with views, practices, and policies of extreme change **d** : advocating extreme measures to retain or restore a political state of affairs <the *radical* right>
4 *slang* : EXCELLENT, COOL

CHAPTER 17

Ya' Can't Say That. Yura Christian.

Around the time I first started working on this book I went to the Luis Palau Association President's Conference in Bend, Oregon. We were doing a *Livin' It Live* event in the same town the next day, so I invited my friend Zorro along for the ride. Zorro is the drummer for his lifelong friend Lenny Kravitz. I wanted him to see what we do in one of our live events as well as introduce him to Kevin Palau and some of my other friends in the Palau organization. But first we went to the President's Conference banquet along with fifty or so potential financial donors and ministry volunteers. Zorro's been leading people to Christ for twenty years, so I thought this was an organization he would click with. Now during this very prestigious President's Conference, Luis Palau shares with these donors and potential donors everything that's going on in the ministry. Then I get up and talk about *Livin' It* and how God is using it.

In the middle of the whole thing Zorro stands up, heads toward the platform and says, "I know I'm not supposed to do this, but can I say something?" I look at Luis and he looks at me and gives a very enthusiastic "Sure." Luis loves people who are young and vibrant and in love with Jesus. So this drummer for Lenny

Kravitz gets up there and starts talking about how all these people in the room have to get excited about what God is doing. Then he says, "Part of my evangelism strategy is to get people excited so that when I talk about the power of God it will scare the crap out of them." Now, when Zorro used the word "crap" in a room full of very conservative, very proper Christians at a Luis Palau President's Conference, you could hear a pin drop. The first thought I had as I listened to him was, "You can't say that to this crowd. You're a Christian." But by the time he was finished, this crowd of very conservative Christians gave Zorro a standing ovation because everything he had to say was dead on right, even if he used the word crap.

WHO SAYS I CAN'T?

Of course Zorro shouldn't have said the word "crap." Everyone knows that. Or should he? I'm constantly running into people who tell me I can't say or do certain things because I am a Christian, and I'm sick of it. Now I'm not saying I should be able to walk around dropping F-bombs. I get that. But hey man, where does it say in the Bible I can't use the word crap? Is it a slang word? Does that mean I shouldn't be able to use it? *You know you are sinning when you use that word, Stephen. That's the language of compromise.* Hey, guess what, I don't believe using the word crap is a sin. What do you have to say to me now?

Why the hang-up on words, anyway? The word bitch refers to a female dog. Does that mean it is off limits for me? Is it a sin for me to use a word that refers to a female dog? I don't know. And ass. An ass is a donkey. Jesus rode one. The King James Bible uses the word, but am I not supposed to? Why? Because someone declared it to be a bad word? Lighten up. That's my message to the body of Christ in America. LIGHTEN UP! If the first thing that comes to your mind when I tell you to lighten up is, *That guy's a sinner*, then you should put this book down because I'm not writing it for you. I'm writing it for people who don't have time to nitpick over words because they are too busy making a difference in the culture today.

Words form only one small part of what gets me worked up. Somewhere along the line the conservative Christian movement came up with this stupid stereotype of what a believer is supposed to look like and sound like and smell like and vote like. We devised this safe little box that every person who claims to love Jesus is supposed to fit into. And you already know what that stereotype looks like. The picture of some guy or girl just popped in your head, and if you are like me, it's a picture of someone you never want to become. But that's the accepted ideal of Christian behavior, and we're all supposed to fit into it.

Too bad because I don't. I've had many Christians come up to me and say, *You're a Christian?* with that tone of voice that makes it clear they don't think I am. And I say, yeah. So on what are you basing the question in your mind? My movies? Okay, I repent. I'm not doing those movies anymore. Do you still believe me? No, they don't. Why? *You have those crazy tattoos on your arms and you look like a skateboarder.* Am I any less a Christian because I have tattoos on my arm? That's the stupidest statement I've ever heard. But some people think it's true. If I really loved God I would cut my hair and laser off my tattoos.

That attitude is exactly what keeps the people I look like, the skateboarders, from coming to faith. If it says in the Book to not judge a book by its cover, why are Christians judging the books by their covers and then wondering why the world is the way it is? These people with the short haircuts have to get over their fear, they have to get over the premeditated notion of what has been taught to them about what a Christian looks like, and approach that fat guy on a Harley who looks like a member of ZZ Top, or that little gnarly skateboarder. God doesn't care how people look. Why should we?

But that's the problem. We don't want to approach those scary people. Then, when non-believers come to us seeking answers to life's big questions, we're left fighting from our backs because we've set so many limitations on how we can interact with them. Some Wall Street broker comes to us but he has a *Maxim* magazine in his hand, and we immediately dismiss him. According to the box, this guy first needs to get rid of his *Maxim* magazine, and then we will share eternal truth with him. Where does it say that in the Book?

Pardon my "French," but that's a load of crap. We don't just need to think outside the box. I want to take that freaking box that tells me what is acceptable "Christian" behavior and throw it on the ground and jump up and down on it until I smash it into a million pieces. That's what I am trying to do both with my current ministry and with this book. I'm sick of that stupid box. This in-the-box thinking keeps us from being relevant to the culture, and as a result, people die and go to hell because we care more about what kind of music people listen to than their eternal souls.

Not long ago I heard a pastor from California on the radio and this bonehead actually said over the air, "I don't know about you believers out there, but I believe if Jesus were around today He would never use rap music to preach the Gospel." He went on to say that rap music and hip-hop are basically tools of the devil. As soon as I heard him say that I called this Einstein and, praise the Lord, I got through and they put me on the air with him. So I get him on the phone and I said to the guy, "I have a question for you sir." And he said, "Sure, fire away." I asked him, "If an inner-city black youth from Harlem who doesn't have a whole lot of opportunity to hear and understand the Gospel message in a culturally relevant way that they can connect to, if this guy hears a Christian rap song, and, as a result comes to faith, doesn't that prove your point is way off base?" Then this brain surgeon preacher replies, "How would putting the Gospel into a rap song be any different from posting a Gospel message in a pornographic magazine?" And I said to this guy on the air, "Hey, rocket scientist, the musicians creating the music are Christians, when obviously the publisher of a porn magazine is not. That's the difference." All the guy could say in response was, "I don't agree with you," and he hung up on me.

Again I ask, where in the Book does it say I can't use rap music and hip-hop to preach the Gospel to those immersed in hip-hop culture? *But I don't like rap music.* Okay. Fine. Then don't listen. It isn't for you, anyway. I don't like country music. So who says your Southern Gospel country music is more holy than my rap? The words? Have you listened to Christian rap? The words come straight from the Word. So now what do you have to say?

What, you prefer hymns? You think songs straight from the hymnal are the only sanctified music worthy of conveying the sacred Gospel of Jesus Christ? Fine. Did you know the tunes of many of those hymns came from bars? One of the most high fallutin' hymns of all time, "A Mighty Fortress is Our God," was a popular tune in German pubs when Martin Luther took it and changed the words. Why is some freaking German drinking song more holy than Christian rap? Give me a break.

It's this kind of attitude that says you can't use rap music in ministry that locks people out of the Kingdom. Again, this is only my opinion, but I seem to remember the Apostle Paul saying we need to become all things to all men so that we can reach everybody. Instead of telling me what I can't do, why don't you pull your head out, look around, and find a way to reach people in a culturally relevant way while there is still time? Of course, that's just my opinion.

Calm down there, Stevie B. Don't get so worked up. How can I not? Listen, all of these stupid rules, this idiotic box of what is acceptable Christian behavior and proper ways of reaching people, are keeping people from coming to Jesus. Personally, I think if that doesn't get you worked up, you might as well call the cemetery and reserve yourself a plot because you're not doing much good here.

TOO NICE TO BE ANY GOOD

I'm constantly shooting my mouth off, and it gets me into a lot of trouble. I hear, *Stephen, you shouldn't say that* so often you might think I would learn to keep my mouth shut. But of course I won't. Not long ago I spoke at a large festival with around twenty or thirty thousand people in attendance. A lot of the people in the crowd weren't Christians, which was the whole point of the festival in the first place. The organizers asked me to speak and share my story of how I came to Christ. So I shared my story. I said something like, "You know I come from Hollywood, and now I am born again, dah dah dah, my life's so different and praise God, I am so blessed and I am so happy and everything is so wonderful."

Up to this point all the event organizers are delirious because here's one of Hollywood's own telling people to come to Jesus. But then I went on to say, "One of the greatest epiphanies I had in my faith was when I discovered there was a difference between God's Spirit being *with* you and God's Spirit being *in* you." That's a biblical statement. The Bible commands Christians to be filled with the Spirit (Ephesians 5:13), which means there is a difference between God's Spirit being with you and in you.

When I walked off the stage one of the event organizers came up to me and said, "Hey, can I talk to you for a minute? Listen, we here in this organization don't want to rub anyone out in the audience the wrong way about that topic. Because there may be denominations out there that might be offended by what you said. So who we are and what we do is to confine ourselves to talking about having a relationship with Jesus, and then trust the Holy Spirit will lead them from there."

That ticked me off, buddy. That was that wussie, safe, thing that Christian ministries have been doing for too long. No wonder we are losing the battle for this culture. I looked at this person and I said, "I don't understand what you are saying." He replied, "Well you said there is a difference between the Spirit of God being with you and the Spirit of God being in you, and we would prefer that you just don't say it like that." Again, I looked at this person and I said, "But isn't it the truth, and if it's the truth, why wouldn't I want to say it?"

I can tell you why they didn't want me to make that statement even though it comes from the Bible. This organization, and most of the conservative Christian movement, is so worried about offending someone that they back off from the raw truth of the Bible. We're too nicey-nice. It's like everyone is afraid to say what the Bible says. Give me a break.

Listen, have you actually read the Bible? Have you ever read the words of Jesus? He didn't play nice. If the truth offended someone, He didn't care. THAT'S WHY THEY CRUCIFIED HIM! One day Jesus walked into the Temple and found a bunch of guys selling sheep and goats and exchanging money. Basically they turned the center of worship into a flea market. Do you know what Jesus did then? He grabbed a whip, turned over their tables, and kicked them out of His Father's house.

Another time Jesus went to the Pharisees, the religious authority in His day, and told them they were all a bunch of snakes that would burn in hell if they didn't get right with God. Later a tower fell over and killed eighteen people. When His disciples asked Him about it Jesus said, "Unless you repent, you too will all perish" (Luke 13:5). Nice guy, huh? Jesus wasn't being cruel, He was simply being straight with people.

Jesus wasn't the first of God's spokesmen to talk like this. I will let you in on a secret: In the Bible, everyone who spoke for God stomped on people's toes with the truth. Don't believe me? Read the Book. Pick up a Bible and read Isaiah, Jeremiah, Amos, or any of the other prophets. They spoke truth without sugar-coating anything.

When I came to faith I was told I needed to read the Bible and do what it says. Why, then, when I say what the Bible says, does someone pull me aside and say, "You can't say that, you might offend someone." If the truth of the Word offends you, take that up with God. Don't tell me to be quiet. I've got a real problem with that. I'm tired of the safeness, the nicey-niceness. I think God is as well.

THE OTHER EXTREME

Speaking the truth doesn't mean going out of our way to make people mad. Ephesians 4:15 says to speak the truth in *love*. To me, it's like hearing bad news from the doctor. It's one thing for him to tell you that you have some horrid disease; it's another thing completely for him to enjoy doing it. I've come across some Christians who seem to enjoy telling people how horrible they are.

Not long ago I was in Toronto shooting a movie for the Sci-Fi channel. I started talking to my driver about God and the two of us connected. In the middle of the conversation he told me this other high-profile Christian actor was in town a few weeks earlier making a film. You would immediately recognize his name, but my publisher advised me not to use it. So, I'll just call him Mike Seaver, which is not his real name. I don't know Mike personally, but I'd heard he was on fire for God, which makes him okay in my book. My driver proceeded to tell me Mike asked him if he'd ever lusted after a woman before. "I told him sure, I guess. Who hasn't?" my driver said. Then this famous Christian actor shot back, "Then you are going to burn in hell." Needless to say, Mike Seaver is making my job a lot harder.

Let me be straight. Looking at a woman with lust doesn't send you to hell. Rejecting Jesus Christ does. That's not my opinion. That's what the Book says. Lust is like every other sin. All of them are symptoms of a life that has rejected God.

That's not even the point. Why would anyone in their right mind think that telling someone he would burn in hell for looking at a woman with lust would make him want to trust in Jesus? Was this high-profile Christian actor trying to scare this guy into heaven? I don't know. Maybe. I know how I would have reacted prior to my conversion. I would have laughed, told the guy he was full of a word I try not use anymore, and gone on my merry way. Being told I was on my way to hell wouldn't make me more curious about a God Who loves me.

So are you saying people should never hear the bad news about what will happen if they don't turn to God? No, not at all. But I am saying this: There is a key difference between offending people with the truth of God's word and offending them by being obnoxious, overbearing, self-righteous idiots. That would be like going to a corner in Manhattan and screaming at people with a Bible in your hand. I doubt if anyone would listen. But hey, that's just my opinion.

WHAT YA GOTTA SAY

Well, Stevie B, you sure told us. Since you're so good at telling us what we're doing wrong, what do you suggest we do instead? The question isn't what we should do but what God is already doing. I believe God is raising up a new breed of radical, hardcore, sold out, pay any price for God group of individuals who will turn this culture on its ear.

These are guys like Brian Welsh, the former guitarist of the group Korn. He came to Christ and immediately walked away from one of the top metal groups in the world. Now he spends his days doing mission work in India.

Another hardcore guy is Paul Anderson who eighteen years ago started a church for skateboarders. Everyone said he was crazy, but guess what? He's reached over two hundred kids a month for eighteen years. Check him out at skatechurch.org. He's making a difference in the culture. Instead of running out to the suburbs to start a church for people who have money, he decided to dedicate his life to a bunch of skaters that no one else really cared about.

That's the kind of people God is raising up in response to the stupid in-the-box thinking that keeps American churches from doing anything but spitting into the wind. God's new breed of radicals doesn't care about denominations and labels and egos. They don't have time for that nonsense. Instead they want to find ways for God to unleash the power of His Holy Spirit through them.

This new breed consists of people like Mike Foster and Craig Gross, two young pastors who share a deep concern for people trapped in the web of pornography. Instead of just standing back and telling anyone who reads *Playboy* or watches dirty movies that they are going to hell, Mike and Craig decided to do something radical. They started a Web site called XXXchurch.com, a site they advertise as the number one Christian pornography site. Both the name and their tag line cause their site to get hits when people Google for porn sites. A lot of people don't get what they are doing. Mike and Craig are constantly asked if they are pro-pornography. What a stupid question. They don't promote porn, they minister to those people who hide in the dark. Instead of pounding on people, they reach out and promote a life of purity, integrity, and an outrageous walk with Christ. The people they reach don't fit inside the box, which just goes to show how ridiculous the stupid box is in the first place.

Another guy is Ryan Dobson. Last name sound familiar? That's because he's Dr. James Dobson's son, and he's got more tattoos than me! He's got the chops to be preaching it way outside the box. All these people are examples of the new hardcore movement of faith God is raising up.

In my opinion, and again, this is only my opinion, what the church in America and all these ministries and all of this Christian subculture that exists in America today better do is they better acknowledge the hardcore movement of faith. And they better do it fast. *But those people are so radical!* Well, so is the Lord. He's more radical than your mind can imagine, which means you need to get radical as well. Instead of telling people what they can't do and having a fit when you see a tattoo or a body piercing, you need to get in line with these people and catch the movement God is stirring up. Yet people don't want to do that.

The other day I heard about a nineteen-year-old kid who came to Christ about three years ago and is completely sold out to God. This kid has read through the Bible, he's gone off on mission trips helping dirt-poor people in Appalachia, and works with little kids in his church. Now he's off at college studying to become a lawyer who will go to remote parts of the world and fight to uphold justice in the name of Jesus. This is a guy who loves God with everything in Him. And yet he catches flak from the "grown-ups" in his church because he has a lip ring. People have actually complained about this sold-out, hardcore, radical Jesus lover being around their kids because he has a hole in his lip with a piece of metal sticking through it. Meanwhile, if a cannibal tribesman from, I don't know, some really obscure place like Oolaybuluahula Island, yeah, that's it, now if he came to your church and told you his story of how he became an intimate lover of Jesus Christ and he had a big ole bone through his nose, ya'll would probably give him a standing ovation. That's what's wrong with the whole conservative Christian movement. Instead of criticizing, the church needs to get on board with the radicals God is raising up.

God is raising up a new generation. We need to get on board with them. Everyone out there reading this book that was either raised in a Christian home or who has been a believer long enough for your enthusiasm to die out, you need to stop and examine your heart. You need to ask yourself:

A) Am I relevant?

B) Am I like Jesus?

C) Is my commitment to Christ my first priority in everything I do?

D) Would I die for Christ today?

E) And will I go out and, to the best of my ability, do the last thing Jesus told me to do before He left this earth? Will I go and make disciples of all nations?

Jesus didn't tell you to go run a hedge fund, make a lot of money, and do some good works on the side on your days off. If you want to obey Christ, working for the Kingdom has to be your first and only priority.

Whoa there Stephen. Calm down. Hold on. You know you're not so smart. You never went to college. How can you discern what God is doing in the world? How can I discern? I'll tell you. Every day I rip out my heart and hold it out before the Lord. I tell Him to take this thing and do with it what He will. I challenge you to do the same. I don't mean to sound holier than thou and I don't want you to think that I believe I'm the only one who has this Christianity thing figured out. I know better. But my heart aches when I see Christians waste so much time and so much energy throwing a fit over things that don't matter instead of living out the radical walk with Jesus they could enjoy.

If you don't agree with me and you don't care about reaching people with the Gospel, God bless you. Go on with your meaningless, mundane life that you think is serving Christ. Go for it. I respect the fact that what I have to say right now isn't for everyone. Some of you think the only way to serve God is to go down to the church and lick stamps and stick them on the church's newsletter. That's valid, if that's what God is telling you to do.

But if just one stamp licker reads this book and realizes that maybe she could make a difference in this culture in a radical way, and she goes into a candy store and brings some ten-year-old to Christ who twenty years later leads fifty million to Christ, that's how we are going to start winning. Don't listen to the people who tell you what you can't do. Stop listening to those who say you have to fit into some box. Get away from those who tell you to sit down and lick those stamps and stuff those envelopes. Stop playing it safe. When you become part of the radical movement of faith God is raising up today, there are no limits.

Today I feel like I just jumped out of a plane without a parachute, and I'm loving it. I live to die serving Christ. That's my experience. I think that should be everyone's experience. And if it's not your experience you have no one to blame but yourself for not having the cajonès to pursue it. Don't blame it on your pastor. Don't blame it on your daddy and your mommy. Shut up and stop whining and complaining and go for it.

You can't tell people that, Stephen. Dude, I just did.

Movement
Main Entry: **move·ment**
Pronunciation: 'müv-mənt
Function: *noun*
1 a (1) : the act or process of moving; *especially* : change of place or position or posture (2) : a particular instance or manner of moving **b** (1) : a tactical or strategic shifting of a military unit : MANEUVER (2) : the advance of a military unit **c** : ACTION, ACTIVITY — usually used in plural
2 a : TENDENCY, TREND <detected a *movement* toward fairer pricing> **b** : a series of organized activities working toward an objective; *also* : an organized effort to promote or attain an end <the civil rights *movement*>
3 : the moving parts of a mechanism that transmit a definite motion
4 a : MOTION 7 **b** : the rhythmic character or quality of a musical composition **c** : a distinct structural unit or division having its own key, rhythmic structure, and themes and forming part of an extended musical composition **d** : particular rhythmic flow of language : CADENCE
5 a : the quality (as in a painting or sculpture) of representing or suggesting motion **b** : the vibrant quality in literature that comes from elements that constantly hold a reader's interest (as a quickly moving action-filled plot)
6 a : an act of voiding the bowels **b** : matter expelled from the bowels at one passage

---

CHAPTER 18

Hold the Cheese

Hey Christians out there, I have a question for you. And this question isn't just for individuals. I ask this of all the pastors reading this and everyone who leads any kind of ministry big or small. Here's my question: How relevant are you in the culture today? How relevant are you? It's been my observation over the past few years that for most of you, the answer is "almost not at all." I see a lot of attempts at being relevant and most of them are a joke. At least that's how it looks from the standpoint of a guy who's spent nearly twenty years in the cultural center of America. Too many Christian attempts at relevance fail to be relevant or they fail to be truly Christian.

Before you grab the pitchforks and torches to storm my house, hear me out. When I ask how relevant you are in today's culture, I'm not throwing rocks at Christians in America. Remember, I'm one of you. I love believers and their churches and ministries. I really do. We're family. I don't know how your family is, but we Baldwins stick together no matter what. That's how I feel about my new extended family in Christ. I love you and I would never do anything to hurt you. But being family means being straight with one another, and that's what I'm doing now.

When I ask how relevant you are to the culture I'm not asking you anything that I don't ask myself every single day. I don't want to wake up one day and find that the world has passed me by. God called me to impact the youth culture in this country. I cringe to think that I might lose my edge and lose the ability to speak to this culture with the Good News in a way they can understand. The thought of it scares the heck out of me, and it ought to scare the heck out of every Christian. The second worst thing that could happen to us is to lose our voice in the world. The worst thing that could happen would be to lose our grip on the message God gave us to deliver. If either of these things happen we might as well check out and get out of the way of those God raises up to speak to this generation.

And make no mistake about it, God will raise up someone to speak for Him. There's even a story in the Bible of how God made a donkey talk when He couldn't find a human being to step up to the plate. That story gives me hope. If He spoke through a donkey, I figure He can use me.

WHAT'S THE BIG DEAL?

The culture constantly changes, and if you want people to be able to understand what you're saying, you have to change with it. You want proof? Back in the eighties my brother Alec made a movie called *The Hunt for Red October* with Sean Connery. The movie, which was based on a book by Tom Clancy, was this Cold War action thriller about a Soviet submarine commander who decided to defect to the United States and bring his state-of-the-art submarine with him. Great movie. It made my brother a household name, which didn't hurt Stevie B's climb up the Hollywood ladder. That movie would look kind of strange if they made it today because the Soviet Union no longer exists. And it hasn't for fifteen years. Back in 1950 everyone was afraid of the communists taking over while the Cold War raged. For a new generation of adults the Soviets and the Cold War only exist in history books.

That's not all that's changed since 1950. Music, television, movies, fashion, you name it, it's different now than it was fifty years ago. Why, then, is the thinking of so many churches and ministries stuck in the fifties? In my opinion, hip-hop is the dominant factor in the shape of the culture today. It hasn't just changed music, it's also changed the clothes kids wear, the way they talk, and their definition of cool. You want to see the power of its influence? Watch the NBA. It's the hip-hop league now. But for a lot of church leaders, hip-hop is a tool of the devil. They're so busy condemning it that the thought that they might be able to use it to reach people with the Gospel never enters their minds. That's the stupidest thing I've ever heard.

Culture change is nothing new. That's why Paul, the man who wrote half of the New Testament, said,

> To the Jews I became like a Jew, to win the Jews. To those under the law I became like one under the law (though I myself am not under the law), so as to win those under the law. To those not having the law I became like one not having the law (though I am not free from God's law but am under Christ's law), so as to win those not having the law. To the weak I became weak, to win the weak. I have become all things to all men so that by all possible means I might save some.
>
> (1 CORINTHIANS 9:19–22)

I think if the guy who wrote this was alive today he would say, "To the hip-hop, I became hip-hop to win the hip-hop. To the Jeff Foxworthy crowd I became a redneck to win the rednecks. To the skaters, I became a skater to win the skaters."

Saint Paul the apostle would never wear those baggy clothes or get a tattoo to appeal to skaters. He would never lower himself to that level!

Oh yeah, then why did he do it in the Bible? And people gave him grief about it. Back in Paul's day the religious establishment considered anyone who wasn't circumcised to be unclean. That meant they avoided them at all costs. Not Paul. Even though he was a Jew, he hung out with the non-Jews, and the Jewish Christians got all over him for it.

That sounds a lot like how religious people treat those who don't look like them or act like them today. Paul told those jerks in his day to get over it. People get after me because I look like a skater. If you have a problem with my tattoos or the way I dress, my message for you is the same Paul had for the people chewing on his butt back in the day, GET OVER IT! And fast.

The other day I heard about a guy who wanted to start a skate ministry for the kids he saw all over his town on their boards. So he went to his church board with the idea, and they shot him down. *We've never done anything like that around here before*, they said. Hey, guess what you geniuses, you never had anything like this back in the fifties, which is where your brains are stuck, because skate culture didn't exist back then. Skateboards were around then, but they were pieces of wood with metal wheels. Kids spent more time scraping their faces off the concrete when those pieces of junk hit rocks and came to a sudden stop than they did on the boards.

The invention of neoprene wheels around the time a drought hit California changed everything. Kids on the new boards experimented in dry swimming pools across Southern California, giving birth to the skate culture and extreme sports. Now more kids ride skateboards than play Little League baseball. So guess what? If you don't want your church to go extinct in the next twenty years, you better figure out a way to reach these kids before they tune you out completely.

This goes back to what I said in the last chapter. Too many church leaders are so busy talking about what you can't do, that they miss what God is already doing. Jesus said you can't put new wine in old wineskins, and that's what's happening here. The old wineskins are the crusty old curmudgeons who keep saying "We never did it like that back in the day." That day doesn't exist anymore. Get over it.

The Bible says, "Do not say, 'Why were the old days better than these?' For it is not wise to ask such questions" (Ecclesiastes 7:10). The old days are over, dude. Hey, don't get me wrong. God blessed the Christian movement in America that has gotten us this far. But, times have changed. Now, what are you going to do?

CONFUSED

I know it must sound like I'm piling on churches and ministries that are already struggling to survive, but believe me when I say that is not my intent. I've spent time in a lot of churches and worked with different ministries across the country. The vast majority really want to make a difference in the world today. Their hearts are in the right place, but they struggle implementing a strategy that might actually work.

A lot of the ministry leaders I've met were real innovators back when they got started. When they stepped out in faith and started the works God told them to start, they stepped on the establishment's toes to get things done. They defined the cutting edge. They were the new wineskins for the new wine of God's new work in the culture. But for a lot of these guys, that was a long time ago. Now they are the establishment. They are the old wineskins. The world changed, but they didn't. Maybe they couldn't, I don't know. All I know is somewhere along the line the stuff they were doing didn't connect with people like it once did. Now it's time for these guys to do what the previous generation of leaders did for them. They need to hand off the baton to the new hardcore movement God is raising up.

I'm not saying every pastor or ministry leader over forty-five is now a dinosaur. Some have kept up with the changing times, even though it hasn't been easy for them. I do a lot of work with the Luis Palau Association. Years ago Luis developed a formula for holding crusades and reaching people. That formula worked for decades. But a few years ago Luis risked alienating all his supporters and completely changed his approach. Instead of weeklong crusades, he now does festivals that incorporate the hottest Christian rock stars and even extreme sports. That's what connected me with the organization to begin with. The change hasn't been painless. I'm sure I drive the guys at the Palau headquarters in Portland nuts. But at least they're trying.

Too many churches and Christian organizations don't try, or if they do they end up producing some cheesy pile of dung that is about as relevant as a Pat Boone song to a hip-hop rapper. The problem is these groups don't know the culture they're trying to reach. A bunch of people who've been in the Christian subculture since they wore Pampers get together and try to figure out what would be cool and hip and cutting edge based on watching a couple of hours of the X-Games. Then they wonder why it doesn't catch on.

The other day I was sitting in church and a promo video for a very popular men's ministry came on. I've gotta tell you, it was the biggest pile of stinking cheese I've seen. Apparently these people want to reach out to a younger audience. So they had some fifty something guy read a script where he comes on the screen and starts saying, "Yo, man, what's up, how ya doing dawg, yeah, how you doing." I guess they figured if he talked like that young men would immediately connect with him. If I was a kid in church and I saw that thing I would fall over laughing. The only reason I would want to attend the event after that is if my youth pastor that I respected invited me to go with him.

Okay, this group is trying to be relevant. Great. God bless them. But instead of relying on a marketing analysis of what attracts younger men, they should have had a young man in the promo instead of some old guy trying to act young. If a twenty-five-year-old gangsta rapper who's fallen in love with Jesus came on the screen and spoke from his heart, that would connect with men both young and old. But they didn't do it. They didn't have some tattooed scary looking hip-hop guy come on the screen and say, "Listen up, yo. There was a time when I believed that I didn't have time for my baby's momma. But then God changed me and the way I think. Then I married that girl and I honored the Lord." They should have found a guy like that to put in their promo. A statement like that would have impacted the rapper and the guy on Wall Street both. Instead the safe, marketing analysis approach just came across as a cheesy joke.

That's the other problem I see with Christian attempts to get relevant. Not only do we not understand the culture, we're afraid of going too far. Make no mistake about it. God has people out there on the front lines that reach every part of society. He's got His radical army out there in the streets reaching pimps and prostitutes and addicts. But established Christian ministries are usually afraid of these people. They would rather stay conservative and play it safe. Their slogan is "Don't get carried away. Don't go too far."

I can just hear Jesus saying that, can't you? He's dragging His cross through the streets of Jerusalem, and about three-quarters of the way to the place where the Romans are going to nail Him to it He stops and says, "Ah, I'm tired. Let's go get a Starbucks."

What if He did that? What if Jesus threw down His cross three-quarters of the way to the place of the skull and said, "You know what, I've changed my mind. I'm too tired. I don't want to do this. I just don't feel like it. I don't want to work that hard. I don't want to be that radical. It doesn't matter." If He had done that there would be no point to this book. There would be no point to my life. There would be no point to Christianity or the church or anything. So, the real question is, how far are we willing to go to make an eternal difference in people's lives? How far are we willing to go? That's my question.

MISSING THE POINT

Christians trying to get relevant can run to an opposite extreme which is, in my humble opinion, even worse than not being able to relate to the culture at all. Christian bands are especially vulnerable. There's this whole industry of Christian music created by Christians for Christian labels with Christian content. But do you know who distributes their music around the world? Secular companies. One company, this huge Christian recording giant, is linked with the same people who brought you *Grand Theft Auto*, a video game with hidden pornography you can unlock with a code. This marriage doesn't make any sense to me. Yeah, I've heard the argument, *This partnership helps us get more music out there, and as a result, the message spreads.* Okay, but what is the real cost?

Now before you say it, I realize this book is published by Warner Faith, an imprint of Warner Books. I'm not saying secular companies are inherently evil. However, there's a problem in the Christian music industry. Christian labels have told their Christian artists to cut back on the references to Jesus and God to make their music more attractive to a crossover market. I can name names in the Christian music business of heads of labels who went to bands they were considering signing and told them, "I listened to your demo. We want to sign you, but you referenced the name of Jesus six times in a song that we think is hip. If you take five of them out we can move forward." That's a problem.

If you cut God out of the music, what's the point of the band's existence? They might make good, clean music, the old "God or my girlfriend" songs that sound Christian to Christians and like plain old love songs to everyone else, but is that why God brought this band together?

Yeah, well Stevie B I noticed you still do secular movies. Didn't I catch you on CBS recently in a movie with Tom Selleck? Sure you did. I'm not saying Christian artists should only play songs about Jesus and never anything else. But you need to let people know who you are and who you are about. I guarantee you, if Warner Books came to me and told me to edit all these God references out of this book, I would find a new publisher.

This problem pains me. I've watched as one of the biggest bands out there, a band I really like, guys who are really cool who I connect with, has fallen prey to this. Their first few CDs were up front about the Lord. Great music. Good message. I pimped these guys to my friends. But something changed when they signed with a mainstream label. They lost all the references to God. You can't find it in their music and you can't find it on their Web site. I've looked. It isn't there. Why? I guess to sell more records. I don't know. Again, what's the point of that? Their songs talk about finding true happiness and they refer to Ecclesiastes on one of the personal sections of the Web site, but where is Jesus? They make reference to a trip they made to Africa and eliminating Third World debt and all of that, but still no Jesus. Why? Apparently they've gone from being a Jesus band to a band that now creatively feels it can have more influence and impact for the Kingdom by talking about poverty in Africa instead of the Lord. In my opinion they're wrong. They are flat out wrong.

Relevance doesn't mean adopting the culture's methods to the degree that you lose the message. You have to stay true to the Gospel and make it clear enough for God to work through it. The band Mercy Me had a huge breakout hit with a song that was all about God. *Livin' It* works because it is a really good skate video, even though it has Jesus all over it. You don't have to compromise truth to make an impact on this culture artistically and spiritually. Real relevance means bridging the gap between God and the culture. If you forget to bring God along on the journey, what's the point of the bridge?

There are other Christians out there in the mainstream that

have an opportunity to make a bold statement for the Lord. I mean, come on, Bono, one of the biggest freakin' names in the music business, is a believer. But, you don't hear it boldly enough in his music. In my opinion you should. Why be so lukewarm about your faith? Hey Bono, how long would it take for you to stop in the middle of one of your shows, bring up the lights, and share the Gospel?

Look, Bono, I am a huge fan of yours. You've got great talent. I just think in my opinion, and it's only my opinion, that you would do far more good if you preached the Gospel of Jesus rather than trying to get Third World debt relief. If you asked me, and you didn't but here it is anyway, I would tell you to preach the Gospel on MTV. God will take care of that Third World country.

Yeah, I know. I'm being too narrow-minded. I have Christian friends who worship Bono's music. They can find every minute, super-duper Easter egg secret reference to God in all of his songs. I ask them, What about the regular guy on the street? What good are the secret references if he can't understand them? If I am a non-believer, even if I figure out a song is about heaven, if I don't understand that Jesus is the only way to get there, what's the point? Are Christian singers supposed to just make great music, or are they supposed to honor the Lord and Savior Who gave them the talent in the first place? I think you know my answer.

INTO THE ARENA

I read a frightening statistic the other day. It said that less than ten percent of all evangelical Christians in America polled believed they would ever lead another human being to Jesus Christ. So out of the branch of Christianity that is supposed to be the most on fire, only one in ten felt inspired enough about their faith to tell someone about their Lord. I'm going to talk more about this in a later chapter, but for now I want to make this point: All this talk about becoming relevant doesn't mean a thing until Christians actually care enough about the souls of people around them to do something. Once that changes, we then need to put our money where our mouths are.

God is already in the process of raising up churches and ministries that are making inroads into this culture. Bob Coy and his church are. He is pastor of Calvary Chapel in Fort Lauderdale, Florida. He doesn't look like a normal pastor. This guy is awesome. He preaches in a Hawaiian shirt and makes faith fun. Maybe that's why 15,000 people attend services there every week.

There are all sorts of other pastors and churches like that out there, churches you've never heard of, but they're led by young, fiery culturally relevant pastors. And they are making a difference. In the last chapter I mentioned other hardcore people and ministries God is raising up. Know this: God isn't going to leave Himself without a voice in this world. He's going to find someone who will do whatever it takes to get His message out. They are already out there. The church is making some progress. Unfortunately, from where I sit it looks like it's coming at a snail's pace.

We can speed it up. God is doing His part, we need to do ours. It's time for us to invest in those ministries that are making a real difference in the world. It frosts me to think that some of the most culturally relevant ministries have the hardest time paying their bills. Old established ministries have lots of supporters who pour in millions of dollars every year, while new, cutting-edge, radical ministries like the Cross Movement are not being given the opportunity they deserve. Let's face it, hip-hop has taken over the culture. Imagine the ministry impact these guys could make if they had the finances.

We need to financially support groups that are making a real difference. We need to get behind ministries like Walking on Water (www.walkingonwater.org), a surf ministry, and King of

Kings Skate Board Ministry (kksm.org). Man, I hate the thought of standing before God one day and having Him ask me why I didn't do more. What kind of lame excuse will we use then? But Lord, I didn't like their music. They played hip-hop. But Lord, the people they were trying to reach had tattoos. But Lord, I thought You wanted me to play it safe and not take a chance on anything radical. Come on. Do you think God will buy any of that? I don't.

Not only do we need to get behind the culturally relevant ministries that are out there, I believe it is time to do whatever it takes to develop and distribute culturally relevant, artistically excellent materials that will make the world sit up and take notice. I don't want to look around at the world and try to copy what other people are doing. Now is the time for Christians to turn their God-given, Spirit-empowered gifts loose.

I had this idea: Let's start a Christian media company where investors donate money to the company to create the materials I'm talking about. We would put together a solid business plan, but the company would be all about making a difference, not turning a profit. I doubt if I would have many people line up to invest in a company where they wouldn't get a return on their money, but I would love to try it. I would love to get a couple of Christian billionaires together and have them invest in a state-of-the-art Christian media company. Then we could change the whole perception of Christian media from a cheese factor to the cutting-edge trendsetters. Is it possible? I know it is, and I'm going to have fun giving it a try.

Wrath

Main Entry: ¹**wrath**

Pronunciation: 'rath, *chiefly British* 'ròth

Function: *noun*

Etymology: Middle English, from Old English *wrǣththo*, from *wrāth* wroth
— more at WROTH

1 : strong vengeful anger or indignation

2 : retributory punishment for an offense or a crime : divine chastisement

synonym see ANGER

CHAPTER 19

Wrath

I started my Christian experience by, in my mind, climbing up on top of the biggest rock I could imagine, and screaming at God, "If You are real, show me!" This wasn't the brightest thing I've ever done, but hey, that's me. I told God that in His Book, Jesus said His followers would do even greater things than He did, and that's what I wanted. "You said this would happen, God, now show me." I wasn't asking for proof of His existence before I believed. I already believed. That question was settled. Now I wanted God to do what He said He would do in His Book.

My part of the bargain was simply this: I pledged to God that to the best of my ability I would do anything and everything He asked me to do for the rest of my life, no matter what. If He wanted me to become a flipped-out Jesus freak standing in the middle of Times Square screaming at people about God and His Word, I would do it. No questions asked. "Point me in the right direction, God, and I will go there," I told Him.

All I wanted was for Him to show me crystal clear, unequivocal proof that I wasn't wasting my time. I told Him if He wasn't real, I didn't want to live any longer because there wouldn't be any point to it. Like I said, shaking a fist at heaven and challenging God wasn't the brightest thing I've ever done. After all, a well placed lightning bolt could have ended both the discussion and me, but I was willing to take that chance.

Several years have now gone by, and my covenant has not changed. I've done what I said I would do and God has done what I asked of Him. Over and over again He has reinforced the reality of this experience. He has shown me He is more real than my puny little brain could have ever imagined. Since the day I stood on that rock in my mind, God has held my eyes open and forced me to see how great and how mighty and how absolutely amazing He really is. I've felt a lot of emotion while this was happening: joy, peace, wonder, happiness. But the biggest emotion I've felt, the one that grips me in places within my soul I didn't even know existed, is fear.

The Bible says the fear of the Lord is the beginning of wisdom. Now I know what that fear is. It is knee knocking, poop running down your leg fear that comes from having the façade of this world ripped off and seeing God for Who He really is. And brother, when God shows you some of the things He's shown me, you will need to change your pants as well.

THE MEANING OF FEAR

Oh, Stephen, calm down. God is a loving God. You aren't supposed to be afraid of Him. You're supposed to enjoy His love and His forgiveness. Yeah, yeah, yeah. Keep thinking that. Keep on deluding yourself and making God out to be something less than He is.

In the Bible, when people caught a glimpse of who God really was, it scared the crap out of them. In the book of Exodus the Lord speaks to the children of Israel from Mount Sinai. They all hear a booming voice giving them the Ten Commandments. Let me tell you, the sound of that voice didn't make them all get goofy grins on their faces and break out singing "Kum Ba Yah." Their leaders went to Moses and pleaded with him to go to God and get Him to keep his distance. They did that because they were afraid God would get too close and they would all die as a result. Based on what they did not long after, they should've been afraid.

People react like this to God all through the Bible. God appeared to the prophet Isaiah in a vision, and the first words out of Isaiah's mouth were, Woe is me, I am a dead man. Let me give you the Stevie B paraphrase of that verse. Isaiah took one look at God on His throne, fell on his face, and cried out, "*Oh my gosh, I'm a goner.*" Why? Because seeing God up close and personal scared the life out of him. That's why.

Jesus' disciples did the same thing a few centuries later. The twelve of them and Jesus were out in a boat in the middle of the Sea of Galilee late at night when a storm blew in. The wind threw their boat around like a bathtub sailboat. Water started pouring over the sides and the sides of the boat shook like the whole thing was falling apart. These guys were fishermen, they knew the boat was about to sink. Jesus slept through the whole thing.

Finally, His whining wimpy disciples woke Him up screaming like little girls, "We're all going to die!" Jesus looked around at the wind and the waves, told them to shut up, the storm that is, not the disciples, and laid back down. As He was drifting back to sleep He told His disciples, "Where is your faith?" The Bible says that when the wind and the waves stopped, the disciples looked at Jesus and were filled with fear.

Five times the Bible says the fear of the Lord is the starting point of wisdom. The children of Israel got a little wiser when fear gripped them at the foot of the mountain. Isaiah got a little smarter when he hit the ground face-first at the sight of God. And the disciples acquired wisdom when they backed up from Jesus in that boat asking one another, "Who *is* this guy that can order thunderstorms around?"

Are you saying we should be scared of God? That doesn't sound like the God I've always believed in. That's exactly what I am saying. You should feel an overwhelming, knee knocking, wet your pants fear of the Almighty God Who spoke the entire universe into existence. The Bible says that in comparison to God, the entire universe barely fills the palm of His hand. Are you telling me you shouldn't be afraid of the One Who has that much power? I bet you would be scared if you jumped in your car and found a guy with a gun in the backseat. How much more so should you be afraid of the God Who holds the entire universe in His hand with room to spare?

Before you start thinking that I burned up too many brain cells back in my substance abuse days, you need to understand that none of this is my opinion. I, Stephen Baldwin, am not the one telling you that you should feel fear when you get close to God. The BOOK says it. The word fear appears over 260 times in the Bible, and the Book specifically tells us nearly one hundred times to fear the Lord. Ecclesiastes even goes so far as to say the whole duty of a human being on this earth is to "Fear God and keep his commandments" (Ecclesiastes 12:13).

Most people only know about God's love. When I open the Bible and show them how often they are told to fear the Lord, they usually respond by saying, I didn't know that was in there. Guess what, I didn't either. I remember cruising through my Bible reading one day and coming across the words, "The fear of the Lord is the beginning of wisdom." I did a double take and said, Whoa, where did that come from?

As I continued reading I discovered the Bible says we are to submit to the fear of the Lord. In my faith experience I've discovered that the more I become willing to believe that God and His promises are real, the more real they are. And the more real He becomes, the more I fear Him. God is such a mystery and the way He works in this world is so far beyond our pathetic ability to understand, that I can't help myself. Yet I find hardly anyone takes Him seriously. I start talking about God and people say, Yeah, sure, whatever.

Most people believe they can make God into anything they want, like He's made of Silly Putty or something. But when I started searching for the real God, I found Him. I shook my fist at heaven and challenged God to prove He is real. He has. He's shown Himself to me in supernatural ways, and the more He does, the more I fear Him. I may not be the sharpest crayon in the box, but I'm smart enough to figure that one out.

I know talking about the fear of God isn't exactly popular. Most people don't want to think about this idea. I know a lot of evangelical Christians who try to downplay the fear of the Lord. I have a friend who debates this with me all the time. All he wants to talk about is God's love. You know the talk, *God loves me, even when I make mistakes He still loves me.* Okay. I agree. That's in the book. But the book also talks about fearing God because God is a God of wrath.

THE WRATH OF GOD

Talking about the fear of the Lord is only the beginning. You probably figured that out already since this chapter is called "Wrath" not "Fear." Earlier in this book I talked about God's calling on my life and the mission He gave me. I firmly believe that part of that mission is to tell people about God's coming wrath.

Now Baldwin's gone completely over the edge. What's next, are we going to see you walking up and down Broadway with one of those sandwich signs that says "Repent" on one side and "The end is near" on the other? I don't know. Maybe. If God told me to do it I would. He hasn't yet, so I haven't started working on a sign. But I understand the reaction. No one wants to talk about God as a God of wrath. No one wants to even think that a day of judgment could literally lay in our future. They make movies about the parts of the Bible that talk about plagues and fire falling from heaven and Armageddon. How can they be real?

Here's the scary part: The Bible says a day of wrath is around the corner, and not even Spielberg or Jerry Bruckheimer or the Wachowski brothers who made *The Matrix* or anyone else who makes the big budget, apocalyptic, disaster movies can come up with anything that even comes close to showing how bad that day will be. And yeah, I really believe that day is coming. Do I sound nuts? Sure, maybe, based on your understanding. But I believe the Word, and what the Word says is if you are down with the Christ, you don't have a problem. But if you're not, you are up for grabs.

Before you fall over laughing at what a nutcase I am, I want you to try to see this from God's perspective. You remember the expression, What Would Jesus Do we talked about earlier? I want you to ask yourself the same question with a little Stevie B twist: What would you do if you were Jesus? What would you do if you were God? Just let that question sink in for a moment, then hang on. It will make sense soon.

I have people tell me all the time that I shouldn't take the Bible so literally. *It's just a book of stories written by men*, they tell me. There are entire denominations out there that have preachers who get up on Sunday mornings and say that. These people tell me, *Yeah, but so and so didn't live seven hundred years. Come on.* I always respond by asking these people if they believe God is real. And they usually say yes. If they don't, the conversation is pretty much over. But when they say they believe God is real, I will ask them if they believe God wrote the Bible. Most of the time they will say something like, *Some of it, but not all of it.* That's a pretty common perception.

Most people out there believe God had a hand in getting the Bible down on paper, but they believe people got in the way and caused it to be interpreted the way it has over the past couple of thousand years. Fair enough. I hear this a lot.

When people tell me this I will ask them again if they believe in God. *Yes*, they say. Then I say something like, when you say you believe in God, you mean you believe there is a higher being. *Yes. There must be, there are too many unanswered questions in the universe.* Do you believe then that this higher power created everything? *What do you mean, Stephen?* Do you believe God created the earth? *Yes.* Do you believe God created the moon? *Yes.* Do you believe God created the stars and the planets and the galaxies? *Yes, I believe that. I don't know how He did it, but I believe He did.* Good. Then I will say to them, don't you think that it took an incredible amount of power to do all of that? Don't you think that the power it took to create the stars and the planets and the galaxies is so great that we can't even comprehend it?

Usually the person will say I am probably right. And then I ask, do you think it is possible that the power that could do all of that could also control your mind? *What do you mean?* Do you think it is possible that the same power that created the universe could have enough power to control you and your life? After a few moments of thinking about this they will usually say they believe that is possible. That's when I hit them with my point. I ask, don't you think, then, that the power that can do all I just described could have controlled the minds of the men who penned the Bible so that every single word on every single page is exactly what that power wanted it to be?

You see, I ain't no rocket scientist, but on a very basic, commonsense level, I believe that any power that could create the entire universe could also write a book. How He did it is still a mystery on a natural, human understanding level, and it always will be because God is God and we aren't. But, on a very simple level, I sleep very well every night because I know that the God Who created the world and the stars and the galaxies and the whole universe wrote the Bible through men He handpicked.

You need to understand this because everything I believe and the stands I've taken are all based on this book, the Bible. I believe every word of it is true. And if it is true, every person on the planet needs to prepare themselves to the best of their ability for the most serious butt-kicking the world will ever see. Now you don't have to like what I just said, but according to the Book, it is coming and there ain't nothing you or I can do about it.

Hold on there, Baldwin. What does the Bible being true have to do with a global butt-kicking? And what does that have to do with that nutty question you hit me with at the beginning of this section? Everything.

According to the Bible, God didn't just make the universe, He also made people. But He made us different from everything else. Out of all the stuff He flung out into every corner of the universe, we are the only thing He made in His likeness. Animals weren't. Angels weren't. Nothing else compares to the human race. We were God's crowning touch, the crescendo of the week of creation.

When He made us, He didn't just make us flesh and blood. The Bible says He scooped up some dirt and breathed into it the breath of life. That means He gave us an eternal spirit. As if that wasn't enough, God dropped the first people He made into the middle of paradise. Then He told them they could have the rest of the planet as well.

He did all of this because He loves us. All He asked in return was for the pinnacle of His creation to love Him and obey Him. And what did the apex of the universe do in response to all of this? We flipped God the bird and told Him to leave us alone.

That's why I ask, if you were God, what would you do? According to the Bible, here is what God did. Since the beginning of time He gave the world so many second chances you'd need a super computer to count them all. That's why He wrote His Book. The Bible isn't just a bunch of cute little sayings to give you a better day. He wrote the Book so we could get back the thing we threw away when we chose sin over God.

When no one listened to His Book, He sent his Son, Jesus,

to die on a cross for us. The Bible says the penalty of sin is death, so God sent His Son to pay the penalty in our place. My mind cannot even comprehend why He would do that. And as if that wasn't enough, Jesus rose from the dead to give us life. Then God sat back and waited for us to respond. He's been waiting for two *thousand* years! Two thousand freaking years!

Again, I ask, if you were God, what would you do? Let's say we wrote a script called the Bible, and your role is Jesus Christ, God, and the Holy Spirit, the tri-unity all in one. You created perfection. You created life in your own image and you told life, Do this.

From that moment until now, what has that life done? From the moment Adam bit the apple until now, what have the children God created done to Him? It's not quantum physics. For the most part, since the beginning of time we have told Him, *Get lost. I don't need You. I don't care what You've done for me, it doesn't matter.* If you were God, what would you do?

If what I am saying is true, then on a commonsense level, buddy, there needs to be a hell. Think about it. C. S. Lewis said all through his life the human animal screams at God, *Leave me alone!* Hell is God saying, You may have your wish. Am I happy about the fact that it is forever? No, but I'm not God.

You can think all of this is a bunch of bull. That's your right. You can slam this book shut and say I don't know what I'm talking about. You can say that the God of love you believe in would never send anyone to hell. You can take that chance if you want. But keep this in mind: A day of judgment is coming. Don't blame me when the lever is pulled and you start falling toward hell.

When that moment comes, and you feel the wind whipping up under your butt, past your ears and over your hair and you get that sensation of falling, you will have no one to blame but yourself. You and you alone will be responsible for the decision you made. All I can say is good luck to you when that day comes, 'cause you're going to need it.

Hey Stevie B, what are you saying? Are you telling me that those four-foot little pygmies in some rainforest in some obscure corner of the world are going to burn in hell because they've never heard of Jesus? Only God knows the answer to that. My question is, why do so many people who have heard about Jesus allow that reasoning to keep them from entering into this relationship?

I just might agree with you that maybe that's not fair, but you know what, I'm not God. The truth be told, in Stephen's way of thinking, if it's between me and the pygmy, I'm looking out for number one. But seriously, I figure if God is smart enough to create the galaxies, He is wise enough to do the right thing when everyone who has ever lived stands before Him on the judgment day.

BRINGING IT ON OURSELVES

If you think I enjoy talking about God's wrath, you are wrong. I don't. But it doesn't do any good to stick our heads in the sand and pretend it doesn't exist. Nor should we point a finger at God and tell Him it's His fault. His fault? There's no way this is God's fault. We as the human race have brought God's anger on ourselves. Who do we think we are?

God dropped us in the middle of this huge vast universe that is so much bigger than we ever thought before, and He put us on a planet where a piece of the ocean floor can shift and stir up a wave that wipes out hundreds of thousands of people on two continents, and where a thunderstorm forms off the coast of Africa and it scoots across the ocean until it parks in the Gulf of Mexico and grows large enough to turn a major U.S. city into a Third World country, and in spite of all of this we have convinced ourselves that we are in control.

I hear this from people all the time. They say we are responsible for our fates, we don't need God. All we need to do is band together and we can solve all our problems. War. Disease.

Poverty. Violence. Global warming. Everything that is wrong with the world we can fix *on our own.*

What is wrong, they say, is that we as a species are not doing enough collectively to correct these problems. But we don't because the Republicans in Congress keep us from doing it or the President has another agenda or the big corporations care more about profit than they do about healing the planet.

Let me tell you something, buddy. If you got all six billion people on the planet together and went to work on all that plagues this earth, all of us collectively still couldn't do enough to fix it because this world and its problems are too big. And that's why we need God. So to all of you out there that think it is all about us, get over yourselves.

This stupid arrogance is one of the things that stirs up God's wrath. Instead of listening to Him we keep ignoring Him and pretending He doesn't know what He is talking about. He sends reminders to try to get our attention. God sends shots across the bow to remind us how small and helpless we really are and how much we need Him, but we don't listen. What choice does He then have but to make His voice even louder?

That's why the Bible says God's wrath is coming. He doesn't do it to exact His pound of flesh. Nor does it make God happy to punish the human race. He does it to slap us out of this delusion that we don't need Him, so that hopefully, just maybe, we will turn to Him in faith.

But I don't think that's fair, people tell me. I always ask them the same thing in response: When you are driving in your car and you come up to a traffic light and the light turns yellow, what do you do? Oh, I slow down, people say. Then what happens? The light turns red. Right. And then what do you do? I stop. Why? Because it is a red light. I understand that. But why, when you are driving your car and you come to a red light, do you stop? Here are the answers I usually get: So I don't get in an accident. Right. Why else? So I don't get injured. Right. Why else? So I don't break the law. And why wouldn't you want to break the law? So I don't get pulled over by the police. Right. And if you got pulled over by the police, what might happen? I might get a ticket. Right. And you don't want to get a ticket because you don't want to pay a fine and have your insurance rates go up and possibly lose your license.

You are willing to adhere to a system of rules that were given to you by men. If you come to a red light and there is nobody around, you could run that red light all day long. But you don't because you fear the repercussions from the authority that made the traffic laws that you are not willing to break. I am telling you there is another rule book called the Bible. That rule book is very specific. In it God says that if you will follow these rules, He will give you this experience of life. But if you don't, you will face certain consequences. We don't question man's wrath, do we? Why then do we question God's right to do the same thing?

The human race has been on the autobahn of sin, blowing through red lights since Jesus left and before that. We have done nothing but put our foot to the floor on the accelerator of the Ferrari of life, flipping the bird at heaven. And if that is true, then hey man, God's been merciful. He should've shut this deal down a long time ago. But as usual we in our selfish arrogant minds have said, "Take it easy there, God. Calm down. We are running this deal down here." That's why we cannot ignore God's wrath. It is coming. And it may arrive sooner than we think.

All I can say is, I sleep good at night because I am totally content in the knowledge that God is in control. And if the world comes to an end tomorrow, I know that I will spend eternity with Him. Why? I believe in Him. I love Him. And I do my best to follow His rule book. Stephen Baldwin isn't special. God offers this same hope to everyone who will quit ignoring Him long enough to believe in His Son.

Normal
Main Entry: ¹nor·mal
Pronunciation: 'nȯr-məl
Function: *adjective*
Etymology: Latin *normalis,* from *norma*
1 : PERPENDICULAR; *especially* : perpendicular to a tangent at a point of tangency
2 a : according with, constituting, or not deviating from a norm, rule, or principle **b** : conforming to a type, standard, or regular pattern
3 : occurring naturally <*normal* immunity>
4 a : of, relating to, or characterized by average intelligence or development **b** : free from mental disorder : SANE
5 a *of a solution* : having a concentration of one gram equivalent of solute per liter **b** : containing neither basic hydroxyl nor acid hydrogen <*normal* silver phosphate> **c** : not associated <*normal* molecules> **d** : having a straight-chain structure <*normal* pentane> <*normal* butyl alcohol>
6 *of a subgroup* : having the property that every coset produced by operating on the left by a given element is equal to the coset produced by operating on the right by the same element
7 : relating to, involving, or being a normal curve or normal distribution <*normal* approximation to the binomial distribution>

CHAPTER 20

What Is Normal?

I never wanted to be normal. I never wanted to conform to a type, standard, or regular pattern. That has never been and will never be Stephen Baldwin. Instead my goal was to never conform, to never be standard or regular or ordinary. I never wanted to be normal. Since normal also means "free from mental disorder," most people would say I reached my goal. Whatever. Yet, when I started exploring the Bible I discovered my old life was very, very normal.

I may have jumped out of airplanes and hung out at the Playboy mansion and done all kinds of other things that most people never get to do, but I still conformed to the norms of the world system. I fell for the lie that says this world is all there is and all you need. I believed in God, but I only turned to Him when I needed help to escape my addictions. Most of the time I lived for Stephen and depended on Stephen alone. I was all I really needed. In the world system, that's a pretty normal approach to life.

THE BACKWARD WORLD

Then I came to faith and started reading the Bible. The more I read, the more I could relate to the character Neo in *The Matrix*.

The Bible was my Morpheus exposing all the lies I'd believed. Slowly I came to realize I was living in a dream world. My whole conception of normal was completely backward. According to the Bible, what is considered normal in the world is actually abnormal; and according to the world, what the Bible calls normal is considered abnormal.

I always believed I needed to look out for number one; that was normal. But the Bible told me, "Do nothing out of selfish ambition or vain conceit, but in humility *consider others better than yourselves*" (Philippians 2:3, emphasis added). Whoa. I knew I was supposed to love other people, everyone knows that. Yet this went WAY beyond doing something nice for my wife once in a while. According to God, normal means I consider other people to be better than myself. In the world in which I grew up, that ain't normal.

Neither is another little tidbit the Bible laid on me. Jesus Himself said, "Love your enemies, do good to those who hate you, bless those who curse you, pray for those who mistreat you. If someone strikes you on one cheek, turn to him the other also. If someone takes your cloak, do not stop him from taking your tunic. Give to everyone who asks you, and if anyone takes what belongs to you, do not demand it back. Do to others as you would have them do to you" (Luke 6:27-31). This wasn't some little full-of-baloney saying Jesus came up with to make us think. He actually meant what He said.

Jesus said it is normal for me to *love* my enemies and for me to do good things for those who hate me. As if that wasn't bad enough, when someone curses me, and with the way I drive in New York it happens more often than I would like to admit in this book, I am supposed to answer their curse with a blessing. That's 180 degrees backward from what I'd always thought of as normal. I mean, how weird is it to think that normal means giving some dude your tunic when you catch him taking your coat without permission?

I get the whole turn the other cheek thing. I've heard that my whole life. But I always thought that if someone had the guts to strike me on the second cheek, and I stood there feeling that thing stinging, whoever slapped me better turn and run because I would be fresh out of cheeks to turn. That's not what Jesus is saying. He's saying I've got to keep turning those cheeks, because that's what He did when the Roman soldiers beat Him to a bloody pulp before He went to the cross. According to the Bible, that is normal.

Believe it or not, that's just the tip of the iceberg. At the height of my Hollywood pursuits I did pretty well for myself financially. I didn't pull down Tom Cruise money, but hey, who does? In acting, and every other career under the sun, money matters. That's normal. But not with God. His book says, "For we brought nothing into the world, and we can take nothing out of it. But if we have food and clothing, we will be content with that" (1 Timothy 6:7-8).

That verse is just weird compared to the world I lived in. *If we have food and clothing, we will be content with that*, are you kidding me? When it comes to stuff, God is saying all I need is some clothes on my back and a meal in front of me. That's it. I should choose to be satisfied with that. In God's economy, that's normal.

Most of us think it is normal to get all worked up over planning our—how do they put it in those investment commercials?—*Our financial futures.* But God says:

> Therefore I tell you, do not worry about your life, what you will eat or drink; or about your body, what you will wear. Is not life more important than food, and the body more important than clothes? Look at the birds of the air; they do not sow or reap or store away in barns, and yet your heavenly Father feeds them. Are you not much more valuable than they? Who of you by worrying can add a single hour to his life?
>
> And why do you worry about clothes? See how the lilies

of the field grow. They do not labor or spin. Yet I tell you that not even Solomon in all his splendor was dressed like one of these. If that is how God clothes the grass of the field, which is here today and tomorrow is thrown into the fire, will he not much more clothe you, O you of little faith? So do not worry, saying, "What shall we eat?" or "What shall we drink?" or "What shall we wear?" For the pagans run after all these things, and your heavenly Father knows that you need them. But seek first his kingdom and his righteousness, and all these things will be given to you as well. Therefore do not worry about tomorrow, for tomorrow will worry about itself. Each day has enough trouble of its own.

(MATTHEW 6:25–34)

Normal financial planning in God's economy is to seek Him first and not worry about anything else. He tells me to look at the birds and the grass. If God can give birds feathers and nests and seeds, and if He can give the grass soil and rain and flowers, He can pretty much take care of anything I might need. In the natural, worry is normal, but not in the spiritual realm.

I don't know if you are ready for the biggest blow to my conception of what is normal. It comes from Jesus in His most famous sermon of all. I'm telling you, when you read the verses I'm about to paste in this book, you will think Jesus is a nutcase. That is, if you think in terms of what the world thinks of as normal. But again, He doesn't think this world is normal. To God, what the world calls normal is abnormal, and to the world, what God calls normal is abnormal. Nothing proves this like these words from the mouth of Jesus Himself:

> *Looking at his disciples, he said:*
> *"Blessed are you who are poor,*
> *for yours is the kingdom of God.*

Blessed are you who hunger now,
for you will be satisfied.
Blessed are you who weep now,
for you will laugh.
Blessed are you when men hate you,
when they exclude you and insult you
and reject your name as evil,
because of the Son of Man.
Rejoice in that day and leap for joy,
because great is your reward in heaven.
For that is how their fathers treated the prophets.
But woe to you who are rich,
for you have already received your comfort.
Woe to you who are well fed now,
for you will go hungry.
Woe to you who laugh now,
for you will mourn and weep.
Woe to you when all men speak well of you,
for that is how their fathers treated the false prophets."
(Luke 6:20-26)

Reading this made my tongue hit the floor. I could barely wrap my brain around what Jesus was saying. "Blessed are the poor, and woe to those who are rich?" That sounds backward. And it is.

Reading the Bible made me realize I'd lived a backward life. I might as well have been living inside a computer simulation of reality, I couldn't have been any more screwed up than I was from living in what I thought was the real world. I've always wanted to live life to the fullest, accelerator to the floor, go for it. In the physical realm I have pretty much done that. But I never even thought that it is possible that the spiritual realm controls the physical and the natural realm, as well as my perspective of what is normal. I never realized how my comprehension of normal in the physical world would change when I pursued it from a spiritual point of view.

NORMAL?

This revelation of what is normal explains why I put everything in this book that I did. Everything in it may have seemed weird and backward and completely out of sync with what you consider normal. Because it is. All of which brings me not to a statement but to a question. I want you to ask yourself, what is normal? People have debated the question throughout the ages. So I ask you, the reader, what is normal?

There is the normal that we think is normal when we get up in the morning and go to the bathroom and then go have some coffee and start our day. Then there is the happy ending to a massage that some men think is normal. And then there is the normal way of thinking in the mind of a woman whose husband doesn't pay enough attention to her. She justifies her flirting with other men, telling herself it is normal because she is a woman and she needs that attention. It's normal. So again, I ask you, what is normal? What in your mind constitutes normal in every part of your life, physically, mentally, and emotionally?

When you stand back and think about the question, there isn't really a lot of finger pointing and judging that can go on. Normal is such a big, broad word. If you get on an airplane and fly off to a jungle in a remote corner of the world, you will find people who eat stir-fried bat and roasted roaches. In your Western mind you will say, Hey man, these people aren't normal. And they will watch you pay four or five dollars for a coffee at Starbucks and say the same about you. In France, it is normal for two men to kiss one another on the cheek when they meet. In Massapequa, New York, from 1966 to 1983 it would have been normal to coldcock any dude who tried laying a kiss on another dude. In Japan, eating raw fish is normal. In Indiana, they call that bait.

Trying to define normal is as broad as there are people in the world. However, I have come to believe that there is a universal starting point for what is normal to the human animal. I believe that innately, in the unknown place of intuition, every human being shares an idea of what the "normal" human pursuits should be.

No matter who you are or where you are from, you intuitively want to pursue happiness, joy, peace, success, love and pleasure. That's normal. But if we don't comprehend that the starting point for these pursuits begins in the spiritual realm, then we are unable to have a genuine perspective on the word normal. These pursuits are normal because God designed us to want them. They are normal because that's how we are made.

The problem is that God's original design for the human race was messed up by a thing called sin. Back when God first made the human race out of dirt, it was normal for them to see God with their eyes and hear Him with their ears. Normal meant loving God, walking with God, serving God. Normal also meant having a perfect relationship with other people, which I guess was easier then since there were only two people on earth. These first two people didn't wear any clothes, but that was normal because they didn't have any shame or guilt. Why should they since they had never done anything wrong?

But, on the day the first man and woman chose to ignore God and listen to a lying talking snake (and yeah, I believe this went down exactly as the Bible says it did), the human animal's perception of normal changed. Adam and Eve stood there next to the forbidden tree and for the first time in their lives they felt guilty for being naked. Shame was now the new normal.

Later in the day they heard God moving through the garden, so they hid under a bush. Being afraid of God was the new normal. When God spoke to them they lied to Him and made excuses for what they did.

Trying to play games with God and shirk responsibility for

your actions became the new normal. As punishment for what they did, God drove the man and woman out of the garden paradise He made for them. From that day forward the human race was forced to scratch out a living by the sweat of their brow. God also cursed the ground, causing it to spring up with thorns and weeds and poison ivy. He even increased the pain of childbirth. Pain and suffering and hardship became part of the new normal of human existence.

You might think I'm whacked and that the story of Adam and Eve is nothing more than a fairy tale. But, if that story isn't true, why then is it normal to want more out of life? Why is it now normal for people like three-time Super Bowl winning quarterback Tom Brady to go on *60 Minutes* and say that all of his success isn't enough, that he thinks there must be something more out of life, but he doesn't know what that is?

Superstar singer John Mayer said the same thing in one of his songs he called, "Something's Missing." Looking for something more out of life than cars and success and fame and houses and hot women is normal. Why? There's only one way I know to explain it: God made us to want more than the physical realm can deliver. Why else would every human being on the planet long for happiness in a world that seems designed to keep us from finding it? *What do you mean, Stevie B?* Just this: Why do we look for happiness on a planet where EVERYONE DIES? Funerals aren't exactly a good time, but that's where we're all headed.

We want peace. Everyone wants peace. That's normal. I'm sick of hearing, "War is not the answer." Of course war is not the answer. That's not exactly a new idea. I would like, then, for someone to explain to me why somewhere in the world a war of some kind has been fought every minute of human history. Whether it's the Romans against the Greeks or the French against the British or the Germans against France and England or the cowboys against the Indians or the Hatfields against the McCoys or the Crips against the Bloods, someone somewhere has been fighting since the dawn of time. I think if something has gone on that long, then who knows, maybe it's normal. I don't know, is it?

What is normal? We want peace. How's this for nuts: People fight wars in an effort to make peace. Is that freakin' hilarious or what? And get this. Do you know what they called World War I? They called it the war to end all wars. Obviously that didn't work out so well. So I guess war is normal and so is hating war and longing for peace. The only way to understand how these two opposites can both be true is to start from a biblical, spiritual perspective. You cannot understand what is normal any other way.

A CHANGED PERSPECTIVE

So again I ask you the reader, what is normal? *No one can answer that, Stephen. You said it yourself, what's normal in the Amazon jungle is flat-out weird in Saskatchewan. So how can anyone say anything is normal?* Shouldn't we instead say everything is normal? I know people who try to say that. *You aren't supposed to judge*, they say. *My normal may not be your normal, but so what? Who's to say which is right and which is wrong?* People usually follow all of this with a proclamation that their lifestyle choices are perfectly normal and that they should be applauded for having the guts to go public with them.

They say they were born that way. Okay. I get that. But I have a question. If you are born a certain way in your mind, does that make it normal? If I was born with six fingers on one hand, does that mean it is normal since I was born that way? And if it is, why then would jaws drop every time I went to shake hands with someone? If I claim I was born a certain way and that makes it normal, shouldn't we then conclude that any and all abnormalities are then normal? I'm telling you, no one can live that way. No one is prepared to say it is normal for a child to be born with a heart so deformed that it only survives an hour or two after birth. We call that a tragedy. A child molester may say he was born with an uncontrollable desire to have sex with children. We don't call that normal. We lock those guys away.

So who gets to decide the answer to the question of what is normal? The answer goes back to where I started this chapter: God. He gets to decide. He is the one who says what is normal and what isn't.

Unfortunately, we live in a world where God's perspective has been so bastardized, so smeared with mud for over two-thousand years, that someone somewhere will try to justify anything by invoking the name of God. Talk about your spin zone. But there is one little thing about God's truth that most people would rather ignore: His truth never changes. His normal has never changed one bit since the beginning of time. So what is normal? Whatever God says. How's that for simple? According to God, normal is however He defines it for us in His Word.

That statement is a little more loaded than you might think. There are people out there who will read what I just wrote and say they agree with it 100 percent. *Get 'em, Stevie boy*, they will say. Hold on before you get too carried away. Here's the thing about God being the One Who determines what is normal: You do not get to cherry-pick only the parts of the Bible you like.

I get into conversations with right-wing, ultra-conservative Christians all the time, people who think they are normal, but they aren't having the skydiving experience with God that I am having. When I point this out they say something like, *Well, that's good for you, Stephen, but that's really not for me.* Oh. Really? I say. *Oh, yes, you see I have a different understanding of what the normal experience of a Christian should be.*

When I hear this I tell these people they are crazy. That usually sets them off. *What do you mean I'm crazy?* they say. I usually follow this up by asking them if they drove their car that day. Now that gets some really weird looks from people. *Of course I drove my car, how did you think I got here?* That makes you crazy, I tell them. What if the brakes on your car had failed? *Come on, take it easy, you're exaggerating.* Am I? I say. Don't people die in America every year from accidents that are caused by brake failures? They say yes. But you got in your car and turned the key and chose to have faith that your brakes would not fail!

At this point they usually get a little frustrated wondering what my point may be. That's when I hit them with it. I tell them, you chose to trust in the brakes on your car that were made by people even though you know that people are not perfect and brake systems have been known to fail. Why then won't you believe and act on all of God's Word which is perfect and will never fail?

I believe it is possible for all Christians to have an experience where it is possible for them to enjoy the gifts of the Spirit. Now I'm not saying everyone should speak in tongues, because the Word of God says these things are not for everyone. But Jesus did say we would do greater things in His name than He did while He walked this earth. In John 14:12 He said, "I tell you the truth, anyone who has faith in me will do what I have been doing. He will do even greater things than these, because I am going to the Father." If that is true, why is such a minute percentage of Evangelicals enjoying the gifts of the Spirit?

Again, I know this isn't for everyone, but it seems to me that there are a whole bunch of Christians that have ingested way more cheese than they have living water. I mean, knowing this, how awesome could your experience be if each and every day you were more willing to give yourself more and more to Jesus in return for His filling you more and more with His Spirit? That's the point. Who knows? Maybe some of you could raise the dead.

See, here's the deal. God decides what is normal and He tells us what that is in His Book, the Bible. According to the Bible, there are experiences all believers should have as a normal part of living by faith. Do you want to know what those may be? Read the Book. Start with the book of Acts. And before you say the stuff in there is not for today, pull your head out of your American sandbox and look around the world. The Gospel is blowing up all over the world, especially in countries in Africa and South America, and things like those recorded in Acts happen every day there. It is normal, just like God's Word says.

That's what it means to let God define what is normal rather than us trying to do it for Him. Back in the garden the first lie ever told was this: You can be like God. The human race has tried to make that lie come true ever since. We can't. Only God is God. And now, for me, normal means obeying God. After all I've been through, after everything I've seen and heard and experienced in this world, and all the things I've done and the places I've been and the motivations thereof, the only definition of normal that makes any sense is God's definition.

I don't say it in any kind of freaky deaky, born again sort of way. I say it in a really kind of simple, commonsense, logical, been-there-done-that kind of way. It wasn't until I started to apply what I understood normal to be based on God's way of thinking that I was able to fully comprehend and start to enjoy my life in a way that I always wanted but was never able.

For me normal is now to love God, seek God, live for God, represent God, and go and make disciples of all the nations. I wake up every single day chomping at the bit of life waiting for God to show me what He has for me, where He wants me to go, what He wants me to do, and how He wants me to do it. That is my understanding now of what normal is. Based on this, I believe God now has a future waiting for me so astronomically beyond the realm of possibility that I cannot contain my excitement.

AN UNUSUAL MESSAGE FROM
AN UNUSUAL MESSENGER

But of course, gang, this is all just my opinion. From the first page of this book to the last, this is just one kooky, little, wing–nut dumb jock from Long Island's point of view based on my experience. But don't let that cause you to dismiss everything I have to say. In my life I've discovered that some of the most profound, brilliant, ingenious, powerful, awesome revelations and epiphanies have come from the most simple people and odd situations. And that pretty much describes me. I am simple and odd. Which, according to God, puts me in the perfect position to be used by God.

As you've read this book I figure you keep asking, *Who are you to say all of this Stevie B?* After all, I'm a tattooed actor who made my reputation by doing some pretty crazy things. That's what makes me the unusual suspect in the eyes of the world. People look at me and say, *This guy's a Christian? This guy's trying to tell me who God is and what God does and how God thinks? That ain't normal.* No, normal would be some clean-cut, respectable, highly-educated, articulate, Ivy Leaguer with degrees in theology, psychology, astronomy, and sociology. That's the world's normal idea of who should stand up and speak for God.

Guess what? God's ideas are about 180 degrees opposite. He said, "But God chose the foolish things of the world to shame the wise; God chose the weak things of the world to shame the strong. He chose the lowly things of this world and the despised things—and the things that are not—to nullify the things that are" (1 Corinthians 1:27-28). According to God, I'm not the unusual suspect. When He went looking for someone to speak for Him, I was just who He was looking for.

But that's not all. The title of the book is *The Unusual Suspect*, meaning the thought that God would use a guy like me is very unusual. But when I think about all God has done, and I think about His predestination and how everything I ever really wanted was God, I come to another conclusion.

Every human being was made with a deep longing that can only be satisfied by God Himself. Yet we live in a world system that we don't even realize keeps us from pursuing Him. So I guess, in the end, God is the real unusual suspect because He is the answer to the question of what we really want out of life. He is the answer to who I am and why I'm here and what is my purpose. And if you would only be willing to open yourself up to the possibility that He may be the answer you are looking for, you too would experience this life I now enjoy.

Epilogue

I had an interesting argument the other day with a guy I've known for years. He's a brilliant guy. He graduated from one of the top schools in the country and now holds a Master's in Marine Biology. The guy is so freaking brilliant he even writes SAT questions. He may be the smartest guy I know in the natural. I don't think he's an atheist, but he might as well be. He hates George Bush. Hates the President's Christian agenda. Thinks faith is crap. Totally thinks the Bible is nothing more than a book written by men.

So the two of us got into it the other day about this faith of mine. We went back and forth for a while. He told me everything he thought was wrong with people of faith, from the President on down. He tried to pin all the world's problems on believers and our intolerance and lack of love. I had answers, but I don't know if they sank in. I even gave him some statistics I got from Ravi Zacharias about how Christianity is the fastest growing faith in places where people are given a choice about what faith they will believe. He didn't listen.

After a while of arguing with my friend I finally said to him, "Okay tough guy. You keep griping about God. I dare you to have the cajonès to pull your pants down and expose yourself to heaven and say to God, 'Okay pal, if you are real, show me.'" He didn't really know what to say to that, so I kept going.

I told this old friend of mine to stop pointing his finger at people of faith and saying *What kind of God would do this and that?* I challenged him to quit hiding behind excuses and actually check out to see if this God is real. I said to him, "I dare you, not in an obvious go and make disciples kind of way. I'm worse than that. I'm sicker than that. I dare you in that way like the guys playing poker on television who go all-in, I dare you in that way. I dare you in the new radical way. I dare you to challenge God to prove His existence is real."

But I didn't stop. I told him that he would have to find out if God was real God's way, which means reading the Bible, applying it to his life, and praying.

Maybe I shouldn't have been so blunt, but I finally got sick and tired of hearing his same old arguments over and over. Do you know what pushed a button with my friend? I was talking to him about all of this, and he said, "Why is Bush going to war if Jesus said we are to be peacemakers and turn the other cheek?"

And I said, "You know what bro, I'm not God. I don't know why all this is happening." Then I said, "You know what I hear coming from you? Everything coming out of your mouth is motivated by hate and anger. So don't point a finger and tell me that I support a cause that doesn't represent peace and love and happiness and freedom and joy, when in fact, all you can spew is hate." At the end of the conversation I said to him, "Until you know God's Word, until you have researched and lived in it and slept with it and prayed on it, you cannot know if this faith is real or not."

That's what I want to say to every skeptic who just finished this book. Don't tell me this faith is a bunch of baloney until you are willing to actually find out if it is real. Personally, I don't care if you agree with me. In fact, if you don't agree with me, I can't believe you made it to this point.

But if you've got the guts I challenge you to do what I did. Over and over I told you how you won't get the experience until you are willing to try it God's way, and that means believing enough to jump out of the plane of life holding on to nothing but Jesus. Now's the time to do it. Like I said before, you can't wait until everything makes sense. You don't get the understanding until you are willing to believe. So what are you waiting for? My prayer is that before you close the back cover you will be willing to take a chance, drop your guard, and enter into this experience I'm having with God. I guarantee you will not be the same if you do.

Amen
Main Entry: **amen**
Pronunciation: (')ä-'men, (')ā-; 'ä- *when sung*
Function: *interjection*
Etymology: Middle English, from Old English, from Late Latin, from Greek *amēn*, from Hebrew *āmēn*
— used to express solemn ratification (as of an expression of faith) or hearty approval (as of an assertion)

Prayer of Faith in Jesus Christ

Father God . . .

I know that I have sinned against You . . . and I need to know the truth. Please, come into my life . . . and change me . . . with your love, peace & joy, which I understand, I can only experience, by believing that You are real, and giving my life to You and accepting your son Jesus as my Lord and Savior.

Father God . . . I need your love, I receive your will, please forgive me for my sins, I forgive myself.

I believe that Jesus died for my sins on the cross, and rose again, defeating death, as only He could, by the power of your Holy Spirit, conquering the spirit of this world.

Thank You God for offering me this truth, setting me free, blessing me with the knowledge and understanding of my true purpose, that You had for me before I was born.

I will love You and serve You, the best that I can, from this moment on, and when I am with You in Heaven.

Thank You Father . . . in the name of your Son . . . "Jesus"

Amen.

Chapter Notes

CHAPTER 7

1. Census Bureau report on *MARITAL STATUS AND LIVING ARRANGEMENTS*, from www.divorcereform.org.
2. Ahlburg and DeVita, "New Realities," 4-12. Cited on pg. 5 of *The Abolition of Marriage*, by Maggie Gallagher.
3. "Walking the Walk on Family Values," by William V. D'Antonio, *Boston Globe*, October 31, 2004, http://www.boston.com/news/globe/editorial_opinion/oped/articles/2004/10/31/walking_the_walk_on_family_values/.

CHAPTER 14

1. "Science of the Heart: Exploring the Role of the Heart in Human Performance," by the HeartMath Institute, http://www.heartmath.org/research/science-of-the-heart/soh_20.php.
2. From *Nexus Magazine*, Volume 12, Number 3 (April - May 2005), by Paul Pearsall, PhD, Gary E. Schwartz, PhD, Linda G. Russek, PhD. You can read the article at http://www.paulpearsall.com/info/press/3.html.
3. Ibid.
4. Pearsall, Paul, *The Heart's Code*. New York, Broadway Books, 1998, pg. 7.

Scriptures You Should Check Out

Amos 9:9–15
Titus 2:11–20
Matthew 11:12–18, 10:34–39
Romans 12:1–2
Ephesians 6:10–18
2 Corinthians 10:3–6
Jeremiah 29:11–14
Psalm 27
Philippians 4:4–8, 2:5–12